KT-440-465

Contents

Data, Information and Knowledge

Welcome to AS ICT — the riveting study of Information and Communication Technology. To start with, you need to be clear on some very basic definitions. Close your eyes and make a wish, and all your ICT wishes will be granted.

Data, Information and Knowledge

The difference between these terms is quite subtle, but really important to understand:

1) **Data**

   Data consists of **characters** that are **stored** and **processed** in the computer. The computer doesn't understand what the data means and it has **no meaning on its own**.

   > **e.g.** Examples of data could be the strings of characters '19091985' or 'VD51FGD' which may be input into the computer, processed in some way and then output.

2) **Information**

   Information is **data** that has been **given a meaning** by being put into context, or data that has been processed into a useful format. If you know what a string of characters means, then it **becomes information**.

   > **e.g.** '19091985' may be a product code for an item or it may be the date of birth of a person (19th September 1985) — it becomes information once you know what it refers to.

3) **Knowledge**

   Information becomes **knowledge** when you use a **rule** or a **set of rules** to manipulate the information.

   > **e.g.** If you know that 19091985 is a person's date of birth (19th September 1985) you can work out that the person is aged 18 or over and so is eligible to vote. You've used a rule which states 'if age>= 18 the person can vote' to get knowledge from information.

Data Sources can be Direct or Indirect

There are two basic, different ways in which we can get data:

1) **Direct Capture**

   Direct data capture is when specific data is collected for a specific purpose (e.g. like on a census form or a tax return). The data is then entered into a computer and processed. (e.g. to find out how many people there are in the country and what the age distribution is).

2) **Indirect Capture**

   Data that is collected directly (e.g. membership details for a gym) may be passed on (with the member's permission) to another company (e.g. a sports shop) and used for a very different purpose (e.g. sending out advertising leaflets). In this case, it's called **indirect data capture**.

Data Sources Need to be Reliable

Data needs to come from reliable sources in order to ensure accurate results. It's common sense really — for example:

If conducting a poll to determine whether a Skate Park should be built in local parkland:

DO ASK: if they're local residents. Get proof of address, and don't ask passers-by without checking if they do live locally.

If trying to research a history essay on-line:

DO ASK: search engines, different websites. However, whenever you use an unfamiliar website, you need to be aware of the source, and judge how reliable that source is. If it is a website written by another student, for example, then you'd need to be wary of its accuracy.

AS-Level
ICT

The Revision Guide

Editors:
Simon Little, Chrissy Williams.

Contributors:
David Astall, Marie Gibbs, Nick Jackson, Gavin Lawrence, June McKenzie, Kate Redmond, Edward Robinson, Karen Scott, Rachel Selway, Sonia Stuart, Barry Thomas, Jennifer Underwood, Richard Vickery.

Proofreaders:
Sarah-Jane Clark, Peter Saunders, Sonia Stuart.

With special thanks to Neil Hastings, whose love of databases and teletext made this book possible.
Also thanks to Peter Spencer, who polished off numerous curly wurlys whilst giving his love and support.

Published by Coordination Group Publications Ltd.

ISBN: 978 1 84146 971 3
Groovy website: www.cgpbooks.co.uk
Jolly bits of clipart from CorelDRAW®
Printed by Elanders Hindson Ltd, Newcastle upon Tyne.

Microsoft product screen shots reprinted with permission from the Microsoft Corporation.
Microsoft, Encarta, MSN, and Windows are either registered trademarks or trademarks of Microsoft Corporation in the United States and/or other countries.

Extract from the "Parrot Scene" taken from: *Monty Python's Flying Circus "Just the words" Volume One, by* Eric Idle, John Cleese, Michael Palin, Terry Jones and Graham Chapman, by permission of Methuen Publishing.

Data, Information and Knowledge

Your **Data** Needs to be **Top Quality**

The **quality** of the data that is input is very important. If it's inaccurate or out of date or unreasonable, then it doesn't matter how wonderful the computer program is; it will still produce incorrect results. You can sum this up with the word: **GIGO**, which means '**garbage in garbage out**'.

	PROCESS	INPUT	OUTPUT
Example 1	find age	Date of Birth 09121883 _this should be 09121983_	person is over 120 years old
Example 2	calculate gas bill	Meter Reading 9009456 _this should be 0009456_	bill is £2,500,000
Example 3	calculate weekly wages	Hours worked 420 _this should be 42_	wage is £2,100

Data must be **accurate**, **up-to-date**, **complete**, **reasonable** and **correct**.

There are **Different Data Types**   *This bit is OCR only.*

When data is stored in a computer, it can be stored in **different ways** depending on what it is used for.

1) The data may be a **number**, in which case it may be a whole number (integer) or have a decimal part (real number).
2) Alternatively, it might be a group of several **characters** (letters and numbers) in which case it is called a string.
3) Thirdly, it might just represent one of two **conditions** (e.g. "true" or "false") — this is called a Boolean type.

Data Types and Examples
Integer   e.g. 2003, 18
Real numbers e.g. 147.35, 0.0034
Strings e.g.   ABC435, Benjamin, CQ117YT
Boolean e.g. True or False, On or Off, 1 or 0

Practice Questions

Q1   Explain the terms data, information and knowledge.
Q2   What is the difference between direct and indirect data capture?
Q3   What does GIGO mean?

Exam Questions

Q1   It is important to be able to distinguish between data, information and knowledge. 21092002 is an example of data.
   a) Give two reasons why "21092002" is a piece of data, not information. (2 marks)
   b) Give one example of what information "21092002" could be converted into. (1 mark)
   c) Explain the process of changing information into knowledge and give an example using your answer to (b). (2 marks)

Q2   A company is carrying out some research about the eating habits of young people. They want to ensure that they obtain good quality data.
   a) Give three characteristics of good quality data. (3 marks)
   b) For each characteristic, suggest how the company could ensure that good quality data was obtained. (3 marks)

Aceing your exams will be a data remember (groan...)

You need to make sure you've nailed the subtle differences between the meanings of the terms 'data', 'information' and 'knowledge'. The examples on this page are just the beginning. Try and think of more real-life examples that might crop up in an exam — otherwise it'll be: data = F, information = ICT AS result: F, knowledge = oh dear I seem to have failed.

Data, Information and Knowledge

Blimey — another two whole pages on data, information and knowledge? Jinkies — this must be your lucky day! Just kidding. It's all good stuff though, so dive in and make with the learning. "If it hadn't of been for those pesky examiners..."

The Data Cycle — Input, Process, Output, Feedback

A **data cycle** is the **overall process** of information being converted into data, input into a computer system, processed, stored, output and converted back into information.

Make sure you **understand the diagram**, and go through the example below carefully so you're clear on all the stages.

<u>Example:</u> *Recording a sale at a supermarket using EPOS (Electronic Point of Sale)*

```
            ┌─────────────┐
            │   Feedback  │
   ┌────────┴─────────────┴────────┐
   │            Data               │
   │  ┌──────┐ ┌───────┐ ┌──────┐  │
 ──┼─▶│ Input│▶│Process│▶│Output│──┼──▶
   │  └──────┘ └───────┘ └──────┘  │
   └───────────────────────────────┘
              Information
```

A. **Data is entered at <u>input</u> stage.** *e.g. Barcode is read and validated.*

1. **Information** is converted into **data** before it is input. *Product details (name of item, size, manufacturer etc) are given numbers.*

2. The **data** may be converted into a **coded form**. *A barcode is produced from all the bits of data, including a check digit.*

3. The data is **input** (scanned) and **validated** (checked) to make sure it has been read correctly. *The barcode's check digit is recalculated and compared to the original: if there is an error, the reading is rejected.*

B. **The data is <u>processed</u> by the computer.** *e.g. Product details are found, stock level is updated.*

1. The **data** is **compared** to a **database** of items. *The barcode is found in the product database.*

2. Data from the database is **read** and **stored temporarily** in RAM. *The product details and price of the item are found.*

3. The data in the database is **updated** and **checked**. *The record of how many items are in stock is reduced, and a check is carried out to see if the product needs reordering.*

4. The **data** stored in RAM is **processed**. *Total bill is calculated after all the items have been scanned.*

C. **The processed data is <u>output</u>.** *e.g. an itemised receipt is produced and items may be reordered.*

1. The **results** are **communicated** to the user. *The total cost is displayed on the till screen and a printed, itemised receipt is produced for the customer.*

2. The **results** may also be **stored** permanently (e.g. hard disk, CD). *The customer's purchases may be stored for analysis if they have a loyalty card. Details of items that need reordering are stored temporarily and then checked at the end of the day.*

3. The **information** obtained at the output stage might then be used as **feedback** to **input** more data.

Information Takes Many Forms When Saved as Data

1. **Recorded Facts**

   e.g. a company worker has an employee number of 475 which is stored as data in his record in the employee database.

2. **Events**

   e.g. Mr. Jones borrows a book from the library and the book number and borrower number are stored together with the return date in the library database.

3. **Transactions**

   e.g. Jim goes shopping and the supermarket takes £35 from his bank account to pay for the items — this transaction is recorded as a debit and Jim's bank balance is reduced by this amount. This transaction is stored in the bank account database.

Data can be Coded

1) When information is entered as data in a computer it is often stored in a coded form.

2) For example, when entering a person's gender into a database it is usually stored in a one character field as either 'M' or 'F'.

3) Other examples of coding that could be used in a library database are in this table:

Information	Data (in code)
Gender	'M' or 'F'
Membership Type	'F' (family) or 'I' (individual)
Book Status	'L' (on loan) or 'A' (available)
Barcode	'1 78082 645 3' (contains product details)

Data, Information and Knowledge

Advantages of Coding

1. **Less memory** is needed to store the data (e.g. M rather than Male).
   2. It's **quicker** and more convenient to enter a code.
      3. Data entry can be **validated** more easily, to make sure that the data input is reasonable.
         4. Coded information can be more **private**, especially for sensitive information.

Disadvantages of Coding

1. It may be difficult to **remember the codes** (though a drop-down list can be used as a reminder).
   2. **Accuracy** may be lost when coding the information (e.g. giving grades for work instead of percentages).
      3. Some codes are difficult to **understand** (e.g. a barcode).

There Can be **Difficulties** with Coding **Value Judgements**

A "**value judgement**" is a judgement made by an individual person.
Coding information that comes from value judgements can be difficult,
because they **aren't mathematically precise**. For example:

1) An Internet researcher (Clive) has to give websites a star grading (from 5 stars to 1 star),
   depending on how user-friendly he thinks they are.

2) This can make it easier for users to choose sites to visit, as they can see which ones did better than others.

3) BUT, different researchers are likely to have different views about each site,
   and give ratings which are different to Clive's.

4) Clive's personal response to websites isn't enough for users to go on.
   It would be better to get a panel's response or a vote from all the users of that site.

Practice Questions

Q1 Draw a data cycle diagram and label it fully.

Q2 Give TWO advantages and TWO disadvantages of coding data.

Q3 Why is it difficult to code value judgements?

Exam Questions

Q1 Data collected using a questionnaire needs to be stored and processed.
   Before this happens some of the data is coded.

   a) Give three reasons why data may be coded. (3 marks)

   b) For each reason, illustrate it with an example from a typical questionnaire. (3 marks)

Q2 Using the example of data collected from a questionnaire,
   explain these three parts of an information processing system:

   a) Input of data. (1 mark)

   b) Processing of data. (1 mark)

   c) Output of data. (1 mark)

If you've got a code, buy an extra large box of tissues...

The data cycle diagram on the opposite page is a pretty fundamental concept in ICT — basically, every ICT system in the whole world... ever... can be looked at in this way (well, pretty much). It's going to crop up again and again and again and again and again throughout the course, so make sure you really understand it. Anyway it's lunchtime now so I'm off for a pie.

Value and Importance of Information

Information is data put into a context. "Yes yes yes" I hear you cry, we only covered this a couple of pages ago. Well, there's no harm in repeating things now and again, especially if your head is made of sand and blancmange like mine is.

Information Can Be Valuable

1)   All information is **valuable to someone** (even utter rubbish can be of interest to somebody random).

2)   Some information is **valuable to everyone**.

3)   The better the quality of the information, the more valuable it becomes.

There is life beyond ICT. That strikes me as very valuable information.

Information Needs To Be Of Good Quality

Information is of **good quality** if:

1)   there is enough of it to help people **make decisions**.

2)   it is **accurate** and **up-to-date**.

3)   it is presented in an objective way that **can't be misinterpreted**.

4)   it is **relevant** to the person who wants to use it.

5)   it is **easy to understand** and isn't buried in loads of useless information.

The classic example is the Internet — there's massive amounts of information on the Internet, but so many hours can get wasted sifting through web pages till you find some quality information.

The Data Protection Act Tells Us When Information Is Illegal

Information is illegal (under the Data Protection Act 1988) if it is:

*   sold or passed on **without the permission** of the person/persons it is about.

*   used for a **different purpose** than it was collected for (e.g. medical information might be collected legally for health records but it becomes illegal if it is sold and used for insurance purposes).

*   **inaccurate** where this could damage the reputation of a person or organisation if the facts are wrong (e.g. if information held about you stated that you have a criminal record when you don't, and it stopped you getting a job or a loan, this data would be illegal).

Information can also be **obtained illegally**. E.g. a hacker might access bank records in order to commit fraud, or personal records in order to blackmail someone. The **Computer Misuse Act** covers this type of use.

Useful Information Can Fetch A Cracking Price

1)   A CD with files on it listing the contents of your cousin Jenny's bathroom probably isn't worth anything (depends on what's in the bathroom), but a CD-ROM containing very **recent**, **accurate** and **full market research data** could be worth thousands to any company that could use the information.

2)   A CD-ROM containing **old data**, with lots of **gaps** and **mistakes**, stored in a **hard-to-access format** might be worth not much more than the bathroom CD-ROM.

3)   Information can be **immensely valuable** to the right person, if it's **useful** to them.

Ensuring Information Is Valuable Costs Time And Money

Organisations keep information that is useful to them, but the information will often have a "use by date" after which it is **too old to be useful**. Time and money have to be invested to keep the information **valuable**.

1)   There needs to be enough staff to **update** the data.

2)   There need to be **security systems** in place to ensure that the data doesn't get changed accidentally or maliciously.

3)   There needs to be **enough storage space** for the data.

4)   There needs to be effective software to **manipulate** and **organise** the data into **useful information**.

Value and Importance of Information

You Can Have Too Much Information

1) Information moves around the world fairly easily these days, but some of it is **uninvited**.

2) We have **junk mail** posted through our letterboxes every day. Similarly, we get **unsolicited emails** (**spam**) in our mail boxes.

3) Spam **slows you down** as you try to separate it from the **useful information**.

4) The **Mail Preference Service** was set up to help people **remove their names** from mailing lists.

5) ISPs and e-mail providers offer **similar services** for reducing the volume of spam you receive.

Good Quality Data Is Reliable, Accurate, Up-To-Date, Complete And Precise

1) Information is produced by **organising data** in such a way that **meaningful** and **useful facts** can be gathered. The **quality** of the information depends on the **quality of the data**.

2) Reliable data is **collected from the right sources**. E.g. it's no good getting data on credit card usage from kids, nor is it always useful to ask for opinions rather than facts, as these are really hard to measure and record.

3) Accurate data is **recorded** exactly as it is and is **protected from being changed** accidentally or maliciously.

4) Up-to-date data is **recorded at intervals**. E.g. surveys on shopping preferences must take place regularly as shopping trends change with the time of year. If winter data is used to influence decisions to be taken about summer stock, the shops might be full of winter clothes in the summer. Just imagine the horror.

5) Data is **complete** when **all aspects are included** and **all possible sources are used**. E.g. a survey of five people is not as complete as a survey of 500, and any survey where many questions are left unanswered will give inaccurate results.

6) **Precise data** has **no possible alternative interpretation**. E.g. the recording of someone's weight is precise if it is measured, but the recording of how much they think they weigh is likely to be inaccurate.

Practice Questions

Q1 Describe four characteristics of good quality information.

Q2 Give three examples of illegal information.

Q3 Give one example of information that could be valuable to a company.

Q4 Describe five characteristics of good quality data.

Exam Questions

Q1 A ski holiday company marketing new ski packages to Andorra in 2005 wants to decide which resorts to promote. The data they are using was collected in 2001.

   a) Give two reasons why the 2001 data might not be useful in predicting the popularity of resorts in 2005. (2 marks)

   b) Describe two of the costs that would be involved in gaining more up-to-date information on what skiers want from a ski resort. (2 marks)

Q2 A mail order company takes new customer details over the telephone. They need the full address of the new customers in order to set up an account. Rather than ask the customer to give their full address, they have bought a database of postcodes from which the address can be read. The customer only needs to give the postcode and door number to complete their address details.

   Give three advantages to the mail order company of using the database, rather than collecting the address information directly from the customers. (3 marks)

The answer to life, the universe and everything — that's valuable information...

...and I just happen to know the answer. And before you say "42! 42! 42!", it's not 42. But I'm not sure whether it's appropriate for me to exclusively reveal to a group of ICT students information of such incredible staggering importance... Oh go on then, here it is — "love". Isn't that nice? Does it give you a warm feeling inside? It's not really that, it's 46.

Capabilities and Limitations of ICT

While it's important to learn specific details to impress examiners with, you need to have an overview too. These two pages will go over the general capabilities and limitations of ICT. You know, things like "makes noise but not jam"...

ICT Systems Can **Create**, **Process**, **Store** and **Transfer Data**

1) ICT, basically, is the use of technology to **create**, **manipulate**, **store**, **exchange** and **transfer** data in a variety of forms (including textual, graphical, audio, video).

2) ICT systems include all types of **computerised systems**, **telephone systems** and **mobile communications systems**.

3) The term ICT refers to the **hardware**, the **software** and the **data** that make up the system.

4) ICT systems **process vast amounts of data** and **produce information** that people can use to make decisions.

ICT Systems Can Do Lots Of **Useful Things**

Browsing for goats at Amazon — what else?

You can store vast amounts of data using ICT

Large ICT systems are capable of **storing millions of items of data**. E.g. online stores (e.g. Amazon or Waterstones) keep databases of thousands and thousands of books and other items. The UK census is now being stored for access online. The census database holds data about millions of people in the UK.

You can transfer data quickly and easily

It's estimated that in 2005 over 35 million people will use the Internet to **access vast amounts of stored information**, **communicate** with each other and carry out a number of **online transactions**. Mobile telephones are capable of accessing web pages, sending and receiving e-mails, text messages and pictures as well as allowing us to communicate verbally. **Fast transfer of data** means **better access** to shared information. Communications systems allow live transmission of news from anywhere in the world, using satellite phones, video links and webcams, which means that news coverage can be broadcast from anywhere as it happens.

ICT systems can give instant feedback on the data they store

Being able to **give instant feedback** makes ICT systems **very efficient**. E.g. **stock control systems** keep track of how many of each item is in stock. As soon as the level drops below a specified limit a reminder is produced so that a company can decide to re-order the item. Another good example is **electronic funds transfer systems** — they allow electronic transfer of money between accounts instantaneously. If someone tries to buy something and they don't have the money in their account, an electronic funds transfer system will report this immediately and a shop can decide to cancel the transaction and not sell the item to the customer.

You can get useful information from combined data

ICT systems can be given specific items to look for, and can **retrieve** these and **combine** them with other items to **produce useful things** such as lists, invoices or mail-merge letters. E.g. you can search a book shop database for all books by a particular author. You can choose different books from the list you're shown, and the system will gather all details to create an order and an invoice for you.

ICT can carry out repetitive processes

ICT systems can carry out repetitive processes like **calculating figures**, **producing lists** or **controlling devices** over and over again without making mistakes or needing a break. E.g. a banking ICT system updates all changed accounts at the end of every day and produces a statement for every customer at the end of each month. Factory robots carry out repetitive tasks such as spraying cars or fitting components on to circuit boards.

Capabilities and Limitations of ICT

But, ICT *Has Its Limitations*

Sometimes the hardware isn't up to the job

1) You can only **store** as much data as the **system has disk space for**.
2) The **speed** at which the system can retrieve and process data depends on the **speed of the processor**.
3) **Hardware failure** can cause loss of data and **disruption** to the whole system.
4) When you need to transfer data quickly, the **connection type** will govern the speed (Broadband is much quicker than a standard dial-up connection for Internet access).

Information provided by ICT systems is only useful if the software processes it effectively

If the software is **badly written** it can mean:
1) It doesn't **retrieve** the data in an **efficient** way.
2) It **can't organise** the data in a way that can be **understood** or is **useful**.
3) It **can't control** what data is entered.
4) It **can't back up** the data safely.
5) It **has bugs** which can cause the system to crash and lose data.

There can be compatibility problems when transferring data

1) **Different types** of hardware and operating systems **store and deal with data differently**, so one machine may not be able to deal with data sent from another machine. For example:
   - **Apple Macs** are different from **PCs** and process data differently.
   - **Spreadsheet** packages often can't open a database file and vice-versa.
   - Many companies now give their employees **laptop computers** with **wireless** capability so that they can work anywhere using e-mail and the Internet. But as many different types of wireless technology have emerged (Wi-fi, 3G, GPRS) a worker will only be able to use their laptop where the right type of wireless access point is available.
2) The **Open Systems Interconnection model** (OSI) was designed to help ICT systems developers work to a common system so that all ICT systems are able to communicate with each other.
   - When you send and receive e-mail, for example, it doesn't matter what type of computer or device you are using or what e-mail software you have in order to be able to send and receive.

Practice Questions

Q1 List three general capabilities of ICT systems.
Q2 Describe two ways in which hardware can limit the effectiveness of ICT systems.
Q3 Describe two ways in which software can limit the effectiveness of ICT systems.

Exam Questions

Q1 ICT systems can input and validate data. Give three other examples of things an ICT system can do. (3 marks)

Q2 ICT stands for Information and Communication Technology.
Explain the term "Communication Technology" in this context. (2 marks)

ICT — but I'm limited by my inability to get near the kettle...

That's because all the other writers, editors, examiners and teachers are hogging it. Oh yes, it's a busy busy morning at CGP central today. The office is humming with activity, and some calming music is being piped in for us. The only down side is that I'm imagining it all and have therefore clearly gone insane after only one section. Oh well, on to section two then...

ICT in Industry and Manufacturing

This section will give your life a much needed dose of salty ICT goodness. Or, to put it another way, it will go through everything you need to know about ICT in the real world, in a very clear and straightforward fashion. Smashing.

Industry **Wouldn't Work** Without ICT

ICT is used in many different ways in manufacturing and industry, from initial design to control and ordering.

1) It is used in **administration** — e.g. payroll systems, clocking on and clocking off, communications (e-mail, telephone, fax), word processing and accounting, general office management and co-ordination.

2) It is also used to order and keep track of **raw materials** needed in the production process.

3) ICT is also used to create **designs** and **models**, and to **test** and **manufacture** them.

CAD stands for COMPUTER AIDED **DESIGN**	**CAM** stands for COMPUTER AIDED **MANUFACTURE**

CAD is Very Useful in the Production Process

CAD is used by manufacturers and engineers to **design** things that will be built e.g. toasters, cars, bridges, buildings. CAD is usually **vector-based** software, which is very powerful and often needs a lot of memory to run.

e.g. a factory production manager may use CAD to model the effect of a particular design on manufacturing schedules.

Benefits of CAD

1) CAD software provides **three-dimensional representations** of designs on a screen (even though basic design may have been done in two dimensions), which can be rotated to be viewed from any angle.

2) It produces useful **information** (e.g. data on parts lists, requirements for different materials and components, wiring schedules etc).

3) **Higher output** because time-consuming tedious tasks are removed (e.g. many calculations are done by the software).

4) CAD software can **create simulations** which help **test** how the product will perform (e.g. in car plants, CAD can simulate car crashes in safety tests).

Drawbacks of CAD

The down side is that professional CAD systems require **complex, powerful** and **expensive** hardware, and the users need to have a lot of **training**.

CAM is when the Machines are Controlled by Computers

If the machines used in manufacturing or testing are controlled by a computer, it is a CAM system.

Benefits of CAM

1) Production of parts is faster and more reliable because machines do not get ill, go on strike or have a bad day.

2) The quality is more consistent.

3) Production can continue day and night, so output is greater.

4) Some difficult or unpleasant jobs can be done by robots.

Limitations of CAM

CAM machines are designed for particular functions, and though they can be programmed (e.g. to cut at a different angle) they cannot be switched between totally different tasks.

Robots / Robotic Arms can do Nasty Jobs for us

- **Dangerous** e.g. involving the use of explosives, welding, working with chemicals, monitoring radiation, cleaning up contamination.

- **Unpleasant** e.g. where working conditions are poor and uncomfortable (e.g. cold or wet).

- **Boring** e.g. jobs which need continuous repetition of tasks (e.g. working on an assembly line).

- Jobs that require **physical strength** e.g. lifting heavy car parts, putting piles of newspapers onto palettes or loading and unloading machines.

- Jobs that need **fine motor control** for example assembling watches or computer microchips.

- Jobs where **delicate objects** are handled. (e.g. Robots are used by Sainsbury's to test whether their aubergines are ready for eating.)

I'll get you for this...

ICT in Industry and Manufacturing

CAD and CAM have Changed People's Jobs

CAD and CAM systems (particularly CAM) have affected many workers all around the world.

1) Many jobs have become **automated** and are either fully or partly carried out by machines. For example, in the car industry, all spray painting of cars is now done by robots.

2) Some jobs have **changed**. The workers produce the **same goods** in a **different way**. For example, where a draughtsman used to produce drawings using pencil and paper, now they use CAD.

ICT in Industry — Positive Points for the Workers

- Sometimes using ICT can make a job **more interesting and efficient**. For example, a draughtsman can use CAD software to produce a drawing and then experiment **easily and quickly** by making changes to find the best solution.

- **New jobs** are created to design, produce and control the machines. (Many of these new jobs are not in manufacturing, but are more likely to be, for example, in IT support).

- Although retraining is often needed when humans doing manual jobs are replaced by robots, **gaining recognised qualifications** can improve workers' employment and salary expectations.

ICT in Industry — Negative Points for the Workers

- Some workers are **too old or uneducated** to adapt to new working practices. Others may **live too far away** from new employment opportunities.

- Some communities which grew up around a manufacturing industry have become 'ghost towns' because people have moved away to find new employment.

- Many industries have become completely **dependent** on ICT. If the ICT fails, the industry cannot go on until the problems have been fixed.

- Some workers **do not like change** and are unhappy with being forced to change the way they work.

Practice Questions

Q1 What do CAD and CAM stand for?

Q2 Describe two different ways CAD is used in manufacturing and industry.

Q3 Give three benefits of using CAD in manufacturing and industry.

Q4 Give four examples of the sorts of jobs robots are used for.

Exam Questions

Q1 Describe, by means of examples, the ways in which the introduction of ICT into manufacturing and industry can eliminate some jobs, transform others and create some new jobs. (6 marks)

Q2 ICT has brought benefits to a number of different areas.
Give two uses of ICT in manufacturing companies and describe the benefits that can be gained. (4 marks)

I want robot arms that will do my homework...

CAD and CAM can get pretty complicated. The good news is that examiners don't want to know if you're a trained CAD system operator. What they want to know is that you understand the processes at work in industry and how they affect the workers. Examiners also want to know how to make their drab, loveless lives better, but that won't help your ICT exam.

ICT in Commerce

Most money transactions, especially purchasing goods and being paid a salary, now get carried out electronically. So, here's a little tip: sticking a tenner in a CD drive won't help you buy stuff off e-bay, though it makes a great noise.

Customers Can Get Cash Any Time

1) In the old days we used to have to carry cash around all the time. If the banks were shut when we ran out, it meant we had **no access** to money and no way to pay for things.

2) Now we have **credit** and **debit cards**, and most banks and supermarkets have **ATMs** (Automatic Teller Machine — i.e. cash machines) so we can get money **at any time**.

3) ATMs have a magnetic reader to read the **magnetic strip** on the back of the card. The user types in their **PIN** (Personal Identification Number), to **verify** that they are the account holder.

4) '**Chip and pin**' cards (which contain an embedded chip that is read) are now **replacing** magnetic strip cards in Britain, although they have been in use in other countries for many years (e.g. America, France).

Customers No Longer Rely on Cash

Cash is readily available, but there are also more options to pay electronically, so we're becoming a **cashless society**.

 Credit and Debit Cards

These allow users to buy goods directly without using cash.

Data identifying the card is read using the embedded **chip** (or the **magnetic strip**).

Money is removed **instantly** from the customer's bank and put in the shop's account, so no physical cash needs to change hands.

These transactions are called "Electronic Fund Transfer" (**EFT**) or "Electronic Fund Transfer at Point of Sale" (**EFTPOS**)

Cheques

These allow users to pay for goods directly without using cash.

UK cheques have a line of **magnetic ink** on them which contains the cheque number, account and sort code information.

This data is read using **MICR** (magnetic ink character readers). The cheque then takes up to 7 days to be verified or "cleared".

Direct Debit and Standing Orders

These are used to pay bills on a regular basis.

They directly **link** individual bank accounts to the company that needs to be paid.

Standing Orders — you tell the bank what to pay.

Direct Debits — you authorise an outside company to ask your bank account for payment.

 BACS (Banking Automated Credit Systems)

This is used by most companies to pay employees' **salaries**.

Employees receive a **payslip** but **no paycheque**, as money is transferred into their account electronically.

An electronic file of the company's payments is produced and transmitted to **BACS** who process the payments on behalf of the company.

This makes the whole process more **efficient**, with less likelihood of delay or loss/theft of money.

Utility Bill Cards

Rather than pay a bill all in one go, users are able to pay a **little bit** at a time.

The user transfers money from his account onto the card. Money is gradually taken off the card by the company providing the utility, as and when that utility is used.

As the amount of money left on the card gets smaller, the user then has to **"top up"** the card with money again.

Online and Telephone Banking

Users can pay bills and view accounts from their **own homes** using the Internet, digital television or telephones.

 Smart Cards

They look like credit cards, but instead of having a magnetic strip which can be read for identification, they have a **chip** inside them which can talk to a computer. The chip can record and store new information.

e.g. some credit cards, health cards, government ID cards

Being a Cashless Society has Advantages and Disadvantages

Advantages	Disadvantages
No need to carry cash	Some transactions incur administration fees
Can shop from home by phone, digital TV or the Internet	Many traders unwilling to install expensive equipment
Less chance of being mugged	Some people prefer cash
Less money in the shops and banks to be stolen	Cash sales are usually quicker
	Security problems with sending money electronically

ICT in Commerce

Loyalty Cards Help Supermarkets to Target their Customers

1) Most supermarkets now issue **loyalty cards** to their customers.

2) The supermarket uses loyalty cards to **keep an eye** on their customers. Every time a customer uses their card, the details of every item bought are recorded (e.g. where, when, in what quantity and how it was purchased).

3) In this way the supermarket can build up a picture about the **spending habits** of their customer base. It can then target individual customers by encouraging them to buy products that match their **shopping profile**.

4) Every purchase gives the customer **reward points** which can be **redeemed** later on for money off or free products. The supermarket can use this to **boost sales** of certain products by offering extra reward points on them.

A "One Card" Society Could Be On The Way

1) At the moment we use lots of **different cards** for different things which is confusing because so many of them can be used in different ways. A plan has been formed to replace all these different cards with a **single card**.

2) The main **problem** with only having one card is that if you lose it or it is stolen, then you **lose your identity** and it becomes much easier for a stranger to get access to all of (not just one area of) your finances.

On-line Shopping is Getting More and More Popular

This allows the user to shop for goods from their home using the **Internet** and **digital television**.

Advantages	Disadvantages
Can shop from home and shop worldwide	Must have access to a credit/debit card
Wider range of goods available	Problems with security/fraud (e.g. people using your credit card details, or unreliable sellers selling products that don't actually exist)
Can often shop around quickly and find better deals	Cannot physically handle the goods until delivery

Practice Questions

Q1 What is meant by a "cashless society"?

Q2 Give an advantage and a disadvantage for a customer of having a supermarket loyalty card.

Q3 Give an advantage and a disadvantage for a customer of shopping on-line.

Exam Questions

Q1 Jago's Surf Shack (a chain of surf clothing shops) has decided to set up an on-line store.
   a) State two advantages for the chain owner of using the on-line store instead of the actual shop. (2 marks)
   b) State two advantages for the customer of using the on-line store instead of the actual shop. (2 marks)
   c) State one disadvantage for the customer of using the on-line store instead of the actual shop. (1 mark)

Q2 A local building society branch has just installed a new Automated Teller Machine (ATM).
   a) State one advantage for the building society of installing an ATM. (1 mark)
   b) State two advantages for the branch's customers of the new ATM. (2 marks)

Q3 A nationwide chain of bookshops has an automatic ordering system between their stores and their warehouse.
   a) Give two advantages for the bookshop chain of using an automatic system. (2 marks)
   b) Explain one advantage of the bookshop chain using an automatic stock control system for a customer. (2 marks)

"Cash in on revision tips for extraordinary results" — yeearg...

I'd be a lot less cashless if I had someone else's identity, I'll tell you that for nothing. Well, get learning all the ideas on these pages, as they're pretty important. If you can answer all the questions above then you're well on the way. Just be sure to remember cashless old me when you're rich and famous, having achieved stardom through extraordinary AS ICT results.

ICT in the Home

Home ownership of ICT devices is growing all the time. You should know about different kinds of ICT and how the use of all this ICT is changing home life. Not like my mum. My mum still thinks she can delete the Internet with one click.

More People are Using **Computers** at **Home**

In 2001, **more than two fifths** of all households in the UK owned a **personal computer**. This figure is growing all the time. The amount that computers get used in the home is also **increasing**. Typical computer use in the home includes:

- **Creating personal data** reliably, e.g. using address books, using spreadsheets to do accounts.
- **Storing information efficiently**, e.g. using computer filing to store documents, using e-mail folders to store important e-mails (such as registration details, or records of on-line purchases).
- **Finding information** easily on the Internet and CD-ROMs, e.g. cinema listings, research for schoolwork.
- As a **word processor** for typing documents, e.g. personal letters, coursework, creative work.
- **Designing web pages**, e.g. to display family photos, as part of a school course.
- **Communicating** with friends, family or others using e-mail, chat and instant messaging (e.g. MSN / Yahoo Messenger). This can range from plain text chatting, to using webcams and software that "speaks" to you, turning the other person's text into speech.
- **Downloading music**, e.g. sites such as Napster or iTunes allow users to legally download songs for a price.
- Used to **play CDs or DVDs** — can be a useful alternative when the telly's being watched by someone else.
- Doing **homework**, e.g. drawing graphs on a spreadsheet program, revising using revision CD-ROMs, researching schoolwork using the Internet, etc.
- **Playing games**, e.g. on-line or on CD-ROMs.
- **On-line shopping**, which lets users compare prices more easily than going round the shops and so can save a great deal of money, time and effort.
- **On-line banking**, which many users find more convenient as they can do it 24 hours a day, instead of relying on the bank's opening times and potentially wasting time queuing at their local branch.

More People are **Working From Home**

1) The number of people working from home is increasing as **communication links improve** (e.g. faster broadband Internet connections, fax machines that display received material digitally, rather than on paper).

2) Many people are able to do all, or large parts, of their work from home using e-mail, telephones, faxes and computers. This is called **teleworking**. In 2001, **7.4%** of all people in employment were **teleworkers**, and this number is **growing**.

3) Working from home means that **less time** is spent **travelling**, so there are fewer cars on the road which means less traffic and less pollution.

4) People working from home have the ability to choose their **own working hours**, are able to **avoid office politics** and also have the possibility of combining **childcare** with work.

5) However, problems can arise with **working conditions**, as many people cannot afford all the luxuries of a modern office, or else simply do not have a big enough space in the house set aside as an office.

6) It is also hard to keep **home life separate** from work life, and working from home can get a bit **lonely**.

Having a **Home Computer** has its **Problems**

1) Some children spend so much time in front of their computers that they don't learn valuable social skills and **lose the ability to interact** successfully with people face-to-face.

2) Unlike in an office, users are **unlikely to be trained** to use the hardware they've bought, and can have great difficulty setting up and using it.

3) Parents can feel **pressurised** to buy **expensive equipment** because they see computers as being able to help their children, and because they want to keep up with the Joneses.

4) A major concern is that **children** are able to **access unsuitable websites** (e.g. pornographic sites) and that parents **don't know** how to stop it happening.

"Baby no want bottle. Baby want 17 inch flatscreen monitor. Wah."

ICT in the Home

Computers are Not the Only Type of ICT Found in the Home

A **large number** of devices found in the home are driven by ICT.

1) **Mobile phones** have a built in microchip to control many functions, e.g. messages (texting), address book, alarm clock. Some include digital cameras.

2) **Games consoles** like the X-Box and PlayStation are powered by microprocessors and use digital media (CD-ROMs and DVDs) to play games, films and music.

3) **Video recorders, DVD** and **CD players**, **digital alarm clocks** and **watches**, **central heating systems**, **burglar alarm systems**, **home security lighting**, **home video cameras**, **microwaves** and many functions in **family cars** (including navigation systems) are controlled by microchips.

4) In **washing machines**, microchips and sensors work together to control the washing cycle. Some washing machines have a wide range of programs and more sophisticated ones allow users to download washing programs from the Internet (though that's just silly, frankly).

Good Things about ICT in the Home

1) It's easier to **select** and **control** the things you want devices in the home to do, e.g. you can set a digital alarm clock using a remote control and you can choose what kind of wake up call you want.

2) The use of **microchips** in devices has made some **cheaper to produce** (e.g. digital wristwatches) so they are available to more people.

3) Cheap technology has led to the development of many devices which can improve our **quality of life**.

Bad Things

1) When microchips break they cannot be repaired and need to be **replaced**. Sometimes it is cheaper to replace the **whole device**. This has led to a wasteful "throw away" society.

2) Some people find it difficult to **adapt** to new devices and prefer the old-fashioned ones they could understand easily.

Practice Questions

Q1 Describe three things that computers are used for in the home.

Q2 What are the main problems with using home computers?

Q3 Discuss the pros and cons of teleworking.

Exam Questions

Q1 A friend remarks, "We don't have a computer in our house. In fact our house is an ICT-free zone". Explain, using three examples, why it is unlikely that their house is entirely free of ICT.　(5 marks)

Q2 Many households now have Internet connections.

a) Give two examples of the ways children might use the Internet at home. For each example, discuss one benefit and one drawback of using ICT in this way.　(6 marks)

b) Give two examples of the ways adults might use the Internet at home. For each example, discuss one benefit and one drawback of using ICT in this way. (Use different examples, benefits and drawbacks.)　(6 marks)

Q3 The use of Information and Communication Technology (ICT) has brought benefits to a number of areas. State two uses of ICT in the home (other than the Internet) and describe the benefits that can be gained.　(4 marks)

I go to work at one, take an hour for lunch, then at two I'm done — I WISH...

Imagine, if you will, working from a tiny bedroom, typing for 20 hours a day just to make ends meet, with cats wandering around miaowing to be fed, and kids mooching about the place demanding their pocket money, and the trains that blast by so loudly, so LOUDLY, SO LOUDDARGGHHHHHHhhhh... Anyway, just make sure you can answer exam questions about it.

ICT in Education

Pretty much everyone uses ICT, from teachers to primary school kids to police officers. Which personally I find weird because in my day, teachers couldn't even work the remote control for the video. Does that still happen? Probably...

ICT is Used in Three Main Ways in Education

1) As a **tool**, to perform specific tasks (e.g. word processing, doing calculations, etc.).
2) As a **tutor**, helping students to learn new information (e.g. learning via CD-ROMs).
3) As a way to **manage, store and communicate information** (e.g. using databases to store pupil records).

ICT as a TOOL

- **Calculations and measurements** — calculators and spreadsheets save time on calculations and retrieval / display of information, graphing programs can produce graphs from numerical data, sensors and automatic measuring devices can be used in experiments, e.g. digital thermometers to record temperature.

- **Research** — classroom computers are connected to the Internet, which can be used as a source of information. E-mail allows pupils to share data and ideas with students from other schools.

- **Coursework / homework** — word-processing improves presentation and makes documents easier to edit, spreadsheets can be used to organise data and produce graphs for coursework reports.

- **Interactive display boards** — these can be used instead of a traditional blackboard to display computerised teacher's notes and presentations. The board is basically a large projected computer screen which can be controlled by moving and clicking a special pen on the screen.

ICT as a TUTOR

- **Teaching programs** on CD-ROM or the Internet can give the students information, or teach skills using games. Students try to answer questions and feedback from the computer helps students improve their knowledge.

- **Integrated learning systems** (ILS) give students their own specific learning programme, set to their own ability. Software (e.g. SuccessMaker) contains full details of the curriculum being followed and records a student's progress, as well as highlighting their learning needs so teachers and the Head of Year are aware of them. However, such software is very expensive and needs highly-trained staff to manage and maintain it.

Teaching programs are invaluable for **distance learning**. The student works from home, being taught directly by specially designed software for the course (e.g. on CD-ROM or the Internet). The student will also use ICT during the course to communicate with tutors and other students, e.g. via e-mail, electronic forums, chat rooms, bulletin boards.

ICT as a way to MANAGE, STORE and COMMUNICATE INFORMATION

- **Databases and computer filing** improves the efficiency of general administration, e.g. student's records can all be kept on computer for quicker access.

- **Communication** — e.g. e-mail / Internet increases students' ability to communicate with each other but also with tutors and people with specialised knowledge. Teachers can also put teaching materials on an Intranet.

There Are More Benefits Than Problems

Benefits	Problems
Students can use ICT in order to **present** their work more **neatly**.	ICT equipment is **expensive** to buy and needs experienced / trained staff in order to maintain it correctly.
Users with **special needs** are better catered for with ICT (e.g. more visual for students with hearing impairments).	
ICT can support many **different formats of teaching**, and so varies the ways in which students can be drawn into different subjects.	Hardware can be **unreliable** and breakdowns lead to frustration.
Some computer use (e.g. teaching programs) provides **immediate feedback** for students which is very useful.	Using ICT can mean that children **don't learn to do things by hand** (e.g. arithmetic and drawing graphs).
Sensors, measuring and calculating devices can help students better understand **mathematical concepts** in subjects like Science.	Use of the Internet in classrooms raises **security issues** (e.g. children accessing unsuitable websites).
Some applications **save a lot of time and effort** (e.g. CD-ROMs that teach French vocab are quicker and more efficient than using paper).	
Using computers often encourages **collaborative work**, so students learn to work together.	

ICT in the Police Force

The Police Force Uses ICT in Two Main Ways

1) Communication

Many different forms of ICT help the police force communicate with:

1) **itself** (on a local and national level) — e.g. file sharing between different regions, e-mail for national communication, walkie-talkies and radios for local officers to communicate quickly with each other.

2) **international bodies** — e.g. sharing information (databases, files, images) with Interpol to help catch criminals.

3) **the general public** — e.g. the police can home in on criminals by getting the public to provide information. Large numbers of people can be shown mugshots, CCTV footage and crime re-enactments on the television or Internet, increasing the chance of getting useful information.

2) Organisation

1) The police use lots of different databases e.g. for storing fingerprint and DNA data. **HOLMES2** (Home Office Large Major Enquiry System 2) is the main database used to pull all the information together into one place. **Details** of all crimes are entered into it and users can **search** and **analyse** the data.

2) Before HOLMES2 was introduced, police officers had to **sift** through large numbers of documents **manually**. Now, HOLMES2 helps officers to **keep track of evidence** and **reduce paperwork,** improving overall **efficiency**.

3) It lets **different forces work together**, providing one big HOLMES2 incident room instead of lots of small ones around Britain, and holds details of all electronically-tagged criminals, so they can be easily located.

Benefits of ICT for the Police

Quicker and more efficient solution of crime:

Faster response times through improved communication.

Quicker at retrieving / sharing information from other agencies.

Forensic investigations more thorough with better technology (e.g. more precise scanning equipment retrieves more evidence).

Improving crime prevention (e.g. CCTV, burglar alarms).

Problems with ICT for the Police

ICT equipment is expensive

Equipment can be unreliable

Hacking is a constant danger — high security is needed so that investigations can't be compromised

Practice Questions

Q1 How does the Internet provide learning opportunities for school children?

Q2 Give three examples of how ICT is used in schools.

Q3 Give three problems of using ICT in schools.

Exam Questions

Q1 The Head of a school decides to adopt an IT package to track pupils' grades and achievements. The package will be used throughout the school.

  a) Identify three different potential users of this package. (3 marks)
  b) With the aid of examples, suggest different ways that each user could use the package. (6 marks)

Q2 The use of Information and Communication Technology (ICT) has brought benefits to many of the public sectors, such as education, medicine, industry and commerce.

  For both of the following, state two uses of ICT, and describe the benefits that can be gained. Your examples must be different in each case.

  a) Education (4 marks)
  b) Police (4 marks)

No Mr Holmes, please don't shoot me — I'm Holmes two...

Shucks. See, back in the good old days I was talking about in the intro, the police didn't know how to work videos either, let alone manage massively impressive databases of the gruesome and gore-tastic. Well, guess you'd better learn all this stuff, if not to improve your exam result, then at least to know what to watch out for when the rozzers are on your tail.

ICT in Medicine

You need to have a good idea of different ways ICT is used in medicine, and understand some advantages and disadvantages of its use in order to do well on these sorts of questions. Nick nak paddy wack give a dog a bone...

Doctors' Surgeries Rely Heavily on ICT

1) **Patients' records** are kept on a computer **database**, making them **quick to find**, **well-organised** and **legible**.

2) This also means that a **hospital** can get **almost instant access** to anyone's records.

3) The **appointment system** is **computerised** so there are fewer double bookings and misunderstandings.

4) If doctors have trouble diagnosing a condition, they can refer to an **expert system**:

> An expert system is an application that combines artificial intelligence with a database of specialist knowledge. A medical expert system can be used to diagnose conditions from a list of symptoms entered by the user. It is programmed with a set of rules that tell it how to analyse the information in its database and form conclusions. It gives the doctor instant access to a vast store of knowledge — much easier than using chunky reference books.

5) Doctors and pharmacists can also refer to **on-line databases** for the most up-to-date **medications** and advice about **prescription levels**. This is useful because all the information is kept in one place and **regularly updated**.

ICT Can Help Unwell or Disabled People at Home

Here is a selection of the many ways that ICT can help people in their homes:

1) Using **self-diagnosis tools** such as the NHS Direct web site (or one of a range of CD-ROMs), people can often **get advice electronically**. They will, however, often be directed to seek out the advice of a qualified doctor as well (e.g. self-diagnosis of a sprained wrist could lead to trouble if it turns out actually to be broken — delayed medical attention could result in permanent damage to the wrist or other complications).

2) **Vital signs monitors** can be used at home to measure things like blood pressure, temperature and blood oxygen level, making it possible to **monitor** patients with a chronic condition or those recently discharged from hospital.

3) **Body chips** (including a microprocessor, sensors or a wireless radio frequency device) can be implanted inside people to monitor and regulate blood pressure, heart rate and cholesterol. Internal pacemakers for the heart also include a chip. This means that people are able to **go on with their daily lives** more normally.

4) Disabled people can use **ECUs** (Environmental Control Units) to interact with and manipulate one or more **electronic appliance** (e.g. television, CD player, lights, fan, etc.). This can be done in different ways, e.g. **voice-activated equipment**, **special switch access**, a **computer interface** and **adaptations** such as X-10 units.

   The **BCS** (British Computer Society — www.bcs.org) does a lot of work in **raising awareness** of disabled people's ICT needs, and runs a support network.

> **X-10 units** act like remote controls for things that are already wired to a switch. E.g. one could be used to turn household lights on and off so that the user did not have to get up to use the switch.

5) Blind or partially sighted people can be helped by **Global Positioning Systems** (GPS) so that they know where they are. E.g. a GPS can be programmed to alert the user that the next bus stop is the one to get off at.

6) There are many ways in which blind or partially sighted people are able to use a computer.

   - Specialist **big screens** are available (up to 30 inches).
   - **Stickers** showing characters in **large print** can be stuck onto the keyboard.
   - **Magnification software** can zoom in on any part of the screen.
   - **Screen "readers"** use speech output to talk to the user and tell them what is on screen, and relay back what is being typed.
   - **Voice recognition software** is available as another way to command the computer.
   - **OCR** (optical character recognition) scanners can scan and "read" most printed text.

7) Many programmes are **subtitled** for deaf or hearing impaired people, and virtually all DVDs supply subtitles.

8) Deaf or hard of hearing people can use **hearing aids** which are custom programmed by a computer to match the person's hearing abilities.

   - An **audiograph** tests the patient's hearing by transmitting sound waves directly to the inner ear.
   - This is used to produce an **audiogram** (a kind of graph) of the test results.
   - The computer uses this information to **programme** the **hearing aid** to give the best hearing improvement.
   - The hearing aid can be **reprogrammed** at any time.

ICT in Medicine

ICT has Many Different Uses in Hospitals

Virtually all hospital **administration** is carried out using ICT.

1) All patients' records are stored digitally by local surgeries, and are shared quickly and easily with hospitals.
2) Patients' records are then **updated** following hospital treatment and returned to the surgery.
3) ICT is also used to **track bookings**, **create appointments**, **write letters**, **update databases**, **monitor stock levels** of medical supplies and equipment and to **order more** when needed.

Surgery is increasingly being carried out with the help of ICT equipment.

1) **Robotics** are used in some medical operations because they allow surgeons to **control their surgical instruments** and require only the smallest of incisions on the patient. The systems usually consist of:

> - Minute cameras that are inserted into the patient to send images back to the surgeon.
> - Surgical instruments mounted on a surgical arm.
> - A viewing console where the surgeon sits in order to manipulate instruments using joystick-like controls.

2) Surgery is also helped by **organ donation**. When an organ becomes available, medical staff consult a national **database of requests for organ transplants** so that they can then send it to the appropriate hospital.

ICT has various uses in hospital **wards**.

E.g. ICT helps nurses to **monitor** the blood pressure and heart rate of patients — input sensors collect data and send it to a microprocessor. If a **problem** is detected, an **alarm is sounded**.

ICT Plays a Big Part in Medical Research

1) Computer models can be used by researchers to **simulate** the effects of a new drug, virus or treatment on the human body.
2) Other researchers use a database of illness and conditions to **track trends** in the country and world wide.
3) ICT can also be used for **data collection** (e.g. using sensors to track temperature changes), data analysis (e.g. using a statistics package) and to present findings (e.g. using a graphics package to show results).

Practice Questions

Q1 Give three benefits of using ICT in doctors' surgeries.
Q2 Give three examples of ways ICT is used in medical research.

Exam Questions

Q1 a) What is meant by the term "expert system"? (2 marks)
   b) Explain how a doctor might use an expert system to assist diagnosis of ailments. (2 marks)

Q2 ICT-based systems exist that enable patients to diagnose their own ailments.
   Discuss the advantages and disadvantages of such systems. (6 marks)

"Doctor, Doctor, can you cure my acne?" — "I never make rash promises..."

Don't worry. The author of that gag has already been taken to the psychiatric ward for treatment. Well there's quite a lot on these two pages, isn't there? This stuff gets quite tricky and technical in places, but it's really important for you to know. You can see from the practice exam questions that some right nasty ones crop up on this subject, so get swotting now.

Information and the Professional

Whatever job IT professionals undertake, they must be able to show a number of other qualities as well as technical skill if they are to succeed in their careers. **Skip these two pages if you're doing OCR.**

There are **Certain Qualities** you **Need** in Order to **Work** in ICT

Good written skills

All professionals must have **good written skills**, as they enhance communication and lead to better understanding. In an IT context, different professionals will need good written skills for different reasons. For example:

- people working on a help desk would need to keep **clear and concise records** of all the problems that have been logged.

- systems analysts need good written skills so they can give users **clear documentation** on the system and make appropriate recommendations in an understandable way.

> In the exam you may be asked to describe qualities an IT professional needs. If you answer the question by writing about "communication skills" then you won't get as many marks as splitting this into good <u>listening</u> skills and good <u>written</u> skills.

Be able to communicate well orally

All professionals need to **communicate effectively**, and **oral** communication is a large part of that. For example:

- ICT helpdesk workers need to be **clear and direct** if giving instructions to users over the telephone.
- Computer programmers need to use more **technical terms** and "jargon" to discuss things at work with **precision**.

Good listening skills

The IT professional must also be able to **listen to users** and **co-workers** in order to find out what problems or instructions they have.

"...and we just CAN'T get it to record Hollyoaks."

Problem solving skills

The IT professional must be able to work in a **logical way** in order to solve problems. Although there are specific ways that specific problems may be solved, frequently they will need to attempt **different approaches** until they are certain what the actual problem is. Being **thorough**, **logical** and **systematic** is important for all IT professionals.

Approachability

Most professionals need to be **approachable** in order to make working with other people easier. For example:

- IT support professionals (in a large company) need to be approachable so users will **come forward** with problems.
- Programmers don't need to be approachable in the same way, but need to be **receptive to comments** from employers, and make superiors feel that he / she is willing to be approached with **feedback**.

Technical competence

The IT professional must have a **strong technical competence**. This may seem a little obvious, but there you go. Another way of putting it is "don't hire a monkey to do an elephant's job."

Patience

Solving IT problems is about **finding solutions** — there is not always an obvious answer or quick fix. It can be a frustrating and time-consuming process, so the IT professional must have the ability to be patient and calm.

Self-motivation

This is important in any job. IT professionals tend to need to be very self-motivated. For example:

- IT support professionals, whilst typically responding to direct queries, also need to take it on their own **initiative** to find and introduce new systems that will better serve the users in the future.
- Programmers can find themselves working on very long projects, and they need to keep themselves motivated in order to continue working on the same thing for such a long time.

Flexibility

Many IT professionals need to be flexible about **when and where they work**. Those providing IT support may need to travel frequently between different sites, while systems analysts may need to work out of office hours when there are no active users accessing the system. All professionals may be called upon to **work extra hours** in order to get a job done.

> You may be asked in an exam to explain what the different types of personal qualities are, or you may be asked to show the qualities required for a particular job. Remember to answer the question <u>in relation to the job named</u>.

Information and the Professional

It's Good To Have **Specific Examples** Up Your Sleeve

Now that you're clear on the skills needed to be a successful IT professional (and I'm SURE you're just dying to become one), have a think about some specific jobs, so you can put all these qualities together in an exam answer.

Help Desk Team Member — Doug   Age 26

Oral Skills

Doug needs to be able to talk to users on the phone. He needs to be able to listen to what their problem is, and then offer advice in a clear and concise way.

Written Skills

Doug will need to log the problem and its solution clearly for future reference.

Patience and Approachability

Doug needs to convey a sense of calm, especially if the user is panicking. The user needs to feel confident in Doug's ability.

Flexibility

Doug needs to think about the user's needs and ability level, and work with them in mind.

Problem Solving and Technical Skills

Doug needs to be able to find the fault in the system as described by the user and solve it.

Systems Analyst — Rachel   Age 31

Oral Skills

Rachel must be able to communicate in a way that is jargon free to the user.

Patience

Rachel needs to explain her findings clearly and patiently to users — they need to understand her conclusions and suggestions.

Approachability

Rachel will be working a great deal with the user and therefore she must be easy to talk to, and make it easy for the user to put trust in her.

Problem Solving and Technical Skills

She needs to be highly skilled and trained so she can observe the current system in operation thoroughly.

> Remember that the explanation is the vital thing in answering these questions — get all the qualities in your answer, but make sure you explain them properly and relate them directly to the job you're talking about.

Systems Analysts and Help Desk Team Members are pretty obvious ones to go for. Of course there's loads of other jobs you could have a think about too. Examples of these are: Computer Technicians, Network Technicians, Systems Administrators, Systems Engineers, Security Engineers, Database Administrators, Programmers / Developers, Webmasters, etc.

Practice Questions

Q1   List three qualities that would be needed by a person working in the IT industry.

Q2   Write an advert for an IT Help Desk Team Member's job, in less than 35 words, listing and briefly describing the qualities you're looking for in an employee.

Exam Questions

Q1   A company called "JP Direct" is recruiting a new member of staff for their support desk. The head of personnel asks the support desk manager to explain what personal qualities the right person for the job will need to have in order to be an effective worker. State, with reasons, four personal qualities that the manager would want a new employee to have.   (8 marks)

Q2   Virtually all companies now work with ICT systems. Many employ users who have little or no understanding of the ICT systems they are using, and who need help from IT professionals.

State two personal qualities that IT professionals should have that will enable them to help such people effectively, and explain why each quality would be needed.   (4 marks)

U nede 2 av gd ritten skilllz if u wanna pas yr xmz — bling bling innit...

Hm. Enough of that painful bling bling rubbish. These questions carry loads of marks — there's never been a question worth less than 4 marks on this topic, so it's really easy to pick up extra points. The questions are pretty similar, so learning the general concept means you'll be able to answer any question set on this topic. Ah — now I feel all warm inside...

The Internet

Hopefully the stuff on these two pages will be familiar already. If not, then where the blooming 'eck have you been? "If you're not jacked in, you're not alive..." That's right, I just quoted Buffy. You got a problem with that? Have you?

Various Things are **Needed** in order to **Connect** to the **Internet**

1) Most people access the Internet using a **computer**, although you can also use other devices e.g. WAP phones or digital television.

2) The computer needs to be **connected to the telephone line** in order to access the Internet. This can either be done with a **modem** or with a **broadband** connection.

3) A **modem** (modulator / demodulator) **changes the computer's digital signals** into the **analogue** signals used by the telephone line, and vice versa, making it rather **slow**.

4) A **broadband** connection uses a dedicated **digital** telephone cable, so there's no need to alter the computer's digital signal. This makes them **much faster** than using modems.

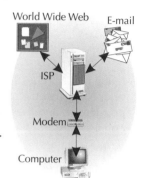

> The speed of an Internet connection is measured in <u>kilobits per second</u> — <u>Kbps</u> (i.e. how much data is transferred every second).

5) The user must also use an **ISP** (Internet Service Provider). ISPs are the companies that create a permanent link to the Internet (e.g. Freeserve, AOL, Demon, One.Tel etc...). They each provide different packages so that each user can choose the connection that's most appropriate for them (e.g. family packages, individual night-time only connections for people who work all day, different speeds and tariffs, etc...)

6) The **computer software** required to view Internet pages is called a **browser**. The two most popular browsers available are Internet Explorer and Netscape.

7) Depending on what websites users try to access, the browser will sometimes need extra pieces of software called **plug-ins** to enable them to watch movies or hear sounds. These are usually easily available to download from the Internet.

Web Page Addresses Are Made of Different Bits

Web page addresses are called **URLs** (Uniform Resource Locators). They're made up of various different parts:

www — **world wide web**. This means it's a website. The "Web" refers to the collection of pages / resources that can be accessed through a web browser like Netscape.

http — **hypertext transfer protocol**. This is the way data is transferred over the Internet. Most browsers will add this bit of the URL automatically.

cgpbooks — **domain name**. This is usually the name of the company that owns the web page (or a name the owner has chosen).

http://www.cgpbooks.co.uk/index.html

html — **hypertext markup language**. This is the programming language used to create most web pages.

co — this is the **domain type**. "co" signifies that the domain belongs to a non-American company.

uk — this is the **country** that the web address is held in.

index — this refers to the **page** that is **being viewed**. In this case, an index / introduction page.

Main Domain Types:	
gov	government site
com	business (mostly USA)
co	business (non-USA)
org	organisation (often a charity)
ac	academic — often a university
net	general, often business

Common Country Codes:	
uk	United Kingdom
ie	Ireland
de	Germany
nz	New Zealand
au	Australia
(if there's no country address, it's probably American)	

The Internet

Search Engines Help Users Find Information on the Internet

1) Today, information can be searched for and sifted through with **digital aid**. It is no longer done manually and laboriously, in person or over the telephone.

2) The basic bits of information that shape our **daily lives** (e.g. bus timetables, cinema listings, car prices, CD prices, holiday destinations, university courses, etc...) are now all just a quick click away.

3) **Search engines** help you find the information you need. They work by storing **details** or **keywords** of different websites. There are lots of **commercial** search engines available, but none of them covers the whole Internet (as it consists of over 3 billion sites) so it's often worth trying **more than one**.

4) The **basic search** is a **keyword search** — you type in a word and the search engine displays a list of sites containing that keyword. A **complex search** uses more than one keyword and links them with logic functions like AND and OR.

5) Many search engines will search for all keywords entered **by default** and have their own **settings** that you can select from (e.g. whether to show only english-language results, or whether to show only pages from the UK, etc...) — different search engines work in slightly different ways.

a search engine

©2003 Google

Intranets and Extranets are Used by Many Businesses and Organisations

1) An **intranet** is like a mini-Internet that runs over a **single organisation's network**. It uses the same protocols as the Internet and has similar facilities, e.g. web pages, but it's kept **private** and can only be accessed by **authorised users** (i.e. company employees).

2) An **extranet** is similar, but it allows people, e.g. external businesses and customers, to **connect from outside** (via the Internet). Users are given **passwords** so that they can access data on the company's **internal servers**. Extranets need **extra security** to stop external users from hacking in.

Advantages of Having an Intranet

1) The intranet can be **customised** to serve the company's needs most effectively.

2) Communication and data retrieval is usually **faster** as everyone is on the same network.

3) It cannot be freely accessed by external users, so the data stored there is **safer**.

4) Data can be **encrypted** easily when sent as everyone is on the same network.

Disadvantages of Having an Intranet

1) It **costs** a lot more to set up and maintain an intranet, than to just let users share files using e-mail or a local network.

2) Only certain users with **specialist knowledge** or training are able to amend or update the intranet.

Practice Questions

Q1 What hardware do you need to connect a computer to the Internet?

Q2 What is an extranet?

Exam Questions

Q1 At first, the Internet could only be accessed by using a personal computer. Name two other devices that can now be used to access Internet services. (2 marks)

Q2 Explain what is meant by each of the following terms:

a) browser

b) search engine (4 marks)

I've heard that the Angling Times needs an Extranet...

Ha haha haha. Cod, that's an awful joke. Well, just make sure you know your plaice — use this revision guide wisely and you're bound to do well. Follow the golden rules: don't get crabby, don't flounder, don't carp on about your troubles — that way everything will work out okay and you'll have a (wait for it) — a — a — a right, cracking, old whale of a time.

The Internet

The Internet has dominated the world of commerce, education and entertainment. It's constantly expanding, bringing many problems as well as benefits. So get your world-domination-problems-and-benefits-caps on and we'll get started...

E-mail is the Most Popular Use of the Internet

1) **E-mail** is used by a huge number of people today. According to IDC researchers, in January 2005 **35 billion** e-mails were being sent every day, and that number is getting bigger.

2) People can send **text** and **attachments** to another person with an e-mail account **via the Internet**. These attachments can take the form of **sound**, **images** and lots of **other files**.

3) E-mail accounts are often provided by the user's **ISP**, which is then normally accessed through their own computer. Most of these accounts will also have an option that lets users **access their e-mail remotely**, so they can access their e-mail on any on-line computer in the world.

4) There is also a huge choice of purely **web-based e-mail** available (e.g. Hotmail, Yahoo etc). Most of these will have an option letting users **forward mail** to an ISP account set up on their own computer.

Benefits of Using E-mail

- It's **fast**, as messages can be sent around the world in a few seconds.
- It's **cheaper** than posting or faxing documents.
- The same message can be sent to **lots of people** at the same time.
- The recipient **doesn't need to be on-line** when the e-mail is sent as it is stored centrally and can be retrieved later.
- Attachments can be sent **easily**.

Problems with Using E-mail

- The people sending and receiving the e-mails must have **their own e-mail accounts**.
- You need access to a computer that has the right software to use e-mail. These things are **expensive** if you don't already have them.
- Messages can get **delayed** by problems with the ISP or with the web-based e-mail provider.
- Messages can become **corrupted** during transit.
- Destructive **viruses** can be sent via e-mail.
- Users often get sent lots of **spam**, despite the filtering and other systems devised by e-mail providers to avoid this.

"Spamming" is when unrequested bulk e-mails containing commercial messages and adverts are sent out.

There Are Lots of Different E-mail Features

Create a message
This lets the sender compose a message to send to another e-mail address.

Send and Receive a message
This lets users send any messages waiting in their outbox, and also check if there are any new messages to download to their inbox.

Forward a message
This lets the user send the message to another e-mail address at the touch of a button.

Attachments
This lets the sender attach sound, pictures, videos etc. to the message.

Prioritising
Messages can be given a high, medium or low priority.

Groups
This lets you create a number of groups of selected addresses so that single messages can be sent to lots of recipients.

Carbon copy (cc)
This sends a copy of the e-mail to another e-mail address — all the recipients can see who it's been sent to.

Blind Copy (bcc)
This sends a copy to another e-mail address, but none of the other recipients realise someone else has been copied in.

Instant Acknowledgement
This lets you know the recipient has received the message. It can be manually or automatically sent.

Bulletin Boards and Weblogs Spread the News

There are other popular ways to communicate over the Internet besides e-mail:

1) People can place information on **electronic bulletin boards** for others to read (and sometimes comment on).

2) For example, a website like www.craigslist.org provides **listings** and **classified ads** for local communities. It's a free, non-commercial website that gives listings of everything from available jobs to pet dogs for sale.

3) **Weblogs** (or "blogs") are also becoming an increasingly popular way to keep an on-line diary or journal, letting users choose if they want to let everyone view their page, or just a select group.

The Internet

Money Changes Hands *Over the Internet*

1) Lots of people shop **on the internet** now. This is called **tele-shopping**.

2) It means customers can buy things from all over the world without leaving home, and companies can **reach a world wide market** with on-line shopping and e-mail facilities (see p. 13 to remind yourself).

3) Tele-shopping is becoming **increasingly popular** as companies continue to make money transactions **safer**.

4) **Tele-banking** is also getting more popular, although there have been some **problems** along the way.

By the way, I'm referring to "e-shopping" and "e-banking" as "tele-shopping" and "tele-banking" because that's what the examiners will call them. There. I'll be quiet now.

Example — The Embarrassment of Barclay's Bank

In 2002, Barclay's Bank had an embarrassing incident when they realised that people who logged out after using their on-line banking service could then access their accounts again just by pressing the "back" button on their browser. This meant that, if their accounts were viewed on a public computer, anyone could gain access to their bank details. Since then, on-line banking has been made much more secure, although stories like this still hit the news from time to time.

5) While some people are still wary of tele-banking, **companies** are using the internet more and more for money transactions because they think it's safer than transferring money physically.

Good Things About The Internet For Companies:

Can advertise and market their goods on-line, increasing their customer base.	Can communicate quickly with suppliers, staff and customers, including via e-mail.	On-line stores save money on cost of staff and of retail outlets.	On-line stores increase sales as they can be accessed by customers 24 hours a day.	**BUT these ventures can be tricky and expensive to set up initially and are at risk from fraud.**

Internet Crime is Hard to Crack

All sorts of crimes are being committed over the Internet:

1) **Fraud** e.g. faking information such as date of birth etc.
2) **Money Laundering** — i.e. transferring money illegally.
3) Targeted / organised **hooliganism** e.g. organising meeting places.
4) Spreading **viruses** e.g. via e-mail attachments.
5) **Copyright infringement** — i.e. downloading music illegally.
6) **Hacking** — i.e. accessing a computer system without permission.
7) Other criminal activities that use the Internet include **terrorism** and **paedophilia**.
8) Criminals who use the Internet have access to a **massive communication system** that lets them create a world wide operation.
9) It's fairly easy for them to hide under **false names / addresses** on-line so tracing them can be very tough.

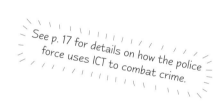

See p. 17 for details on how the police force uses ICT to combat crime.

Practice Questions

Q1 Give two advantages and two disadvantages of using e-mail over normal post.
Q2 What is "tele-shopping"?
Q3 Give three illegal activities that criminals use the Internet for.

Exam Questions

Q1 A friend remarks that they send all their letters by normal post. Suggest two reasons why they might consider sending e-mails instead. (2 marks)

Q2 Explain two ways in which a company can make use of the Internet and explain how each use could benefit the company. (4 marks)

I blog, you blog, he/she blogs, we bloog, you bleg (pl.), they blaggered...

Blog's such a stupid word, isn't it? Can't imagine Jane Austen keeping a blog. Or William Shakespeare. Course that could have something to do with how they didn't have computers back then. I did click on David Beckham's blog recently though, and all it said was "how do you turn this thing off?". So yes. Blogging. E-mail. Make sure you know it all. NOW.

Other Communication Systems

Now you've gotten to grips with the Internet, it's time to take over the animal kingdom... as my auntie Mavis used to say. These next pages look at some of the other ways we crazy things called human beans like to communicate.

Communication Systems are Taking Over the World

This handy blue table lists the **different communication devices** that are looked at on the next four pages. Learn the facts about all of them, as you never know what might crop up in an exam.

Grandma was very proud of her mod-cons.

Communication Device	Home / Personal Use	Office Use
Fax	✓	✓
Voicemail	✓	✓
Teletext	✓	✗
Viewdata	✗	✓
Digital television	✓	✗
Teleconferencing	✓	✓
EDI	✗	✓
Mobile / video phones	✓	✓
Remote databases	✓	✓
Telematics	✓	✓

Fax Machines Use a Telephone Line

The fax machine **scans** a document, **encodes** the data and **transmits** it down the telephone line to another fax machine.

Uses

Fax machines tend to be used in open offices and are used to send **non-personal documents** in business (e.g. invoices that originate on paper, pencil sketches / design ideas that are on paper). Some people still use them **at home**, particularly if they do not have a computer.

Advantages

A hard copy is immediately received by the recipient which **cannot be electronically altered** (very useful for legal documents).

Disadvantages

You cannot **receive** documents unless the fax machine is **switched on** and **connected** to the telephone line.

The **quality** tends to be poorer than in e-mail.

Copies can't be sent to **multiple recipients** in one go.

Problems with the **hardware** can cause delays (e.g. paper jams).

Voicemail and Call Routing are Useful

Voicemail (also called voice messaging) is a **computerised answering service** that automatically answers your call, plays a greeting in your own voice and records a message. After you retrieve your messages, you can delete, save, reply to or forward the messages to someone else on your voicemail system. This is very useful for individuals, or for small businesses who need to be able to record messages people leave for them out of office hours.

Call routing is used more often in bigger companies — it's a **digital answering service** that uses a **central storage system**. This means incoming callers can listen to the menu choices, press the **appropriate keys** for who they want to speak to, then be directed to the right person.

Some systems are more complex, e.g. the Odeon Cinema phone line lets you book tickets without talking to a human being, or some banks guide you through security checks and let you transfer money via an automated call routing system.

Call routing is an efficient, automated system which means **less time is wasted** on the telephone.
But, it is very **impersonal**, and callers can get stuck within **complex menus** when they have a query.

Transport Systems Give Information to Drivers

There are various different types of transport system that help give information to drivers quickly and efficiently:

1) **Matrix signs** on motorways warn drivers of delays and weather conditions.

2) Up-to-date information about traffic flow, accidents and weather can be **texted** to your **mobile phone** (though you'd need a passenger to read the information as UK drivers aren't allowed to use mobile phones in cars).

3) Sophisticated **in-car navigation systems** use GPS (Global Positioning System) and map data to pinpoint your location and can give you directions to your destination. They can sometimes access live traffic information from special transmitters to guide you around traffic jams. This is very useful but is usually pretty **expensive**.

Other Communication Systems

Good Old *Teletext* Still *Has Its Uses* — at the *Moment*

Teletext is the **television information service** that uses the spare lines on a TV receiver to receive a wide range of information based pages (e.g. TV listings, flight information, local events listings, horoscopes etc).

Uses

It provides a **public information system** in the home.

Advantages

It's **free**, assuming the user already has the correct type of television set.

It contains a lot of **information** and is **updated** very regularly.

Disadvantages

It's very primitive by today's standards — the graphics are poor and it can be **very slow** in downloading pages.

You **can't cycle through** blocks of pages manually, and have to wait for them to update themselves.

Pages can easily become **corrupted** due to poor signals.

Viewdata is the *Commercial Form* of *Teletext*

Viewdata is like teletext, but is found in **businesses**, not at home. It uses a **telephone connection** instead of spare TV lines. The data stored on a viewdata system is not general public information, but relates to a **specific company**.

Uses

It is used in business to **connect company offices together** or to give specific information about **company products** (e.g. Tote Racing, Thompson Holidays).

Advantages

The **speed** at which pages can be received is high and it is fairly secure.

Pages can be selected by number and / or via the menu.

More pages can be stored than on the teletext system.

Disadvantages

It uses the same chunky, **old-fashioned graphics** as the Teletext service.

Due to the telephone system the **cost** can be high.

The information it gives is **limited** as it only relates to one company.

Digital TV is *Taking Over*

Digital Television allows viewers to use the TV set as both a **communication device** and a way of **controlling what is seen**. Digital TV uses **satellite or cable technology**, although a simpler service can be used via the television aerial.

Uses

As well as watching TV shows, interactive digital TV also has **other features** (e.g. choosing which of the camera angles to watch a football match from). It can also be used to listen to the radio, carry out tele-shopping, tele-banking (and in the future, tele-voting) as well as accessing general information (like a more sophisticated teletext).

Advantages

It produces a **better quality picture** than analogue sets.

It provides viewers with **more choice**.

It allows the viewer to use the television as a **communication device**.

Disadvantages

It needs a **digital receiver** to decode the signal, some of which are really **expensive**.

Practice Questions

Q1   Give two disadvantages of using a fax machine.

Q2   Give two examples of transport systems that give information to drivers about traffic flow.

Q3   Give two differences between viewdata and teletext.

Exam Questions

Q1   Some car manufacturers have installed in-car information systems which can give up-to-date details of traffic problems across the country. Explain two benefits of having these in cars.   (4 marks)

Q2   By 2010, all analogue television services will be switched off in favour of digital television. Give three benefits of digital television over analogue.   (3 marks)

Video killed the radio star, and digital is sweeping the floor with analogue...

I think it's great that we're ditching analogue TV — digital's much better. I watched "Finding Nemo" with my baby brother and he actually tried to climb into the TV so he could go swimming. Actually, I take it back. I don't want digital TV, I want a swimming pool in my living room. By the way, learn everything on this page, 'kay? There's lots here but you need it all.

Other Communication Systems

Well, this has been a pretty short section. Just two pages left and there's nothing to it. Which reminds me, I saw Eastenders last night. There's nothing to that either, is there? They're just one step away from a plot involving aliens...

Mobile Phones are Really Popular Now

1) Mobile phones and videophones use **microwaves** to contact another mobile phone system.

2) Mobile phones have become massively popular, and as technology improves they are merging with other communication systems to create brand new systems.

3) However, phones have recently been **banned** from being used by car drivers when they're driving, as they distract the driver.

4) Video/camera phones have recently been banned from court rooms and examination offices to avoid illegal filming

Uses	Advantages	Disadvantages
They allow people on the move to **contact** others. Their use is extensive and world wide. **Features** can include digital cameras, WAP (Wireless Application Protocol) technology giving access to the Internet, and sound and video links to other phone systems.	They can be used **virtually anywhere**, by anyone who can afford one, as long as they are in an area where network coverage is available from their service supplier. They are **light** and easy to carry around.	It can still be more **costly** to send messages by mobile phone than with other devices. Many people are concerned about the possible long term health risks due to the radiation they give off. Messages can easily be **hacked**.

Teleconferencing and Videoconferencing are Very Useful

1) **Teleconferencing** is a way of connecting one set of users to another **over the telephone**, making it feel as though everyone is sitting round the same table.

2) **Videoconferencing** is very similar, but also allows the users to see each other.

Uses	Advantages	Disadvantages
They are mostly used in **business** to allow multinational companies to hold meetings with employees in different locations. **Home use** is also increasing, with web cams giving users visual communication as they chat on-line. An up and coming use is in education, where several schools can combine to have joint lessons with other schools. This reduces the need for specialist teachers and could result in classes of 200 or more — eek.	It saves on **travelling costs** as users don't need to meet at a common meeting place. Meetings can be held **at any time**.	**Expensive equipment** is needed. The technology is still **not perfect**, so synchronisation can be poor (especially with video conferencing). Even a good quality service is still no substitute for direct **human interaction** — sometimes it's difficult to feel people's moods accurately.

Teleworking Lets Employees Work From Home

1) In most companies, workers don't work alone — they need to **communicate on a regular basis** with other members of their team, or with **part-time** and **freelance** workers.

2) These days, many employees work from home and send their work to the office using ICT — this is **teleworking**.

3) They can communicate with fellow workers using a WAN and teleworking software.

Uses	Advantages	Disadvantages
Teleworking refers to the use of **any communication device** in order to transmit work to the head office, so it includes e-mail, ftp sites, fax, phone, webcams etc.	Employees working from home can work flexible hours and are often more **satisfied employees**. Companies require less office space, which cuts costs.	Workers can feel **isolated**, and lonely because of lack of personal contact with co-workers. There is no clear separation of work and home life, which some people find **stressful**. There are often more **distractions** at home, e.g. housework, children.

Other Communication Systems

EDI is basically a Giant Electronic Mailbox

1) **Electronic Data Interchange** (EDI) is a way of sending documents from one company to another, using a **telephone network**.

2) The sender's computer can talk to the receiver's computer, regardless of what machines or software are being used by both. EDI is an electronic mailbox, taking data straight off one computer and putting it on another.

Uses	Advantages	Disadvantages
This is used primarily in business to **transfer items** like orders, letters and invoices. It has also recently been used to transfer **exam results** from the examination boards to schools and colleges.	It's very **straightforward** and can transfer massive amounts of data at once. Nothing has to be printed off and posted, so it cuts down on **paper waste** and **postage costs**. It **cuts down on human error** — data goes straight from one machine to another and is processed on-line.	EDI software can be **too expensive** for small companies.

Remote Databases are used Mostly in Business

Remote databases allow users to connect to a company's database via a WAN (e.g. via the Internet).

Uses

You often connect to remote databases **through the Internet**, e.g. when you're finding train times and booking tickets, searching a library catalogue, buying theatre, cinema, plane tickets etc...

Remote databases are frequently used in **business**, (especially leisure and tourist trades) allowing customers to know exactly what is on offer and to have their booking confirmed straight away.

Advantages	Disadvantages
Since you connect directly to the database, the information is always **up-to-date** and you can make bookings **immediately**. It's **cheap** for businesses as it "cuts out the middle man".	There's always a danger of data being **hacked** as it is transferred to the computer system. When the database is open to many users (e.g. a website booking system), it's easy for **mistakes** to be entered and hard to **spot** them.

Practice Questions

Q1 Mobile phones have recently been banned from some public buildings. Give a reason for this.

Q2 What is "teleworking"?

Q3 Explain what EDI means.

Exam Questions

Q1 A sales representative for Puppet Publishing is working on her laptop in a hotel away from the office. Describe two ways in which she can use ICT to send a report to her office. (4 marks)

Q2 A firm of UK engineers is designing a new bridge with an American company. It has been suggested that the best way the two companies can stay in contact during the project is to use videoconferencing.

a) Explain what is meant by the term 'videoconferencing'. (4 marks)

b) Give two advantages and two disadvantages to the companies of using videoconferencing to discuss project progress instead of arranging actual meetings. (4 marks)

Have you seen ma wicked new phone? — Oh no, I forgot to bling it...

Well, bang goes another section — just make sure you know it inside out. It's pretty easy to pick up marks on these communications questions, as long as you know what you're talking about and don't wander off the point into a large hedge where there's a bird I used to talk to my friend Tracey about but she lives in London with my — oh look a penny.

Malpractice and Crime

Computer crime is very serious, and every year the "man" is finding more and more ways to crack down on people who abuse technology.

Computer Crime Is Any Illegal Use Of An ICT System

1) **Unauthorised access** to computerised information systems is an **offence**. If information systems are illegally accessed their data could be **altered**, **lost** or **used for illegal purposes**.

2) Computer crime is an increasingly big problem. Offences range from **malpractice** to **serious crime**:

- **hacking** into a system to **look** at its data
- **hacking** into a system to **destroy** its data
- **theft of data** from an information system
- **theft of money** carried out by transferring money electronically
- **theft of goods** by re-routing them
- **illegal use of software** by copying or using it on more machines than there are licences for
- **internet fraud** e.g. unsecure sites where criminals can get access to your credit card details
- **introducing viruses** into a system to deliberately cause damage

Malpractice Means Professional Misconduct

Malpractice means acting in an **unprofessional way**, that leads to **unauthorised use or loss of data**. For example:

- Staff might **forget to log off** or turn a workstation off, leaving it open for someone else to use.
- Staff might leave password details **lying around** somewhere easy for a criminal to find.
- Staff might access unsafe software or websites and **introduce viruses** which can destroy the data in a system.
- The organisation might not have a **good back up system** and if there is a problem such as a power cut or a system crash, they will lose their data completely.
- The information system itself **might have faults** that allow anyone to get in, in which case the malpractice would have been by the system developer.

  E.g. there was a case recently where a major bank's system allowed people to access other people's accounts.
- An organisation might **inadvertently process data** in a way that **causes distress or damage**.

  E.g. a sales system user might accidentally record a payment to a wrong account so one person seems to have paid too much and another too little. One customer will be asked for a payment they have already made and will be inconvenienced by having to prove it.

Computer Crimes Are Committed By Hackers and Crackers

A **hacker** is someone who uses their technical knowledge to **access a computer system without permission**.

- Some hackers might access a computer system **just to show that it can be done** (some companies employ hackers just to test the security of their systems).
- Some hackers access a system to **use the software**.
- Some hackers access a system to **read or copy the data**.

A **cracker** is someone who uses their technical knowledge to **crack codes**, like passwords and other encrypted data.

- Some crackers **find out a password** then pass it on to a hacker, or use it to access a system themselves.
- Some crackers **translate encrypted code** that was being sent from one system to another.

Trojan Horses Can Destroy A System

1) **Trojan horses** are programs that **seem** to be doing something **useful** but are actually doing something **malicious** in the background.

2) Hackers use Trojan horses to **get access** to a system while a user is doing **a particular task**.

Malpractice and Crime

Viruses Are Designed To Inconvenience Or Seriously Damage Systems

Viruses can **replicate themselves** and **change data** so that it becomes unreadable.

1) A **worm** is a type of virus that replicates itself throughout a system very quickly. E.g. the MyDoom e-mail virus comes as an attachment disguised as an undelivered e-mail and sends itself to everyone in the recipient's address book. Zafi-D is a worm that arrives as an e-mail and replicates itself by e-mail and through files on a local network.

2) **Logic bombs** and **time bombs** are small programs that become activated when the user does a particular thing, or at a particular time. They often cause damage to data or security systems. E.g. boot sector viruses are designed to activate when the system boots up, and the Friday 13th virus was designed to become active on Friday 13th.

Organisations Can Take Measures To Protect Their Systems

The weak points of an IT system are often **its users** and the **points at which it meets the outside world**. **Hardware** can also be a weak point if it is not regularly maintained or is not up to the job.

Things an organisation can do to help protect their ICT systems:

- Staff must **follow strict procedures** when accessing the system, including logging off properly, not disclosing their password, and not downloading from unsafe websites or using illegal software.
- Systems should have **strict levels of access** so that users can only change or view data if they have the right access levels.
- Having an **effective back up system** will prevent complete loss of data.
- Equipment like **uninterruptable power supplies** (UPS) help to ensure that complete **hardware failure is less likely**. Regular equipment maintenance also helps.
- Any data that is transferred within and outside the company can be **encrypted** so that it is not easily readable.
- The organisation can use **firewalls** — a combination of hardware and software that monitors all access to a system from outside, and so helps to reduce the risk from hackers.
- They can use **virus protection software** to detect and eradicate worms, logic bombs, time bombs and known Trojan horses.
- They can **protect the hardware** from physical theft or access using guards, locks, CCTV, etc.

Practice Questions

Q1 Give 5 examples of computer crime.
Q2 Define the terms "malpractice", "hacker" and "cracker".
Q3 What is a Trojan horse?
Q4 List 5 things a company could do to help protect its computer system.

Exam Questions

Q1	Describe three ways in which a company's staff can undermine the security of its information systems.	(3 marks)
Q2	Describe three ways a company can prevent malpractice in the use of its communications network.	(3 marks)
Q3	Give an example of an external threat to a system and suggest a measure that can be taken to reduce the threat.	(2 marks)

Crime doesn't pay — unless you don't get caught...

But seriously, it's not a good idea to indulge in any illegal activity. Prison's a pretty nasty place. I hear that Hitler's dog is there, and one of the Lassies is there (which one? the evil one...). Hang on. I'm actually just referencing an episode of the Simpsons where their dog is having an operation. How did I get on to that? What I meant to say was — this stuff is serious.

Legal and Ethical Issues

Well, this isn't a page for the faint-hearted. Of course, there's no weighty discussions of abortion or vegetarianism, but in ICT-land, this stuff is pretty important. The bad news is you have to learn it all for your exam, so get ready:

The **Internet** Is **Wide Open** To **Malpractice** And **Crime**

All potential malpractice and crime **needs to be dealt with** and can be **reduced** or **prevented** with appropriate measures:

Malpractice / Crime	Preventative measures
Introducing viruses (malpractice) Employees might access non-work related web sites at work and could introduce **viruses**.	Internet **filters** can block sites or monitor who is accessing what. **Virus protection software** can detect and eliminate viruses if they appear.
Hacking and cracking (crime) As data travels around the Internet it can be accessed by **hackers** and may be decrypted by **crackers**. Hackers might use logic bombs or viruses, embedded in web sites, to break through security systems and access or destroy data.	**Firewalls** installed between web servers and the Internet can provide some security from hackers, and **good encryption systems** might deter crackers.
Publishing inaccurate, libellous or offensive material (malpractice or crime) Information on the Internet is **not regulated**. Inaccurate, uncensored and potentially damaging information can be displayed to many people. Sites of this type often appear in search engine lists in response to different keywords.	This is tricky. The monitoring of web sites is a **potential answer** to this. The **Information Commissioner's Office** is a government department that will deal with any web site that displays data of this sort, if the creators can be traced.
Using the Internet to recruit for illegal groups (malpractice or crime) Illegal groups can use the Internet to **recruit** members from all over the world e.g. terrorist groups, groups engaging in organised football hooliganism and organised crime groups.	Again, **monitoring** by appropriate authorities is used.
Hiding your identity (crime) Users on the Internet are anonymous. An e-mail address is not based on a physical location and gives no details about the real person using the address. Users can give **false personal information** in order to commit fraud or other crimes e.g. paedophiles can use the Internet to groom potential victims.	**Publicity campaigns** warn people of the dangers of contacting people whose identities can't be verified. Internet **filters** in schools and at home reduce the number of places children can contact others.
Blackmail and stalking (crime) People can use the Internet for stalking or for blackmail because it is so easy to **communicate quickly and anonymously**.	**Publicity campaigns** and **filters** (see above).
Bogus web sites and credit card fraud (crime) Bogus web sites allow their developers to commit **fraud** by gathering personal and financial details. Credit card fraud is made easier by the Internet as the data can be hacked and card details decrypted.	**Public warnings** about the need to be careful when giving out sensitive data.
Money laundering (crime) Money can be moved electronically and transactions can be **very difficult to trace**. Stolen money can be made to look like it has come from a legitimate source.	**Monitoring** by the authorities.
Buying and selling illegal items (crime) The Internet can be used for buying and selling illegal items such as firearms.	Need for **monitoring**. It is sometimes possible to look at **cookies** to see which websites have been accessed by a particular user.
Illegal downloads (crime) Illegal **copying** of music, pictures, software.	Internet **filters** can block or monitor access to sites that offer free downloads of copyrighted material.

Legal and Ethical Issues

Internet Access Can Put Children At Risk

When children access the Internet they can be exposed to:

- **inappropriate material** including pornography, sites expressing extreme opinions, sites showing graphic scenes of violence, etc.
- **stalking**, when they use chat rooms and set up contacts with people who might not be who they say they are.

An **Internet filter** such as Net Nanny or Cyber Patrol lets parents and teachers block and monitor children's use of the Internet.

When children use the Internet extensively they can run up **very high telephone bills**. Schools will often make children sign an **Internet usage policy** and some may charge children by the minute for Internet access. These will also help to reduce the risk of children ordering goods on-line or maybe even running a business.

Bogus Web Sites Can Be Used For Fraud...

Bogus websites **look like official websites** but are really just a means of **getting personal information**.

1) Bogus financial websites exist that ask for detailed financial information while pretending to need the data to make a recommendation. This practice is called "**phishing**".

2) After the 2004 tsunami, a number of **bogus charity websites** appeared that collected money from unsuspecting users, supposedly for the relief effort.

...And So Can Auction Sites

Auction sites like eBay allow people to **buy and sell on-line**.

1) It is always **possible to falsify information** when using this type of site by giving a false address or telephone number.

2) eBay have policies to cope with this when it happens but it would be impossible to completely prevent it.

3) A falsified address might mean that once a sale has been made, a seller can't then get their money because they can't contact the buyer.

4) Also, on-line auctions let people **falsify information about what they're selling**. They can make things look better than they really are, give incorrect descriptions or might even be advertising non-existent goods.

5) There's no guaranteed safeguard against this — each user has to weigh up the pros and cons for themselves.

Practice Questions

Q1 List eight crimes that can be committed using the Internet.

Q2 Name two things that an Internet filter does.

Q3 Give three problems that are possible when children access the Internet.

Exam Questions

Q1 Describe two examples of Internet crime, suggesting how that crime can be prevented or reduced. (4 marks)

Q2 A school wants to start a lunchtime club allowing pupils Internet access. Describe three concerns related to giving children full access to the Internet. (3 marks)

Why did the criminal get lotht in Chelmthford? — he had trouble with Ethics...

Ethics — you know, like "Essex"? And Chelmsford is IN Essex? See? You see what I did there? Bah... My talent is totally wasted here... Anyway it could have been worse; I was thinking of making an Essex/Ethics girl joke. Hm. That would definitely be a little inappropriate. Speaking of Essex, make sure you learn all these details for the exam — it's important stuff.

Software and Data Misuse

Right then me hearties, time to knuckle down and learn a few specific legal things. No more of yer swashbuckling, timber-shivering parrot talk — I'm talking about real life, honest to goodness piracy. I mean computer crime laws.

The **Computer Misuse Act** Makes **Computer Crime Illegal**

If you hack into a computer system you can **read private data** or you could **copy or damage it**. Reading data isn't a serious crime like theft, but it is an invasion of privacy, and **laws are needed** to make sure that people don't do it.

1) General computer use grew during the 1970s and 80s, leading to **an increase in computer fraud** (e.g. stealing money out of people's bank accounts by changing data) and a new problem — **how to deal with deliberate access or damage to data**.

2) The term "hacking" became used for **breaking into someone's system without permission**. This is sometimes just people proving that they could beat the system for fun, but often it's to **steal** data or to damage a system.

3) **Prosecuting hackers proved to be very difficult** as existing legislation relating to theft, criminal damage and intercepting telecommunications **didn't cover hacking**. One such failed example was Crown v Gold where two journalists were acquitted of unauthorised access to the BT network in the 1980s.

4) This prompted a **Private Members Bill** that became law in **1990** — the **Computer Misuse Act**, which identifies three levels of offence:

Level 1 Offence: **Unauthorised access to computer material** — e.g. 'hacking' and piracy. This means viewing data you are not permitted to see, or illegally copying programs. The **maximum penalty** is **6 months** in jail or a maximum fine of **£5000**, or both.	**Level 2 Offence:** **Unauthorised access with intent to cause a further offence** — e.g. fraud and blackmail. This means gaining unauthorised access with the intention of committing a more serious crime (one that would get you a jail sentence of at least 5 years). It covers things like fraud, blackmail and deception. The **maximum penalty** for this is **5 years** in jail and maybe a **fine** too.	**Level 3 Offence:** **Unauthorised changing or deleting of files** — e.g. planting a virus. This means modifying or deleting the content of any computer with intent to cause damage to programs and / or data (including deliberately introducing a virus). This can get you a **fine** and up to **5 years** in jail.

In order to prosecute someone, it has to be proved that they:
- **intended to gain access** to data or programs
- **didn't have authorisation** to do so
- **knew and understood** that they didn't have authorisation

In 2004 a British university student was given 200 hours community service for the "unauthorised modification of computer data and impairing the performance" of a computer system at the US Department of Energy. The student had used their disk space to upload movies, software and games, which slowed down their system.

But There Are **Lots Of Loopholes**

Some legal experts believe that the Act is too full of **loopholes** to be a real and useful deterrent.

1) Organisations often want to **hide** the fact that there is a **problem with their security** from the public — revealing this could damage public confidence in them and harm their reputation. As a result, companies often **avoid** involving law enforcement agencies and instead deal with matters **themselves**.

2) It's actually quite **hard to prove intent** — it's easy for hackers to argue that their actions were accidental.

3) The Computer Misuse Act is now at least 15 years old and it was written **before** the Internet became so **widely used**, making it a bit **out-of-date**. The person to be prosecuted is often a citizen of a different country to the one the computer system is in, making the process very difficult and confusing.

The British university student who hacked into the US Department of Energy system was prosecuted under British law even though the system was American. The same won't necessarily apply to a foreign national who hacks into a British system.

Software and Data Misuse

The Copyright, Designs and Patents Act Covers Illegal Copying

This law makes it **illegal** to copy a file without **permission** from the owner or copyright holder. It was introduced in **1989**. Individuals and organisations who break this law risk an unlimited fine.

Here's the main ways the law gets broken:

1) **Using software without a proper licence.**

   e.g. if you have a licence to use a word processor on one stand-alone computer, but then you install it on all the machines in a network, you're breaking the law.

2) **Software piracy.**

   e.g. professional criminals producing hundreds of copies of games software and selling them.

3) **Illegally downloading material from the Internet.**

   e.g. downloading MP3 files from illegal sites to avoid paying for them, or copying text or images from the Internet and using them without receiving the copyright owner's permission or saying where you got them.

When You Buy Software, You Buy A Licence For It Too

Single-user licence
You'll need one of these if you're buying software to use on just one computer e.g. on your home PC.

Multi-user licence
Companies need these when they want to use a piece of software on several different machines. The licences usually specify a maximum number of users who can use the software at any one time — it limits the numbers of active users, rather than the number of copies of software that are installed.

Network licence
This allows a company to share software with users over an internal network.

Site licence
This lets a company have an unlimited number of users of the software, within a particular location.

What do you mean "am I operating this car without a licence?"

Different licences cost different amounts. You're likely to pay a fair whack more for a 30-user licence than a single-user one.

Practice Questions

Q1 Give an example of an offence for levels 1, 2 and 3 of the Computer Misuse Act.

Q2 What is currently the maximum sentence you could get for deliberately gaining unauthorised access to files, if it's proved that you didn't intend to commit any further crimes?

Q3 State three problems with the current Computer Misuse Act.

Exam Questions

Q1 Briefly explain three ways in which the law can be broken under the Copyright, Designs and Patents Act. (3 marks)

Q2 A small company has a multi-user software licensing agreement for a spreadsheet package specifying that there must be no more than 5 copies in use at any one time.

   a) Describe what is meant by a "software licensing agreement". (1 mark)

   b) Would the company be breaking the agreement by installing the software on 5 PCs and 3 laptops? Explain your answer. (2 marks)

Johnny Depp's been illegally downloading MP3s — It's a piracy issue...

Phew, good to get these pages out of the way. It's important to learn all about the legislation that's in place to deal with computer crime, even though it does have its loopholes. Criminals have been prosecuted successfully though, and it's only a matter of time before the law tightens up on these issues. But Johnny Depp can be exempt. Because he's a stunner.

Data Protection Legislation

Ooh, more jargon on these pages. I know it's a right pain in the donkey, but learning all the proper words will make you sound much better in the exam. Anything's better than writing things like "him who did that thing with the wotsit..."

Data Is Vulnerable To Mistakes And Misuse

Lots of information is **stored** and **processed electronically**. Good information systems aim to process data to make it:

- **easily accessible** from many different access points
- **easily transferred** from one system to another
- **available** in very large quantities
- **organised** in a way that is **easy to understand**

1) These qualities make the data **vulnerable**. If it's easily accessible, it means it can potentially be accessed by people who shouldn't do so. If it's well organised, it's more useful to those who shouldn't really be using it at all.

2) When the data is **directly related to a living person** and they can be identified by that data, this is a real **threat to that person's privacy**.

There Are Specific Acts Covering The Use Of Personal Data

1) Data protection legislation was brought in to **prevent the misuse of personal data** and to give **basic rights** to the individual whose personal details are stored in an information system.

2) The **Data Protection Act 1984 (DPA)** was brought in to cover all personal data held on electronic media.

3) It was replaced in **1998** with the current Data Protection Act (see page 39).

4) The **Freedom of Information Act 2000** was brought in to allow individuals to access official information (often held on information systems).

There Are A Few Specific Terms You Need To Know

1) A **data controller** decides how the data will be collected, created, stored, organised and used.

2) A **data processor** is the person or organisation who retrieves the data under the authority of the data controller (this could be the organisation that collected the data, or it might be a third party).

3) A **data subject** is the individual person who is identified by the data.

The Information Commissioner Is Independent From The Government

1) The **Information Commissioner** is an independent official, appointed by the Crown, to oversee the Data Protection Act 1998 and the Freedom of Information Act 2000. They must report to parliament once a year.

2) Their office maintains the **Public Register of Data Controllers**.

3) Any organisation that wants to process personal information **must be placed on the Public Register**. It's a criminal offence to keep and process personal data if you are not on the Public Register.

4) **Before 1998**, the **Data Protection Registrar** maintained the register and **dealt only with the DPA**. The Information Commissioner has **wider responsibilities**.

- The Information Commissioner is responsible for making sure that the **Data Protection Act is enforced** and that **all data controllers comply with it**.
- They give **advice** on issues relating to the Act.
- They give **examples of good practice** and **consider complaints** from data subjects.
- They ensure that the **Freedom of Information Act is enforced**.

Anyone Can Look At The Public Register

1) The **Public Register of Data Controllers** is available online. It holds details on **who keeps personal data** and **what they do with it**.

2) **Data controllers give notification** of what data they will hold and the processing they will perform on it.

3) **Data subjects** must **give their consent** to data being held unless the organisation is legally obliged to keep it.

4) They may, however, need to **give consent to some of the processing** if it is not a necessary part of the organisation's activities and it directly identifies individuals. Whether or not consent is needed depends on the type of processing that will be done.

Data Protection Legislation

A Data Subject's **Consent** Is **Not Always Needed** For **Data Processing**

Consent may not need to be given by the data subject, if:

- the data is necessary for **setting up a contract** (e.g. credit references)
- the data is necessary **by law** (e.g. attendance records in schools, production of accounts, details of donors to charitable organisations)
- the data **helps protect** the vital interests of the data subject (e.g. missing persons register)
- it is necessary for **administering justice** (e.g. National Police Database)
- it is required by **government** or it is in the **public interest** (e.g. tax records)

Sometimes **consent is implicit**, e.g. if you fill in a form, you know the data will be stored.

If some of the data is **sensitive** then you must be **asked explicitly** for consent, e.g. when it is about the racial or ethnic origin of the data subject, their political opinion, religious beliefs, trade union membership, physical or mental state of health, lifestyle or it relates to alleged or proven criminal offences.

The **Data Protection Act 1998** Has **8 Principles** For You To **Learn**

The principles are stated below in a slightly simpler form than in the Act itself — you need to learn them all:

Principle 1) Data must be processed **fairly** and **lawfully**.

Principle 2) Data must be obtained only for one or more **specified purposes** and must not be processed in any other way. The purpose stated on the Public Register is the **only purpose** for which the data can be used.

Principle 3) Data must be **adequate**, **relevant** and **not excessive** in relation to the purpose.

Principle 4) Data must be **accurate** and, where necessary, **up-to-date**.

Principle 5) Data must **not be kept** for longer than is necessary for the registered purpose.

Principle 6) Data must be **processed** in accordance with the **rights** of the data subject.

Principle 7) Appropriate **technical and organisational measures** must be taken against unauthorised or unlawful processing and against accidental loss of, destruction of, or damage to, personal data.

Principle 8) Data **must not be transferred** to a country or territory **outside the European Economic Area** unless that country or territory ensures an adequate level of data protection legislation. Countries within the EU have similar legislation to the UK but other countries may not have legislation. Data can only be transferred to an area where there is **adequate data protection legislation** in place.

Practice Questions

Q1 Define the terms "data subject", "data controller" and "data processor".

Q2 Give four responsibilities of the Information Commissioner.

Q3 What is listed in the Public Register?

Exam Questions

Q1 A charity keeps data on all people who have ever donated anything to them. Their Public Register entry shows that they will keep data about the money and services that donors have given, along with identifying data such as name and address. The register also states that the data will be used for accounting, management analysis (of monetary information only) and direct marketing, and that the data will not be transferred to any other countries.

Explain which parts of the register entry may need the data subject's consent and which parts may not. (4 marks)

Q2 Data can be easily transferred from one system to another, regardless of where in the world those systems are.

Name two principles of the Data Protection Act 1998 which relate to the transfer of data between systems and explain how they do so. (2 marks)

I always carry data protection — a big stick to hit researchers with...

You may think it's all over now but OH you'd be wrong. There's a whole two more pages on data protection legislation coming right up, so you'd best turn over and get stuck in to them while it's all fresh and sticky in your head, like some sort of gorgeous, jam-filled, honey-coated, lard-battered doughnut of ICT delight. Mmmmmmmmmmmmmmmm... doughnuts...

Data Protection Legislation

Here we go. These are the last two pages about data protection legislation, and the last two horribly jargony pages in this section. Jargony. Hm. That's not a real word. But you know what is? Slouchy. How weird is that...?

Some Data **Doesn't Have To Be Registered**

Personal data is used for a **wide variety of purposes**. All of them are covered by the Data Protection Act in some way, and some data is identified as being **exempt from the need to register**. Exempt data includes:

1) **data processed by an individual** only for the purposes of that individual's personal, family or household affairs (including recreational purposes).

2) data processed for use in **journalism**, **literature** or **art** as long as its use is **in the public interest**.

3) data to be used for **research purposes**, or to produce **statistics** (so long as it does not identify any particular individual).

4) data used for **accounting purposes** as required by law.

5) data held in the interests of **national security** (e.g. information about members of the armed services, the intelligence service, judges, etc).

6) data used for **producing mailing lists** and **containing only names and addresses** (but only if the individual does not object).

Everyone Has The **Right** To See **Any Data Held On Them**

Everyone has the right to ask to see data that is held about them. This is called **subject access**. If you were to find that the details held about you were incorrect, you could:

- ask for the details to be **altered**.

- **claim compensation** if the error caused you loss, inconvenience or distress (you might have been turned down by a potential employer because the record of the number of days absence from work was incorrect).

Some Data Must Be **Registered** But Is **Exempt From Subject Access**

Some registered data is **exempt from subject access**. This includes data that might:

- affect a **criminal investigation**

- affect the outcome of a **court case**

- affect a **tax assessment**

- **identify another person** (unless that other person has given their consent).

If data is exempt from subject access, then the data subject has **no right** to ask to see what's stored.

Storing Criminal Records Has Lots Of Problems

The **Criminal Records Bureau** (CRB) is the **data controller** for all **criminal records** held on computer systems.

Any organisation that needs to check the criminal record of someone before employing them or allowing them to take part in activities can get the person **to sign a request for a copy of their records**. This is called **disclosure** but the data is very sensitive and there are some **potential problems**:

- a search could find details of the **wrong person** because they happen to have the same name.

- the record of one person could be **linked to another** just because they lived at the same address, even if it was at different times.

- some records can **identify other people involved in a crime** — these are exempt from access.

- some information might be used to **interfere with the process of investigating**, prosecuting or preventing crime — this data is exempt from subject access.

- The CRB only holds convictions records, and **not crimes under investigation** — they only record if a person was caught and convicted. So, if the disclosure was obtained before conviction, **no criminal record** will be reported so the employer thinks there is no problem. The employer can try to **request police records**, but lots of this data will be exempt because it might interfere with the investigation if released.

Data Protection Legislation

The Data Protection Act Was Rewritten In 1998

The 1984 Data Protection Act was rewritten in 1998, and a number of changes were made in order to bring the Act up to date. The table below explains the most important changes:

1984 Act	1998 Act
Data was covered if it could be **automatically processed by electronic equipment**.	Data is covered if it is **stored in any order and in any way**, including manual filing systems.
A **Data Protection Registrar** was employed by the government to keep the register of data controllers.	The **Information Commissioner** is now the person who keeps the register. He / she is **independent of the government**, and has **extra responsibilities** under the Freedom of Information Act 2000 as well.
Data was only protected by law while it was **kept within the UK**.	All European Union countries have data protection legislation. Data must now **not be transferred out of the EU** unless it's to a country with a similar level of data protection legislation to ours.
Employers could **force applicants to apply for disclosure** of criminal records, and if an applicant refuses they might be refused the job.	Employers **can no longer force applicants** to apply for disclosure of criminal records where there is no **reasonable need** for it.

1984 data protection ideas were a bit out of date...

Also, **extra rights** were given to data subjects to allow them to **ask for their details** in an intelligible form and to object to processing that would **cause distress**, that would be used for **direct marketing** or that would be used for **automatic decision making** (without being reviewed by humans).

Practice Questions

Q1   List five types of data that are exempt from the Data Protection Act.

Q2   Explain what "subject access" means.

Q3   Give three problems that arise from storing criminal records.

Q4   List the five major changes to the Data Protection Act when it was rewritten in 1998.

Exam Question

Q1   Give **two** examples of data that is exempt from **each** of the following. State the reason why each is exempt.

a) the need to register   (4 marks)

b) subject access   (4 marks)

Have you heard Cliff Richard's latest album? — that's a criminal record...

It's encouraging to think that the law has found ways to deal with technological criminals, but it's still not exactly awe-inspiring. Make sure that you always behave responsibly around your own systems, so you can minimise the risk of getting royally shafted by criminals. Anyway, only two more pages left until the end of the section... Keep going, you can do it.

Health and Safety

There are a few different health problems associated with computer use, and there is legislation to help protect people from these. The most important thing to remember though, is that this is the last double-page of this section.

There Are **Guidelines** To Help Us **Fix Health Problems**

1) Lots of the health problems caused by computer use can be prevented or reduced with **simple actions**.

2) Some actions are just recommendations, but some are covered by the **regulations set for employers**.

3) There are also guidelines for hardware and software **developers** to consider the health and safety **of their users**.

There Are **Different Ways To Help** With Each Problem

Problem	Causes	Prevention/reduction
eye strain (can cause blurred vision and headaches)	• **concentrating on the screen** for too long • constantly **refocusing eyes** between screen and paper • **glare** from light reflecting on the screen • sitting too **close** to the screen	• Take **regular breaks** from working at the screen — about 15 minutes every hour • **refocus eyes** every 10 minutes and make sure work areas are well lit • use blinds to **reduce glare** from the sun • sit at least one metre from the screen
repetitive strain injury (RSI) (can lead to carpal tunnel syndrome, ulnar neuritis and neck problems)	• Repeated **similar movements**, such as clicking mouse buttons or typing	• use **wrist guards** when typing • take **frequent breaks** • have the keyboard at the **right height** • press keys and buttons **lightly**
back and neck problems	• can be caused by **repetitive movement** • also **bad posture**, especially when sitting for long periods at a computer	• maintain **good posture** • take **frequent breaks** and **move around**
deep vein thrombosis (forming of blood clots in the veins)	• **sitting still** for very long periods of time	• take **frequent breaks** and **move around**
epilepsy	• screens which **flicker** at certain frequencies • **strobe effects** on screen displays	• **screen filters** can reduce flicker

Good Posture And A Well-Designed Workstation Are Important

1) You need to sit upright, keep your **elbows and knees at 90°** and your **feet flat on the floor**.
2) Your **chair** should provide **back support**.
3) Your chair should also have **wheels**, to allow easy movement away from the computer.
4) Your eyes should be at least **1 metre from the screen**.
5) Your **keyboard** should be at the **correct height** (allowing you to keep your arms at 90°).

Hardware Should Be Chosen With Health And Safety In Mind

Hardware can be chosen to **minimise health problems**. For example:

• there are **ergonomic** mice and keyboards

• screens should be an **appropriate resolution and size** for the software they are used with

• printers and copiers should produce the **required quality** of document (e.g. if A3 is needed, an A3 copier should be available, rather than A4 being joined together manually)

• all equipment should work **within acceptable time limits**.

Ergonomic means that it's designed to minimise discomfort and injury.

Health and Safety

Employers Must Meet The Regulations For Health And Safety

The **Health and Safety at Work Act 1974** and **Health and Safety (Display Screen Equipment) Regulations 1992** cover **employers' responsibilities**, especially where employees work with computer systems. Employers must:

- pay for **regular eye tests** and pay for glasses if they are found to be needed
- ensure **electrical equipment** is safe and **provide workstations** with space for movement and comfortable working
- provide **chairs with height adjustment** and **back support**
- ensure working conditions have **adequate light**, **reduced glare**, **good ventilation** and a **comfortable temperature**
- plan work so that **regular breaks** can be taken
- provide **health and safety training** (e.g. lifting techniques) and fire and **emergency training** for employees
- ensure the working environment is **safe** from **fire hazards** and **obstructions** e.g. trailing cables, boxes of paper
- provide **trained first aiders**
- allow **pregnant women** to work **away from VDU equipment** if they choose to (because the radiation levels have been linked with increased chance of miscarriage).

Some Health Problems Can Come From Software

1) When new software is designed, there are **guidelines for the developers** covering health and safety factors linked to **poor software design**.

2) Changing to new software can cause **stress**, and this can lead to **fatigue** and **health problems** — the changeover should be as **smooth** as possible.

3) If **training** is required, it should be **available** to all who need it and should be **comprehensive** enough to allow users to be **confident** in using the software.

4) If the **user interface is too complicated**, this can cause stress — the user interface should be designed to be as **easy to use** as possible.

5) However, **experienced users** will become **frustrated** with a user interface that is too simple. An easy to use interface may feel slow for the experienced user and this may cause frustration and stress. **Shortcuts** can be useful in reducing this stress.

6) The new system must be **as good as**, or better than, **the old system**. A user can become frustrated if tasks that worked well in the old system are replaced with ones that are slower or more difficult.

7) **Losing important work** is another cause of stress. Systems should be designed to allow work to be recovered in case of accidental loss through hardware or software failure.

8) Movement of the mouse, number of mouse clicks and number of keypresses should be **kept to a minimum** and a user should not be required to focus on one particular area of the screen for too long.

9) There are also guidelines explaining that **some colour combinations** place **less strain on the eyes** than others.

Practice Questions

Q1 List five health problems associated with computer use.

Q2 What responsibilities does an employer have in protecting the health and safety of his or her employees?

Q3 What considerations should be made with regard to health and safety when designing new software?

Exam Questions

Q1 Explain what health-related design features should be considered when recommending and developing a new computer system for an experienced user. (3 marks)

Q2 What measures can a user take to protect their own health when using a computer system at home? (3 marks)

As long as you've got your health you're fine — but I'd rather be rich...

Take the money and run, so long as you can run. I know it's easy to joke when you're feeling fit and healthy, but before long you'll find yourself in a work situation where you're basically just sitting totally still for 8 hours a day, and then all this information will come back to you with a vengeance. Learn all this stuff well — not just for the exams, but because it's useful.

Software Drivers

What did the software driver say to the software? "Get off my bus, your ticket's clearly already been used and if you're not going to buy a new one then stop wasting my time." Or... "it's important to understand what drivers do".

Software Drivers *Can Also Be Called* Device Drivers

Computer systems are made up of many devices (e.g. CD drive, printer, network card). A software driver (or device driver) is a program **designed to control input, output and storage devices**.

1) Drivers allow **communication** between the operating system and these devices.

2) They also mean the devices can be **configured** by the operating system to work as intended.

Drivers Are Used Everywhere — For Example...

Home PC

A user may decide to install a new DVD drive on his/her PC. The manufacturer provides **drivers on disk** to set up the device. These need to be installed before they will work properly (for example, so it will show the movies in the correct format).

Business PC

A company wants to print address labels for a mail shot to potential customers. The correct **printer drivers** enable the printer to be set up with the appropriate size and orientation for output needed.

Local Area Network

Most schools run computers on networks. Drivers will have to be installed for the **network cards** in each machine to behave accordingly. Without these there may be problems with devices communicating with each other and the server.

Peripheral Drivers *Tend To* Load Automatically

Most computer systems are moving towards 'Plug and Play', which means that drivers are **loaded automatically** when a new **peripheral** is installed (peripheral means an input, output or storage device).

The most important roles that peripheral drivers play are shown below:

Output:　**Printer drivers** can be used to:

　　1)　set up defaults such as orientation and paper size.

　　2)　make sure that printed copy is output as expected
　　　　e.g. line spacing on paper is as it appears on screen.

　　3)　send error messages back to the computer and output to
　　　　the user if there are problems such as ink shortages.

Monitor drivers can be used to:

　　1)　set up display options such as resolution and colour.

　　2)　fix the refresh rate.

Input:　**Scanner drivers** can be used to:

　　1)　set up defaults like the colour depth (dpi — dots per inch).

　　2)　send messages about the progress and completion of scan.

Web cam drivers can be used to:

　　1)　run tests on the camera to see if it's working properly.

　　2)　set up defaults, such as how the camera manages colour.

Storage:　**CD/DVD R or R/W drivers** can be used to:

　　1) provide information on the speed at which the device reads and writes.

　　2) set defaults like volume levels for CDs, or regional information for DVDs.

Utilities

Learn The Difference Between **Systems Software** And **Applications Software**

Systems software is a set of programs that organise, utilise and control hardware in a computer system.
Applications software is designed to make use of the computer system for specific purposes.

System Utilities Are **Programs** That Perform **Specific Functions**

System utilities can perform several **types of function**:

Compression

System utility programs **convert data into a format** that takes up far **less memory space**. Compression software is particularly useful when data is being sent from one computer to another. Communication of data is faster when the file size is reduced.

File conversion

Each file saved on computer has a **file extension**, e.g. .doc, .xls. The extensions are **related to the specific application** used to create the file. A utilities program enables other applications to **open** a file with a **different extension**. For example, MS Word can open a .wps file created by the word processor in MS Works even though its own files have an extension of .doc.

Looking at configuration files

These contain **information on system parameters**. When a program is run, it may need to look at configuration files to see what conditions it should **adapt** to.

There Are **Other Systems Tools** To Learn About Too

This bit's for OCR only.

Translator

A utility that **converts programs into machine code** so that the computer can run them.

Linker

An **editor** that brings together code and commands written separately (modules) to form a **larger executable program**.

Loader

A utility that an operating system uses when necessary to **retrieve programs from storage devices** and store them in its memory.

Practice Questions

Q1   What do software drivers do?

Q2   Name two output devices that require drivers and give examples of what they do.

Q3   Write one sentence to explain each of the following terms: compression, file conversion and configuration.

Q4   Define the following terms: translator, linker and loader.

Exam Questions

Q1   When a Desktop Publishing program is set up, it is important that the attached printer has the correct drivers installed.

Explain what a printer driver is.

(2 marks)

Q2   An operating system is software that controls and monitors all applications. There are often many system utilities supplied with an operating system.

Describe two examples of system utilities likely to be included.

(4 marks)

Dear old Mary needs a new driver — Driv'er? But I 'ardly know 'er...

Because most drivers load automatically, a lot of computer users don't tend to ever know what they are or what they do. But you get the extra special pleasure of finding out, because you're doing AS ICT. It's hardly the most thrilling topic in the world, but just think how impressed your friends and family will be next time you tell them all about what you've learnt...

Operating Systems

It's easy to take Microsoft Windows for granted, but don't forget that there are other successful operating systems too. Some of them are named after fruit. But I don't like Apples. Why couldn't they call themselves Banana, or Coconut?

The **Operating System Controls** All The **Applications**

1) An operating system is essential computer software that **controls and monitors all the applications**.

2) It provides an **interface** between the **user**, **software** and **hardware** and is sometimes called the "heart of the system".

There Are **Three Main Operating Systems** For The **PC**

1) **Microsoft Windows**, the most popular operating system, provides a **Graphical User Interface** (GUI) for the user. This was originally based on the **Disk Operating System** (DOS) developed by Microsoft. MS-DOS is still used behind the GUI in older versions of Windows, providing some of the control and monitoring.

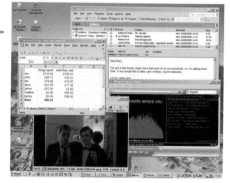

2) **MS-DOS** is a **command driven interface**. This operating system doesn't have features that can be controlled by mouse like in a Windows environment. So, users have to **type in specific commands** to control the software.

3) **Linux** is a rival operating system to Windows. Although it's nowhere near as popular, the fact that the basic system is **free to download** and **open to development** by end users has led to its growth.

An **Operating System** Does **Various Different Things**

1) **Allocates internal memory**

When several applications are running at once there are often great demands on memory. An operating system handles the **allocation of RAM** to try and maximise scarce resources.

2) **Schedules programs and resources**

Again related to several applications running simultaneously, **processing has to be prioritised** to prevent programs freezing and to allow the computer to run efficiently.

3) **Monitors the systems input and output devices (IO)**

An operating system may have to **prioritise various input and output devices** so that they work efficiently, e.g. being able to display characters on screen as they are typed on a keyboard while at the same time another document is being printed.

4) **Logs errors**

Although an operating system tries to cope with all this multi-tasking, there are situations when memory is insufficient and applications or devices fail. An operating system has to provide **error messages** to the user.

5) **Checks for unauthorised access**

Different access privileges such as read only, read / write can be granted to users. An operating system controls the **granting of these privileges** and **regulates users** accordingly.

Operating Systems

Don't Forget About Apple Macs

1) Considered by some to be **more stable and efficient** than Microsoft Windows, the Apple Mac operating systems provide serious competition to PCs.

2) These work on a completely **different processor and systems architecture** to PCs.

3) Apple Mac computers are used extensively in the **graphic design industry**.

Operating Systems Can Multi-Task

1) Because lots of programs need to be run at once (especially in a Windows environment), operating systems need to be able to **multi-task**.

2) Multi-tasking makes it appear as if multiple programs are **running simultaneously**, but actually that's just an **illusion** caused by the fast processing speed of the CPU.

3) What actually happens is that the CPU **divides its time** between various tasks — it performs part of a task on one application, followed by part of a task on another application. It then returns to the first application, and so on.

The tools used by the new operating system were getting curiouser and curiouser...

There Are Different Types of Operating System

1) **Single user system** is the name given to operating systems where one user has access at a time. These are the familiar operating systems usually associated with PCs.

2) **Multi-user systems** allow more than one user to access and use the computer at the same time. This can be seen in Local Area Networks (LANS), with computer servers that are accessed by multiple users.

3) **Distributed systems** use more than one computer system to run an application. These are common to networks, particularly LANs where one application has to be run at different sites.

4) **Batch processing** is where data is first collected together into batches before being input into the system at a later time, usually when there isn't a great demand for processing from other areas.

   For example, banks usually collect cheques that have been paid in throughout the day in various branches. They batch these and process them overnight.

Practice Questions

Q1 Describe the differing characteristics of Microsoft Windows, MS DOS and Linux.

Q2 Name the five main things an operating system does.

Q3 Define multi-tasking and explain why it is useful for an operating system to be able to do this.

Q4 Name four different types of operating system.

Exam Question

Q1 A neighbour is purchasing a new PC. Included in the purchase is software including an operating system. She is only a novice user.

   a) State three tasks that are performed by an operating system. (3 marks)

   b) What type of operating system would you expect to be supplied with the PC and why? (2 marks)

Dr Foster uses leeches and a pump — it's not a great operating system...

Betcha by golly gosh wow gee blimey bananas... That was an action packed double page, wasn't it? Okay, okay. No. It really wasn't. But you know what (yes, I know, you've heard it all before) but it really is useful information. Loads of people who use computers every day don't know this stuff — crazy... It's up to you to learn it all, so you're not one of them.

Human / Computer Interface

A Human Computer Interface (HCI) lets users tell the computer what to do, and allows the computer to ask the user for input or display results. It's like show and tell, only with text prompts and error messages instead of fun.

The **User** And The **Computer Interact Through The Interface**

1) Users use an input device to **tell the computer what they want it to do** (usually a mouse or a keyboard).

2) The computer will **respond** to the user's requests and **ask for input** when it needs it (usually on a screen).

3) The interface is what **connects** the two.

A **System Designer** Will Aim To Create **A Good Interface**

A good HCI will:

- be **easy to use** for inexperienced users.

- give information about what **processing** is happening.

- be **consistent** so that the user becomes familiar with it quickly.

- have facilities for more experienced users to **customise** the interface.

- always do **what the user expects**.

- respond to user instruction in a **reasonable time** and **report on the progress** of a process.

- be **clear**. The user shouldn't have to think about what is required — it should be **obvious**.

- not require too much **effort** on the part of the user (e.g. minimum number of keystrokes, minimum mouse movement).

- reduce the possibility of mistakes by **checking** the user's input.

- have **help** available for the user when they need it.

- not require the user to **remember many commands**.

- take the user's **health and safety** into consideration (e.g. use colour schemes that are easy on the eyes, use screen layouts that don't require too much eye movement, minimise the number of times the user is required to click on things, use pre-emptive text to reduce the amount of typing required).

Interfaces can be of three kinds — **menu-driven**, **graphical** or **command line**.

Menu-Driven Interfaces Guide The User

1) Menu-driven software works with **windows-based operating systems**, such as Windows or MacOS, and with **command-based operating systems** such as DOS or UNIX.

2) A menu-driven interface **guides the user** through a set of menus, letting them choose what they want to do.

3) Many **call centres** use this interface for directing telephone calls. When you phone the call centre, the system gives you choices and asks you to press a number for the one you want, then you're given a new set of choices.

Many Systems Have A Graphical User Interface (GUI)

A GUI will often have:

1) **Windows** — all input and output happens in a window which can be closed, moved, resized or minimised to help keep the screen clear.

2) **Icons** — buttons, check boxes, options buttons, etc. can be clicked on to change settings or to give instructions.

3) **Menus** — users can select instructions from menus.

4) **Pointer** — a pointing device (mouse, touch screen, trackerball, light pen) moves a cursor around the screen so that the user can control the windows, icons and menus.

Human / Computer Interface

Graphical User Interfaces *Are Great For* **Beginners**

1) Graphical user interfaces tend to be **intuitive**. This means that once you know about buttons, scroll bars and other controls, you can generally guess what you need to do next.

2) There is often **context sensitive help**, and the interface will be designed to make it as easy as possible for the user to enter data.

3) Because of all the features added to make the GUI easy to use, the actual software can sometimes be **quite slow** as processing time is taken up by the interface.

4) Also, in order not to confuse the user with too much information, **many commands are hidden** and must be found using help manuals.

Command-Line Interfaces *Can be* **Powerful** *And* **Fast**

Command-line interfaces consist of a simple prompt screen into which the user types commands for the computer to carry out. A good example is MS-DOS.

This kind of system can very **quick** and **flexible** if you know what you're doing.
It's good for computer programmers and other IT specialists who really understand how the system works.

But they're no good for your average computer user with no programming knowledge.

It's **Much Easier** *When* **All Our Software Looks Similar**

1) Many Windows applications use a **common interface** so that they all become easier to use.

2) For example, they all have similar File and Edit menus and some shortcut keys (Ctrl+X, Ctrl+S) do the same in all applications.

3) This means that when you get a new application, a large part of it will already be familiar, making it quicker to learn.

Natural Language Interfaces *Understand* **Human Speech**

1) **Natural language interfaces** are designed to **understand human speech** and to give prompts and responses in natural language.

2) This **should be the easiest** type of interface for any of us to use and shouldn't require too much training.

3) However, it has **some problems**.
   - The processing is quite intensive and this can make the software **slow**.
   - **Regional accents** mean that many people say the same words in very different ways.
   - People use **different phrases** to mean the same thing, so it's hard for the software to understand everything.
   - Also, people often **don't like the sound** of computerised speech.

Practice Questions

Q1 Define the term "Human Computer Interface".

Q2 State five features of a good Human Computer Interface.

Q3 Name the three different types of HCI.

Exam Questions

Q1 Describe three features that should be considered when designing a HCI for complete beginners. (3 marks)

Q2 Give two advantages and two disadvantages of GUIs (graphical user interfaces). (4 marks)

After my PC crashed for the thirty-third time, the HCI I used was a mallet...

Tra-la-laaa... Oh wouldn't it be nice, just once, to be able to let loose on a dodgy PC with a mallet? Like a rock star? Or to throw a monitor out of a window after it's been playing up? Oh the fun we'd have. Of course, that sort of thing results in criminal prosecution and, from what I hear, that's not a very good thing. Hm. Perhaps I'll just sit in and revise instead....

Software Upgrade and Reliability

New systems are being produced all the time. Some are brand new systems built to replace old ones, and some are new versions of existing ones. Everyone likes an upgrade — it's as inevitable as death and taxes, and reality TV...

You Might Want Your Software To Work A Little Faster

1) The **speed of processing** is determined by a number of different factors but one major factor is the **clock speed**.

2) All instructions carried out by a processor take place on the **pulse** of the **system clock**.

3) There is **one pulse every clock cycle** and a processor clock might operate at **millions of cycles per second**.

4) A **166MHz (megahertz) clock** generates **166 million pulses per second**.
A **1GHz (gigahertz) clock** generates a **billion**.

Speeding Up The Clock Makes The Software Work Faster

1) Speeding up the clock might make the software work **a little faster**, but it'll only work as fast as the **slowest component** it uses. (All software uses input devices, storage devices and output devices while it's working.)

2) Speeding up the processor clock **doesn't speed up the devices used**, but allows them to work **at their fastest**.

There Are Other Ways Of Speeding Up Processing

1) Some systems have **more than one processor** working together, so the processing can be done more quickly.

2) **Co-processors** (such as maths co-processors) are **fast processors** that can take some of the processing away from the main processor. They can really speed up software that needs to do lots of calculations, e.g. Computer Aided Design (CAD) software (see page 10).

3) **Parallel processors** carry out **the same type** of processing, but share it out so that it can be done more quickly.

4) Using two processors instead of one **won't necessarily double the processing speed**, as input and output devices can't work any faster and some time is needed for the processors to transfer the data between them.

> <u>Example</u> When you're running an Internet application on your home PC, it will run as fast as it is able using your processor. Even if you increase the speed of processing on your machine, the application may not run any faster because it can only process data as quickly as it can get it over the communications link.

Systems Can Be Upgraded To Improve Performance

Even if systems work satisfactorily, at some point they will all be **replaced** by newer, better, faster systems.
Upgrading can involve a number of different things and can sometimes have **problems**.

Upgrade	Technical Problems	Human Implications
New **hardware** might be introduced.	• It must **work** with the **existing software**, or the software might need to be **upgraded** as well.	• Users will need to **learn to use** new hardware. • Some familiar functions might **not be available** on the new hardware.
New **software** might be introduced.	• It must **work** with existing **hardware**, or **new** hardware might be needed. • It must be **compatible** with any other software it will be used with. • It might require data files to be **converted**.	• Users will need to **learn to use** new software. • They may be **unfamiliar** with **new features** of the software and will need time to adjust. • New systems can cause **stress**. • **Time** is needed to **transfer data** to the new systems. • Old familiar functions may now **not be available**. • Some **staff** might **no longer be needed**.

Software Upgrade and Reliability

All **New Systems** Must Be **Reliable** — They Need **Testing**

The only way to know that a system is **completely reliable** before it is used, is to **test it** in every possible way.

Testing is carried out to make sure that a system:

- **functions correctly**.
- **performs within acceptable limits**, e.g. it must be able to cope with large volumes of data if required, and must be able to produce results in a given timescale if required.
- **recovers** effectively from any type of **system failure**, e.g. data is backed up, data is saved automatically.

Testing Must Be **Exhaustive** For **Large** And **Complex Systems**

Exhaustive testing covers **absolutely every possibility**, but this is **very difficult** to do.

In order to get somewhere near testing everything, a **test plan** needs to be created. The test plan will include:

- a **schedule** for testing where each section is tested at an appropriate time (e.g. after another section that produces its data).
- all **types** of testing — functions, performance and recovery.
- a **set of test data** including **normal** data, **erroneous** data and **extreme** data (see p.129).
- a list of **every possible action** to be tested.
- expected results.

The testing was exhaustive in the worst possible way...

The test plan will be used to **ensure** that **every possibility has been covered** before the system is considered nearly ready to be used.

The **Developer** Tests The System, Then The **Customer** Tests It

After the initial testing by the system developers, there are **three more stages of testing** that involve users.

1) **Alpha testing** — a restricted number of users within the software production company will use the software extensively and give feedback on how it performs. The feedback is used to improve the system and test it again.

2) **Beta testing** — a selected number of clients are given the system to use extensively for a while. They give feedback on how it performs. The feedback is used to make final amendments to the software and to do final testing.

3) **Acceptance testing** — the final system is tested when it is handed over. This form of testing is used to prove to the customer that the system works correctly and that it works with the "live data" that the customer will use.

Practice Questions

Q1 Explain why speeding up your processor clock won't necessarily speed up all your software.

Q2 Give three potential problems that could arise when introducing a software upgrade to your system.

Q3 What three things are looked for when testing a new system?

Q4 List the types of test data that will be used to fully test a system.

Exam Question

Q1 An insurance company has a computerised database system. They enter details about customers and their insurance quotes, retrieve information quickly when a customer needs it and print many insurance quotes and certificates. The system is not always as fast as they would like.

   a) Describe two ways in which the company can increase the speed of its system. (2 marks)

   b) Describe the human implications of introducing new database software. (2 marks)

   c) Explain how a new database system should be fully tested before the users see it. (3 marks)

I can't speed clocks up, but stopping them with my face is a family speciality...

Not that I'm saying I'm not gorgeous but, you know — if you get close enough to a small clock, you can pick it up by the leg with your mouth, and shake it 'til it breaks. Rather like systems developers. Ah the poor little things. They'll never satisfy us completely — and every time we end up picking them up by the leg with our mouths, and shaking them 'til they break...

Generic Software

Right-o chaps. There's an awful lot about software in this section that you'll need to run up the old flagpole. You'll need to learn the differences between generic, specific and bespoke software, so be sure to keep your wits about you. Pip pip.

Software Packages Can Be Generic or Task-Specific

1) **Generic software packages** are for everyday use and are very common. They're things like word processors, spreadsheet applications, desktop publishing software, database applications and presentation packages.

2) They can be used for **lots of tasks**, not just one specific job. For example, spreadsheet packages can do lots of different things like sort numbers, produce simple databases, create charts and graphs, etc.

3) **Task-specific** software packages can only be used for **one particular purpose**, e.g. payroll software can be used to process wages, but you can't use it to write a letter or draw a graph.

4) Task-specific software is usually used for a **specialist application**, so the user needs training in both the software and the subject area, e.g. CAM / CAD or music editing.

Users Will Need a Combination of Generic and Specific Software

Organisations often need to use a number of different generic packages, (e.g. spreadsheets, databases, word processors, etc). Rather than buying all these separately, they can choose an **integrated package** or software suite e.g. Microsoft Office Suite provides Word, Excel, Access and Outlook.

Generic software packages tend to have the same **common features** e.g. copy, cut, paste, delete, search facilities, etc. These common features make it easier and quicker to use different applications side by side and transfer data between them.

However, most organisations will need some task-specific software **as well**.

Example — Schools

Schools will need generic software for general administration and communication.

They'll need also task-specific software for things like budgeting and payroll, computer aided learning, multimedia training systems, and electronic library catalogues.

Example — Businesses

Businesses will need generic software for general administration and communication.

They'll also need task-specific software for things like budgeting, diary systems, payroll, stock control, banking, booking systems, customer records and accounts.

Software Can Be Custom-Written (Bespoke) or Off-The-Shelf

1) Just to confuse things, users can also **commission** software that is **custom-written** for them and tailored to their specific needs. This is usually task-specific software (although it might also contain some generic elements). Custom-written software is normally referred to as **bespoke software**.

> E.g.
> - **editing software** might be commissioned by a music recording studio,
> - **utility billing systems** software for large domestic utilities companies,
> - **route finders** and **travel timetables** for travel companies, etc.

2) **Off-The-Shelf** software is software which has been written for the mass market, is readily available in the shops, and can be used by many users to complete many tasks. This can be either generic or task-specific software.

You Need To Think About What You Want From Your Software

As well as knowing **what** the software does and what the software company's **reputation** is like, there are a few other things it's important to **consider** when getting software.

1) It should have a **range of features**, suitable for both the novice and the experienced user.

2) You should be able to **upgrade** the software when a new version is available.

3) The software should be **compatible** with your other software and hardware. You should be able to import and export data from and to other packages. This might be to other applications, or it may mean transferring data between different brands of the software package, e.g. from Microsoft Excel to Lotus 1-2-3. This is called **data portability**.

4) You should be able to **customise** the software (see pages 54-55).

Generic Software

Learn The Differences Between **Off-The-Shelf** and **Bespoke** Software

Feature	Off-The-Shelf	Custom-Written (Bespoke)
Purpose	The software may not match the user's requirements perfectly, and it's likely that there will be certain features that they've paid for but will never use.	The software will fit the purpose precisely and do exactly what is asked. Of course, there may be some problems if the original analysis was wrong, and if features don't get specifically requested then they won't be there.
Choice	There's lots of competition between software companies, which means there's usually lots of choice between products.	It doesn't matter that you can't pick and choose between different packages because you get to pick who will write the software and have constant communication over exactly what you need.
Availability	Usually available immediately.	It'll take time to complete the initial analysis and design the software. This could be months or possibly years depending on how complicated the software will be.
Cost	Either a one-off cost or a yearly licence cost. Costs can spiral for office use, as you need to keep buying additional licences for each workstation that needs to use the software.	Need to hire the company/person to write the software. This is usually very expensive. You do own the software at the end and have the possibility to sell it on to recoup some of the costs.
Testing	It will have been tested worldwide by many individuals, and patches are regularly released by the company to fix problems reported by users.	It will only have been tested by a few people and there may be many bugs — it can take a long time to correct them all.
Support	There's lots of support available: discussion groups and forums, on-line help from the company, books and training courses.	You can only get support from the people who wrote the software — problems may arise if they choose not to support it or go out of business.
Upgrade	Software is likely to use a standard file format and the company is likely to release upgraded products. Still, having to constantly upgrade your software does add to the cost on a regular basis.	This is not automatic and will mean paying more to the software developers in order to upgrade it.
Staff	You're likely to find staff are already familiar with software that is widely available.	All staff will need training with the new software.
Memory	Likely to have a larger memory footprint than software that's been specially designed for the company.	Likely to have a smaller memory footprint as it's been specifically designed for the company. *Memory footprint means the amount of memory space taken up by the software.*

Practice Questions

Q1 Explain the difference between generic, task-specific, off-the-shelf and bespoke software.

Q2 Discuss three considerations that should be taken into account when choosing a new software package.

Q3 Give two disadvantages for a company of commissioning bespoke software.

Exam Question

Q1 Applications software can be described as being generic, task specific or bespoke.

Describe the characteristics of these three types of software and give two examples of each.
(The use of brand names will not gain credit.)

(9 marks)

Quiet in the back there — speak when you Bespoken to...

Haha just a little joke of mine. Sorry it's not funny. It's my OH SO SUBTLE way of trying to hammer in to you that bespoke (pronounced like "kiss-spoke" with the real emphasis on <u>poke</u>) means "custom-made" or "custom-written". Bespoke software means the same as custom-written software, only with a stupid word instead of just stating the obvious. Typical...

Capabilities of Software

Right then me hearties... Firstly 'ere's some examples of generic software to get your taste buds going, and then we'll move on to the more exciting things that you can do with them. Oooh arrr I can't wait, Cap'n. Pieces of eight and rum and such...

Database Packages Help You Work Systematically

Database packages can be used to systematically **store, search and sort data**. Most databases are relational, where the data is stored in tables and relationships are created to enable the data to be manipulated by the user in a useful way. It is easy for a user to:

1) add new records

2) amend existing records

3) delete unwanted records.

Name	Colour	Favourite Expression	Type of Accident
Blackie	White	Affronted	Hit by car
Jack	Tabby	Plaintive	Sat on by Jim
Nicola	Ginger	Stoopid	Sat on by Jim
Ginger	Black	Smiley	Sat on by Jim

Databases can be linked with word processors to complete a **mail merge procedure**. For example, a personalised letter can be sent, using mail merge, to all customers whose records are held in a database who have a birthday on 26th February.

For more on databases see section 10.

Spreadsheet Packages Do More Than Handle Numbers

> You need to talk about the major pieces of software BUT you mustn't use brand names. E.g. talk about a **spreadsheet package**, not Excel or Lotus 1-2-3.

Spreadsheet packages **display and process data**. They can perform a wide range of calculations and are often used to process numerical data.

Spreadsheet packages can also handle **text** and generate **graphs and charts**. They are very useful in data modelling and analysis.

Example of How Spreadsheets Can Be Used As Models

1) A spreadsheet model can **calculate** the **potential profit** of a stall selling umbrellas and hats over the Easter holidays.

2) You can use a spreadsheet to carry out **'what if' analysis**. You can change the variables, in this case, the number of sunny, cloudy and rainy days to see the **effect** on the **output** of the model.

3) You could use a **logic function**, such as this **IF statement**. The function is =IF(F17>1000,"Go For it!","Not worth it") meaning if the condition 'F7>1000' is met, then display ,"Go For it!", otherwise display "Not worth it".

4) You could present the output of the model as a **graph** or **chart** to make the predictions of the model easier to interpret and understand.

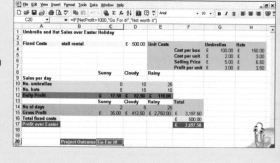

You Need To Know Other Examples of Generic Software

Word Processors

These are used to create, edit, format, store and print **text-based documents**, like letters, memos, reports, labels and newsletters. They can also **import** files from other sources (e.g. graphics, tables, sound and video files) and create **templates** and **indexes**. They can also be used for **mail merge** (see page 99).

Presentation Software

Presentation software lets users create a computerised **presentation**. These can accompany a **talk** given by a speaker, or presentations can be run **automatically** with pre-set timings or with manual, **user intervention** (called "self-running" presentations). Presentation software is often used for **multimedia** presentations that combine text, animation, sound, videos, etc.

Desktop Publishing (DTP)

Desktop publishing software allows you to create **professional documents** like flyers, brochures, invitations, business cards, and posters. Any document that uses lots of **graphics** or a **complex layout** should be done with DTP software.

Capabilities of Software

Object Integration Lets You **Share** Information **Between Applications**

Object linking and embedding (OLE) allows information to be shared **between applications**,
e.g. if you create a spreadsheet, you can **import** it into a word processor. This is also called **object integration**.

1) A **linked object** is where the original information is still stored in the source file, i.e. the spreadsheet in the example above.

2) An **embedded object** means that when you integrate the object into the document you are working on, it is then **saved in that document**. It can still be edited in the original software package by double-clicking on the object. However the main difference is that if you open up the **original file** in order to edit the object, the document you imported it into **won't update** automatically.

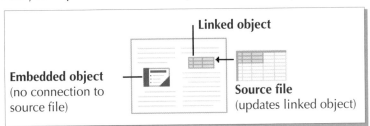

Linked object

Embedded object
(no connection to
source file)

Source file
(updates linked object)

They knew the object must be linked, but how...?

Macros Make Life Easier

1) A macro lets you **automate** tasks that get performed on a regular basis, making repetitive tasks quicker and less tedious.

2) Most generic software packages will let you **customise** them by **recording macros**.

3) For more fantabulous information on macros see p.54.

Application Generators Give Users More Options

1) Lots of modern software packages have the ability to **generate applications** with a minimum of programming knowledge.

2) This usually takes the form of an in-built **wizard** that helps you automate certain procedures and automatically generate the necessary code for them. More on wizards on p.57.

Practice Questions

Q1 Name five types of generic software.
Q2 Explain the difference between linking and embedding an object.
Q3 What is an application generator?

Exam Question

Q1 The manager of a small newsagent uses a mail-merge process to produce reminders for each customer that owes money on their account. Generic application software is used for this task.

Identify two advantages and two disadvantages of using generic application software in the running of a newsagent's shop.

(4 marks)

I don't care how many macros you're using — you're still ages in the shower...

I suppose this page is a bit annoying in that there's lots of descriptions of things but no real meat to get between your teeth. Well, the good thing is that you're never going to be expected to describe the intricate inner-workings of macros. However, you do need to be able to go: "A-ha! Macros! They automate repetitive tasks and make them less tedious! A-ha!" Okay?

Customising Applications

Whenever I think about what I'd like to customise in my life, it's normally things like hair, weight and complexion, not system interfaces. Then again, I guess my face is sort of a system interface for my brain. Then again, maybe not...

Generic Applications Can Be Customised

Generic applications can be **customised** using buttons, forms, menus and macros to make them **easier** and **faster** to use.

1) **Buttons** can be added to take the user to a **specified page** or **run an action** or **command**.

E.g. you can add a command button to the user interface of a database to run a search or to sort or edit data. A button can also display pictures or text. When the user clicks the button, the software runs that procedure.

2) **Forms** can be used to **input data** into a database or spreadsheet. Features like drop down menus and boxes that fill in automatically make things easier for the user.

E.g. when the user enters the postcode and town, the street and county automatically appear.

Input forms can also include **validation code**.

E.g. the form will tell you if you've filled in an impossible date of birth or if you've not filled in one of the boxes.

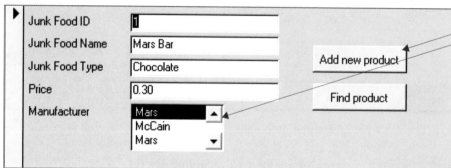

This database form uses buttons and a drop down list to make it quicker and easier to use

3) **Menus** can be used to **hide the inner workings** of the software from the user, and to make it more user-friendly. There are three main types:
- full-screen
- pop-ups
- pull-down

Each type of menu gives the user a **choice of actions**. Some options may not be available and these are usually 'greyed out'.

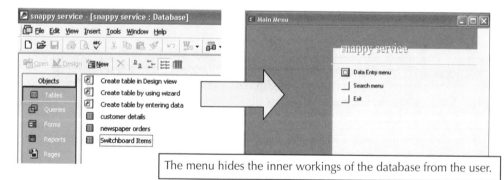

The menu hides the inner workings of the database from the user.

4) **Macros** let you **automate tasks** that you perform on a regular basis. This is done by **recording a series of commands** that you can run whenever you need to carry out the task.

E.g. you could record a macro to add your name to a header in all your documents.

Macros make repetitive tasks **quicker** and **less tedious**. Using macros also reduces errors, as the instructions are run automatically and are the same every time.

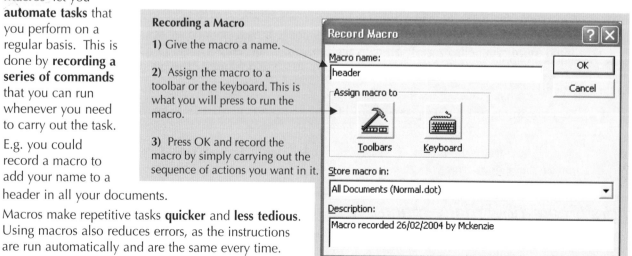

Recording a Macro

1) Give the macro a name.

2) Assign the macro to a toolbar or the keyboard. This is what you will press to run the macro.

3) Press OK and record the macro by simply carrying out the sequence of actions you want in it.

Customising Applications

Having A Customised System Interface Has **Benefits** and **Disadvantages**

Benefits of Having a Customised System Interface:

1) It makes it **faster** and easier to enter data, so users make less mistakes and are more productive.

2) The system is more **user-friendly** which makes it easier for inexperienced users.

3) The Interface can be set up so that data is **validated on entry**, reducing errors.

4) **Technical support** is easier as the complex interface is removed, making it easier to fix.

Disadvantages of Having a Customised System Interface:

1) If options have been **left off the interface** (due to poor planning) then users won't be able to do tasks that they could do with a generic interface.

2) A high level of **technical knowledge** is often required to create and test the interface.

3) If the software on which the interface is built is **upgraded** there are **no guarantees** it will still work as required.

Using Templates Saves Time

A template is a standard document with **pre-set layouts and formats** — it determines the basic structure and settings of a document.

Templates pre-set things like:

Formatting — font size, colour, style

Page setup — margins, size, layout

Text — standard wording,
date / time, headers / footers etc.

Graphics — standard logo, correct position

Every word-processed document is based on a template. When you create a new blank document you usually opt for the package's pre-set 'normal' template.

Most packages also give you the option to choose from a range of templates including **memos**, **reports**, **letters** and **faxes**. These are ready formatted, and you just have to enter the text.

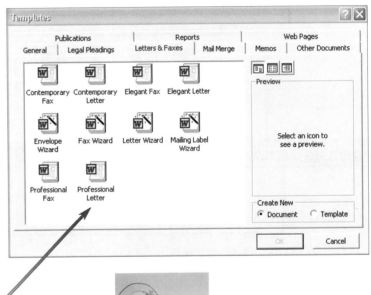

Huw wasn't sure just how these ten plates were going to help with his word processing...

Practice Questions

Q1 How can tailoring generic applications software packages make them easier to use?

Q2 Give 1 advantage and 1 disadvantage of using a customised system interface.

Q3 Give 3 examples of standard document templates found in a generic Word Processing package.

Exam Questions

Q1 Describe three ways to customise the interface of a generic software package to make it more user-friendly. (6 marks)

Q2 A spreadsheet package has macro capabilities.

a) Explain what is meant by the term "macro capabilities". (2 marks)

b) Give two examples of situations where the use of macros would be appropriate. (2 marks)

Washing your socks regularly means a nicer interface for the feet...

Yes folks, you heard it here first — washing your socks means your feet will smell less. Unless you have naturally foul smelling body odours of course. In other news, AS ICT examiners have been found to cause 85% more boredom in pupils than Theatre Studies examiners. That's a statistic I just made up, but it feels true, doesn't it? Anyway, learn all this stuff, etc...

Templates, Style Sheets and Wizards

My mum's a witch. No really. A real life proper witch. She can fly. She has a black cat. She eats babies at halloween. She's really scary and doesn't have anything to do with AS ICT. Anyway, here's a couple of pages that mention wizards...

Creating Templates *is Incredibly Easy*

Creating your own templates is usually pretty straightforward and goes something like this:

1) **Open** a new document.

2) **Edit** the new document so that it looks like the template you want. Design everything from text and graphics to margin sizes and page orientation.

3) When you're happy, **save** it as a template.

Now every time you want to use it you simply open your template and away you go.

  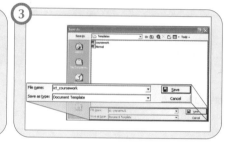

Handy hint — try not to make your coursework look like it's been done by a five year old...

Using Templates Has **Advantages** *and* **Disadvantages**

Good Stuff About Templates

1) Templates are already set-up, so users **don't have to waste time** formatting documents.

2) Templates make sure that documents have a **consistent style** and 'look'. This is especially useful in businesses that need employees to work in a **house style**.

Not-So-Good Stuff About Templates

1) If generic templates aren't satisfactory, then users need to **spend time** creating their own.

2) The **design is limited**, so if layout needs changing then this has to be done manually.

3) Documents can become **boring** as users don't bother thinking about new designs.

Style Sheets *Are Templates For* Desktop Publishing

1) Style sheets are a bit like word processing **templates**, but are used in **desktop publishing programs**.

2) They're used to set the **layout** and **format** of certain publications. They can also be called **master documents**.

3) Style sheets are **more complex** than word processing templates because the software is **more powerful** and has more functions.

4) When setting up your own style sheets, the **user has more control** over the details. E.g. they can drag the page number to wherever they want, or they can layer different objects and text together to form titles or headers.

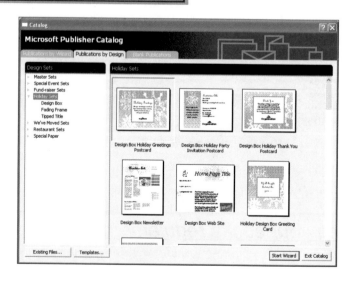

Templates, Style Sheets and Wizards

Using Style Sheets Has **Advantages** and (guess what) **Disadvantages**

Good Things About Style Sheets

1) They **save time** on designing pages.
2) They make sure that documents and publications can be produced in a **consistent house style**, even where they're being produced by lots of different members of staff.

Bad Things About Style Sheets

1) The documents and publications can end up all **looking the same**, making them less interesting and effective.
2) Someone must be **paid to develop the style**, and this will be money wasted if the style isn't followed.
3) It's hard for documents produced using style sheets to be **adapted** for different audiences.

A **Wizard** Can **Help** With **Tricky Tasks**

Lots of different programs have wizards which help you carry out certain tasks.

1) In word processors and DTP programs, wizards can help you with the **design** of your document or publication.

   Wizards have their own **preset layouts and styles** you can choose from. You just select the type and style you want, the colour scheme and details to include, and the wizard will **design and build it for you**, saving you time and effort.

2) Wizards can also be used to **create complex applications** or documents in very user-friendly ways.

   For example, a wizard can be used to build, search and design reports in a database package.

3) The down side is that you're **limited to the options available in the wizard**, and can't be original.

   You also run the risk of your documents looking just like everyone else's.

Example — Using a Fax Wizard

1) Selecting the fax wizard opens up this dialogue box to guide you through creating a new fax.

2) It asks you to fill in all the important information (e.g. sender / receiver details).

3) It even asks you to pick one of their pre-set templates, just to make life easy.

Practice Questions

Q1 Give one advantage and one disadvantage of each of these: templates, style sheets and wizards.

Q2 How do master documents, style sheets and templates help when working in a team?

Exam Questions

Q1 Give two advantages and two disadvantages of using a wizard to create a weekly publication in a desktop publishing package.   (4 marks)

Q2 Clep Co is about to open offices across the UK as part of their expansion programme. Explain two features of generic software packages that could be used to ensure that all the company's documents have a consistent house style.   (2 marks)

Anyone writing Harry Potter jokes will be gagged — with the help of a wizard...

It might seem as though templates, style sheets and wizards are all the same thing, but there are differences between them that you need to understand. So, don't go on to the next page 'til you're sure you know everything on this one. Then, you have to learn the rules of Quiddich. Then you have to find the one ring to rule them all — oh wait, that's the wrong book.

Types of Processing

Here's a little section all about processing information. There shouldn't be anything too stressful here — it's just going through the different types of processing. And remember — you're nearly halfway through the book now. Hoorah!

Booking Systems And Payroll Systems Use Transaction Processing

1) Ticket reservation systems, airline booking systems and invoicing systems are all **transaction processing systems**.

2) It's important that all booking or invoice information is **checked** and **correct** before the booking is made.

3) In a transaction processing system, each transaction is processed **before** another is started. This means that double-bookings (e.g. of seats) is impossible.

A customer can check whether space is available but can't book that space until all the details for the booking have been entered and checked. If two people were trying to book the same seat on a flight, they might both be told that a seat is available, but only the person who **submits their full details first** will get the seat. The second customer would then have to wait for the first customer's transaction to go through before theirs would get processed.

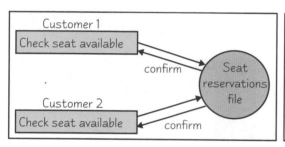 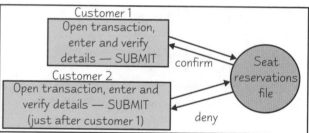

The Method Of Processing Is Chosen To Suit The Purpose Of The System

There are **two** distinct methods of **updating a system's data**:

1) **Real-time systems**
2) **Batch processing systems**

A Real-Time System Processes Data Straight Away

1) Real-time systems update data files regularly enough for there to be **no apparent delay** for the user.

2) **Airline booking systems** use real-time processing. Once you've entered your details the seat is booked straight away. This means that information about which seats are available is always up-to-date.

3) Some real-time systems are designed to respond quickly enough to **control the outcome** of an activity.

> E.g. an **air traffic control system** must constantly monitor the height and position of aircraft in its flight zone. If two aircraft start on a collision course it must react immediately to alert the traffic controller to the problem and allow them to react before it is too late. This is a real-time system.

A Batch-Processing System Processes Data at Regular Intervals

Batch processing systems work by collecting transactions together and updating the main data **all at once**. They're great for when a company has large amounts of data to process at regular intervals.

> E.g. when a **gas company** reads meters they will collect all meter readings together with details such as the address or number of the gas meter. Once a set of readings have been collected the data is input into the gas billing system all in one go and a set of gas bills are generated. When the bills are being generated there is no input from the user at all.

Types of Processing

There Are **Other Methods** Of Processing

Interactive processing systems respond to actions from the user — you **interact** with them.
An interactive system is often **a front end** to a transaction processing system.

E.g. when we **shop on-line** we are using an interactive system. We can check if an
item is in stock, check the price and can place an item in the basket and view
what's already in there. Once we place the order we're making a transaction, which
then updates stock levels and billing information files.

Systems Can Use **More than One** Method of Processing

You've probably realised by now that a lot of common systems use more than one method of processing — e.g.
online booking systems use transaction processing, which takes place in real-time, and probably has an interactive
front end. Still, there's usually a good reason for choosing a particular type of processing for a particular task:

Method	Examples	Reasons for using this system
Batch processing	production of gas bills, electricity bills, bank statements, credit card statements, invoicing, payroll	All transactions are processed together when the system is not busy, often overnight or at the weekend. This means access to the master data is always available during main working times. However, data becomes out of date until the next update.
Real-time processing	air traffic control, flight control, process control, robotics, booking systems	The response to changes in data is fast enough that the user won't notice any delay. Some real-time systems can be expensive, e.g. if they require specialist hardware to monitor physical data.
Interactive processing	on-line booking systems, on-line banking systems, games software, design software	The user can check the state of data at any time and it will be up to date. Allows the user to control a system (e.g. a computer game) as the system responds to each user action. In an online booking /ordering system, it allows the user to look up and check information, e.g. prices, billing address, etc. before submitting their booking / final order.
Transaction processing	booking systems, invoicing and ordering systems, stock control systems	Transactions are made one at a time, which prevents two processes changing the same data, e.g. double booking a seat on a flight. However, there's no feedback from the system until a whole transaction has been submitted (unless it has an interactive front end).

Practice Questions

Q1   Explain what a real-time system is and give an example.

Q2   Explain what a batch processing system is and give an example.

Q3   Explain the difference between the following: a) transaction processing and b) interactive processing.

Exam Question

Q1   For each of the following systems, recommend a suitable method of processing and say why that method is most suitable.

a) a flight booking system.   (2 marks)

b) an end of month invoicing system.   (2 marks)

c) a nuclear reactor monitoring system.   (2 marks)

It doesn't take much real-time processing to work out Big Brother's rubbish...

*The data changes constantly, especially if you watch it 24/7, and instantly the information gets processed by my brain and
out pops the result from my mouth: "Big Brother's just a bit rubbish really, isn't it?" Anyway, apologies to any BB fans out
there but really, wouldn't you rather be learning about different types of information processing? Don't answer right away...*

Processing Different Data Types

Computers can process lots of different kinds of data, as long as they know what they're looking at. It's a bit like watching German television — I'll watch anything that's on, but I really need a programme guide for it to make sense.

Computers Need To Know **What Kind Of Data** They're Processing

Computer systems can **process various types** of data as long as the system knows what type of data it is. The data might be:

- **Text** — processed by applications like word processing, databases and e-mail.
- **Numbers** — processed by applications like spreadsheets and databases.
- **Graphics** — processed by applications like digital imaging, computer-aided design and drawing.
- **Sound** — processed by applications like multimedia.

All Data Is Stored As **Sets Of 0s And 1s**

1) The 0s and 1s are called **binary digits** or **bits**. The **way** the 0s and 1s are **organised** determines the type of data.

2) **Text** data includes **all the keyboard characters**.

> Text is often stored using the ASCII code. Every possible keyboard key has a special code assigned to it. This code is 8 bits long. An example of an ASCII code is 01000001, which represents the letter A. All applications on all systems recognise ASCII code.

3) **Numbers** are stored using **binary codes** to represent particular **numbers**.
Some binary codes represent **whole numbers** and are stored using **binary representation**.

Binary representation of whole number									Whole number
bits	= 128	64	32	16	8	4	2	1	the whole number represented is the sum of the column numbers containing a 1
00000100 = 0	0	0	0	0	1	0	0		4
00000011 = 0	0	0	0	0	0	1	1		3
00000110 = 0	0	0	0	0	1	1	0		6

4) Some binary codes represent **fractional numbers** and are stored using a system called **floating point binary representation**. Some binary codes represent **negative numbers** and are stored using a system called **two's complement binary representation**.

5) As long as the application reading the data knows **what type of data to expect**, it will **interpret it correctly**.

Each **Dot** In A Picture Is **Stored As A Set of Bits**

1) Digital pictures can be **photographs**, **'painted' pictures**, or **line drawings**.

2) Photographs and 'painted' pictures are stored as **sets of dots**. Each dot is stored as a **set of bits**.
The bits represent the colour, shade and brightness of that particular dot. 111111111111111111001100 is an example of picture data — a pale yellow colour. The more bits used, the more choice of colour there is. The number of **individual dots per inch** is the **resolution** of the picture. The higher the resolution, the more dots, and the larger the set of data.

3) A **bitmap** is the **simplest type** of picture file. The whole bitmap needs to be stored and processed together.

4) The file size for a high-res, full colour bitmap can be **huge**. **Compression techniques** can make the file **smaller**. The formats they create include JPEGs and GIFs.
Compression techniques include finding series of consecutive dots that are all the same colour and replacing them with one dot and a number indicating how many to put back in. JPEG and GIF are used by lots of different kinds of software and can be displayed in many other applications including Web browsers.

5) **Vector** or **object-based graphics** consist only of lines and solid shapes. It requires relatively few bits just to store data about the lines and shapes (e.g. where they start, where they finish and their properties). Each shape or line is treated as an object and any changes to part of the object are applied to the whole object. See p103.

6) Applications may have **their own way** of storing vector graphics, so it's often harder to transfer vector graphics data between different applications (e.g. a drawing made with CAD software often can't be opened by a slide show application).

Processing Different Data Types

Data Needs To Be Encoded Using A Standard Format

1) Sound data is also stored as a **series of bits**. Each set of bits represents a sound at a **particular pitch** and **amplitude**.

2) Like pictures, there are a number of different standard ways to store **sound data**. MIDI is one standard, developed for dealing with the output from **musical instruments**. MP3 is another standard, used generally for **recorded music**.

3) Any system can interpret data as long as it knows what type of **data** it is. When data is created it is **encoded** into the required **format**.

- When you type text into a word processed document it will be encoded using the ASCII standard.

- When you take a digital photograph it might be encoded using the JPEG standard.

- Many existing recordings have been encoded using the MP3 standard so that they can be played by applications such as 'iTunes'™.

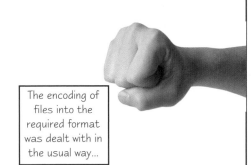

The encoding of files into the required format was dealt with in the usual way...

Applications Are Often Designed To Deal With Many Different Types Of Data

A Microsoft Office document may contain text, pictures, vector graphics, numbers and even sound. A document will be encoded **using different standards** for **each type of data**. **Tags** will indicate where data is of one type or another so that the application can deal with it correctly.

A database application will again deal with **different types** of data. A data table may contain text data or numerical data and each will be **stored** and **dealt with differently**. A spreadsheet application deals with numbers of different types and will create charts and graphs. You can even paste a bitmap picture into a spreadsheet.

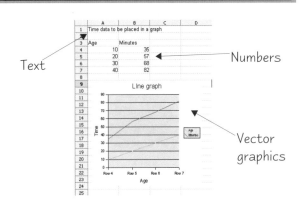

Practice Questions

Q1   What are the common types of data that can be stored?

Q2   Define the term 'bit'.

Q3   Describe the formats used for storing photographic images.

Exam Questions

Q1   Describe how data representing each of the following might be stored:

   a) text   (2 marks)

   b) sound   (2 marks)

   c) lines and shapes   (2 marks)

Q2   Explain how a digital imaging application might encode the picture data it stores.   (2 marks)

Oooh I do like "bits" — on the right person that is...

These pages are starting to look a bit like a maths book, aren't they? Not to worry, there's not much more of that. Make sure you understand it all though — it's no good being woolly-headed about this stuff. Go over it again and make sure you know it all. Then have a little think about all the different kinds of jokes you can make using the word "bits".

Formatting Data for the End User

Of course, it's always the end user that dictates how we process information — you'll need to manipulate files to suit them, which I think is well cheeky. The end users do no work, but they call the shots... Humph. I'm going to rebel...

Users' Needs Come First When Designing Information Systems

A user needs an information system to produce **useful information**. That information must:

- be in the required **format**.
- **not be hidden** in lots of other information.
- contain exactly what the user **wants**.
- be **presented** in the most appropriate way.

When thinking about the **output format**, you need to consider a number of things:

1) **Who needs the information?**

This may tell you **what format** the output might take. The output could be graphical, in a table or text.

2) **What information do they need?**

There might be a lot of information produced by the system but the user only needs **some** of it. What should be left in and what left out?

3) **When do they need the information?**

Should information be displayed **regularly** and updated as it changes, or should it only be displayed once all updating is **complete**?

4) **Will the information be needed for another part of the system?**

If so, does it need to be **stored** in a particular way? Does it need to be sent to another computer **on a network**? Will it be displayed on screen, printed or sent over the Internet? Will it be opened by **another application**? The way the output is presented will differ depending on where it has to go.

There Are Many Different Possible Types Of Output

Insurance	£80	per year
Stationery	£165	per year
Rent	£75	per month
Rates	£250	per year
Wages	£120	per week
Motor expenses	£55	per month
Stock	£2764	per 3 months

Tables

Information can be put into a table. This helps to put it in **order** and it can be read fairly easily. **Database** and **spreadsheet** applications often produce table output. **Word processing** and **slide show** presentation applications can also produce this type of output.

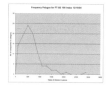

Graphs

Some **numerical data** is easier to understand if it is represented as a graph. We use graphs to show **statistical** information. **Database** and **spreadsheet** applications are particularly good at producing graphs from stored data.

Graphics

Information is often better given as a **picture** than as long pieces of text. **Picture buttons** on web pages are often better than textual links.

 Home

Reports

The best reports show all the required information and **no more**. Choosing the right **search criteria** helps to make sure that the right **amount** of information is found. Once the information for a report has been retrieved, the **presentation** needs to be considered. What information will go where? What order will the records be presented in?

Video, Animation, Sound

Other formats allow you to present information in more **entertaining** ways.

Different People Want The Same Information Presented In Different Ways

The way a piece of information is presented will depend on its audience — different audiences need different presentations:

Sales Director	...needs to use the figures for analysis	...wants the figures in a table
Managing Director	...wants to look at the overall picture	...wants the information in a graph
Shareholders	...want to see how the company is doing	...want the sales figures and graph incorporated into a slide show presentation
Customers	...want to see that they are buying from a successful company	...want something entertaining, like a video including sound and animation.

Formatting Data for the End User

You'll Need To Consider How To **Produce** The Output **Effectively**

The user will want to know that the output is **what they want**, and they'll want to produce it in the **easiest** way possible. They might also want to **save** the output and use it **in a different application**. There are a number of techniques designed to make these requirements **easier to achieve**:

WYSIWYG — What You See Is What You Get

Most applications will provide this. Getting the output right is *easy* if what you see on the screen is what you get on the printer. Where there are differences between the screen and the printed output, most applications will provide a **print preview**.

Mailmerge

Mailmerge allows the user to produce one document in a word processing application and then to use a database of names and addresses and to output **one personalised document for each name**.

Standards for encoding

There are **many different standards** for encoding the output from applications. If an application uses a known standard to create a file, then it's likely that any other application will be able to read it. Examples of standards for encoding are ASCII, JPEG, GIF, MPG, floating point binary, two's complement binary, MIDI, MP3.

Output **Doesn't Just Go To Screen Or Printer**

The output from an information system is very often displayed **on the screen** or **printed**, but there are **other forms of output media**.

1) Some output is **saved to disk**. This output might be used again by the same application or it might be used by a different application. If it is needed by a different application, it must be encoded in such a way that the other application is able to read it.

2) The output might be **sent to another system**, over a network or over the Internet. This output must be created in such a way that it is able to be sent and can be understood by the application at the other end, even if it's not running on the same type of computer. Standards for encoding the data are vital to make sure that applications at each end see the information in the same way.

3) Another type of output media is a **projection screen**, used for video conferencing and presentations. Output designed for projection screens will need to be of a good enough resolution to make it usable on a large screen.

Practice Questions

Q1 What is the primary consideration when designing output?
Q2 Describe five different types of output.
Q3 Make a list of different types of output media.

Exam Questions

Q1 The accounts department of a large company produces yearly accounts for the tax office, for the company directors, for the company shareholders and for potentially important new customers.

How might the annual accounts be presented for each of these **four** purposes? (4 marks)

Q2 A web page may contain many different output formats.

Describe three formats you might expect to see on a web page. (3 marks)

Rex the dog processes food — the output goes on to the pavement...

Well isn't that a nice mental image to end the section on? Hm. Maybe I should go with something a little more upbeat. Well, why spoil the general tone at this point in the book? Seriously though, make sure that you've understood everything in this section before you go on to the next. Make sure you remember to think about alternative output media too, okay?

Hardware — Input Devices

Every computer system takes input from input devices, performs some processing and produces some output. And you know what else — the sun is hot, snow is cold and my neighbour's dog has a tail as long as my arm. So there.

Different Systems Need Different Types Of Input

All systems need **instructions** of some sort and these generally come **from the user**.

- Some systems need **text**. This can be typed in by a user or read from a document.
- Some systems need high-quality **pictures**, and some produce line drawings and need accurate input of lines.
- Other systems use **video** images, and must be able to receive these images.

Input devices are chosen for their **quality** and **ease of use** in dealing with the type of input required.

All Systems Use One Or More Input Devices

Device	Type of Input	Characteristics and Limitations
Keyboard	• text • numbers • some cursor movement	• Most conventional computer systems have a QWERTY keyboard with a numeric keypad and function keys — people are **familiar** with them and they are **versatile** for experienced users. • Most **instructions** can be done **from the keyboard**, although some can be quicker with a **mouse** (e.g. most keyboards have arrow keys to move the cursor through text, but it's often quicker to use the mouse).
Mouse	• cursor movement • click/double click • drag • scroll	• Most conventional computer systems have a mouse or other pointing device — people are **familiar** with them and they are designed to **fit easily** in your hand. • They are easy for **beginners** to use with a graphical user interface. • **Extensive** use can cause repetitive strain injury. • Most instructions are **slower** with the mouse **than with the keyboard** (e.g. to copy and paste requires at least four mouse clicks whereas it only requires two keystrokes, Ctrl+C and Ctrl+V). • Mice are also quite prone to picking up **dirt** and this affects their performance. An optical mouse is less prone to dirt but can have trouble on some surfaces.
Scanner	• images • text	• A scanner uses reflected light to **read data** from a paper document. This data might be a picture or text, in colour or in black and white. • **Special software** is required to interpret what the scanner reads, especially if it is text. • The **quality** of the input depends on the **resolution** of the scanner. A high quality picture needs a high-resolution scanner.
Touch screen	• press • drag	• Touch screens are often used on terminals in **public places** and on notebook PCs. • The user **touches** one part of the screen with their finger or a pointing device, and this acts the same way as clicking a mouse. • Using a touch screen means that a **surface** for a mouse is **not required** and means, in a public place, that the **input device can't be removed**. • It is **difficult** to **pinpoint small areas** on a touch screen and so buttons, menus, scroll bars, etc. must be large enough to be accessible.

Hardware — Input Devices

There Are Also **Other Types** Of **Pointing Device**

Graphical user interfaces make use of pointing devices, such as a mouse or touch screen, as a way for the user to **give instructions**. Other types of pointing device are:

- **Trackball** — this is like an **upside down mouse**. The ball is on the top and you use your finger or the palm of your hand to move the cursor around on the screen. There will be **switches** around the trackball, which act in the same way as mouse buttons. Trackballs are often used on **laptop** computers so that the user doesn't have to plug in or provide a surface for a mouse.
- **Trackpad** — these are also used on **laptop** computers. The pad is sensitive to the **movement** of a **finger** over the surface and the movement of the finger moves the cursor on the screen. Again, **buttons** are provided like mouse buttons and there is no need for a mouse or surface.

Both these devices can be difficult to get used to if you are used to using a mouse.

Some Systems Use **Special Types Of Keyboard**

1) A PC keyboard usually has a set of QWERTY keys, a numeric keypad and a set of function keys. This makes it **very flexible**, but **quite big**.

2) Some systems **don't need all these functions** and so they only have **part** of the keyboard.
   - A **cash machine** will only have a numeric keypad as only numbers will be entered.
   - A **mobile telephone** (or touch tone telephone) uses a numeric keypad but assigns letters to each key to allow text input as well.
   - **Touch tone telephones** are used to select from menus on computerised call systems.

Concept Keyboards Don't Have **Traditional Keys**

1) A concept keyboard uses **sensitive areas of surface** rather than actual keys.

2) Different areas of the surface will **input different commands**.

3) Concept keyboards are useful in areas where dirt or liquid makes it **impractical** to use a conventional keyboard.
   - Many **fast food restaurants** use concept keyboards for entering customer food orders into their system.
   - Concept keyboards are used in computer controlled diagnostic systems for **testing car engines**.

4) Special areas of the keyboard will perform a **particular function** depending on the software it's used with.

5) This type of keyboard is very **specialised** and will be used with one particular system. It's not flexible enough to be used like a conventional keyboard.

Practice Questions

Q1 Make a list of the main types of input that can be used by different computer systems.
Q2 List three types of pointing device.
Q3 Give three different examples where keyboards are used as an input device (other than traditional QWERTY keyboards).

Exam Question

Q1 The World Wide Web is a collection of information often accessed by navigation through a graphical user interface. People can access the Internet from many different systems, including their home PCs, laptops, mobile telephones and public Internet terminals.

For **two** of the systems mentioned above, give an example of an input device that could be used to navigate a web page, and evaluate its use.

(6 marks)

Have you seen my new concept trousers? — they're a bit of a hard wear...

Hardware is a bit of an odd one — in theory, you already know it all. I mean, everyone knows how to use a keyboard and a mouse, don't they? Well... it's not quite that simple. You have to make sure you can remember all the ins and outs of all the different kinds of hardware input devices. It's easy to pick up marks on these questions, as long as you've learnt it all.

Hardware — Input Devices

Some input devices, like keyboards and mice and scanners, are general purpose — they provide a range of different types of input. Other input devices are designed specifically for one type of input. Like badgers. No, wait... What?

Scanners Are Used To Read Different Types Of Input

1) Scanners are used to **read** information from documents and **store** it in a computer system.

2) The data is read by the scanner and **interpreted by software**.

3) If the document is made up of **text**, it might be scanned then converted using **optical character recognition** software. This does the best it can to translate the image it gets into text but it **doesn't always get it right**. Even so, with large volumes of text it is still often **quicker** to scan and edit the text than to type it in.

4) **Bar codes** are scanned by specialist scanners. The scanner is driven by **specialist software** that interprets the bar code. A bar code reader will **only** be able to read bar codes.

Special Devices Are Used To Input Pictures And Drawings

A **graphics tablet** is used to input line drawings (e.g. engineering plans) into a computer. The user has a **stylus** (like a pen), which draws on a **graphics pad**. Drawings can be done from scratch or can be traced by moving the stylus over an existing drawing. A graphics tablet can only input lines but the tablet may have special areas for **giving instructions** for changing colour, line thickness or other features.

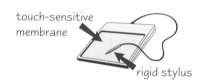

touch-sensitive membrane

rigid stylus

A **light pen** is a pointing device used to point to a position on the screen. It's especially useful for the input of line drawings — it works by drawing the line **on the screen** rather than on a tablet.

- For photographic images a **digital camera** will capture an image and input it into a computer.
- For video images a **digital video camera** can feed a series of images into the computer. The **resolution** of the camera in both cases will determine the quality and size of the image it captures.
- A **webcam** is designed to be connected directly to a computer system so that it can feed its video images straight to a web site, rather than store them first and then upload them.

Some Devices Are Designed For A Very Specific Purpose

Some data is stored in a way which means it can be input **straight into the computer** as long the **right device** is used.

1) Magnetic strips on credit card or train tickets hold data identifying card details or ticket details. A **magnetic card reader** is able to read the strip and decipher the details.

2) A **chip and PIN** card has a small integrated circuit which holds similar details to a magnetic strip, but also holds the PIN number of the card so it can be authenticated as it is being used. A **special reader** is used to read the PIN from the card.

3) Magnetic ink is used on some documents and a special **Magnetic Ink Character Recognition (MICR) device** is used to read the magnetic characters. This system is extensively used in banking systems where magnetic characters are printed on cheques to give the cheque number, sort code and account number. The characters are read by a machine so that bank operators only have to enter the date and the amount of the cheque and the person it is to be paid to. This also makes cheque forgery more difficult.

4) An **optical mark reader** is designed to read marks made at particular points on a form. The reader knows what parts of the form give particular information and uses reflected light to see if there is a mark in any of those places. Common uses of OMR are on National Lottery tickets and school registers.

Hardware — Input Devices

Some Devices Are Designed For Use *Without Human Intervention*

1) Environmental control systems, engine management systems and process control systems use a **variety of sensors** as input devices.

2) These sensors might sense heat, light, movement, humidity, magnetism or pressure.

3) Computer systems can **take the inputs** and **act appropriately**. For example, if a heat sensor gives a temperature reading below what is required the system might turn on a heater.

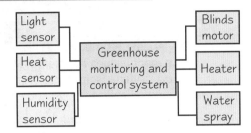

Physically Disabled People Sometimes *Need Special Devices*

Physical disabilities can prevent people from being able to use **conventional input devices** like keyboards and mice. A range of devices has been designed to cater for **different disabilities**:

1) A **foot-mouse** is a mouse controlled by the user's feet rather than their hands. This device has the same capabilities as a conventional mouse but is designed for those who are unable to operate a mouse using their hands, or to reduce the risk of injuries such as carpal tunnel syndrome caused by extensive mouse usage.

2) For blind users, **voice-recognition** devices to allow speech input.

3) **Concept keyboards** are also very useful for disabled users who can't use the conventional keyboard and for very inexperienced or very young users. Large areas of the keyboard have particular functions, often indicated by a picture to help the user.

4) People who are unable to make any movement will need very special devices to communicate with the computer. Some examples of these special devices include:

- **puff-suck switches** used in place of a mouse button and operated by exhalation and inhalation.

- **eye-typers** allow their user to select keyboard keys by staring at particular places for a given time.

Practice Questions

Q1 Make a list of input devices that can be used to input graphical images.

Q2 Explain how MICR devices work.

Q3 What sort of input devices might be used in an environmental control system?

Q4 Give three examples of input devices designed to help physically disabled users.

Exam Questions

Q1 A photographic company wants a computerised system to store new and existing photographs so that they can be printed on T-shirts along with a slogan requested by the customer. They buy a T-shirt printing machine and a thermal printer capable of producing photo-quality output.

Name **three** input devices they will they need and say what each will be used for. (3 marks)

Q2 Describe one benefit and one limitation of concept keyboards. (2 marks)

Input devices? Frankly my dear, I don't give a damn...

Make sure you know all these — we're moving on to output devices next. So go over them until you've got them all down. It's all pretty straightforward though, and none of it's too taxing... Which means that I have a few minutes to ask you what goes black-white-flag black-white-flag black-white-flag? Simple — a nun rolling down a hill with union jack pants on...

Hardware — Output Devices

An output device is any hardware used to communicate processed data to the user, e.g. monitor, speakers, printer. Printers are probably the most popular ones, so we've got a WHOLE page on them. *sniff* I'm just so, so happy...

Inkjet Printers Are The Cheapest

1) **Inkjets** are the most popular printers for domestic use. They use small jets of ink sprayed on to paper as it is fed past the print head.

2) There are **three** different ways of **controlling the flow** of ink. In some printers the nozzles are controlled by crystals inside the printhead which change shape when an electrical current is passed through them. In others, the ink is heated so it expands and pushes through the nozzles onto the paper. Continuous flow printers squirt ink continuously from the nozzles, then the unused ink is electrically charged and diverted back by charged plates.

Laser Printers Are Ace But A Bit More Expensive

Laser printers are the **most versatile** output device. They set up pages in full before printing, and have four main parts:

1) **Electrostatic rotating drum** — has an electrical charge.

2) **Laser** — etches onto the drum a negative image of the page to be printed. Where the laser hits the drum the electrical charge is removed.

3) **Toner cartridge** — contains ink. When the drum passes over the toner cartridge the ink is attracted onto the charged areas of the drum. The ink is then transferred onto the printer paper.

4) **Fuser unit** — heats the paper to fuse the ink onto it.

The User Needs To Think About What They Want From Their Printer

Speed

Laser printers have a high page-per-minute print rate, although the best inkjet printers can also print very fast.

Resolution

When looking for documents of a high quality, laser printers offer resolution with a high dots-per-inch (dpi). Some inkjets are pretty good too though.

Initial Cost

Ink jets are very cheap to buy. At the moment a colour laser printer is still fairly expensive, but the cost of laser printers is coming down all the time.

Running Costs

Laser printers are often more cost effective than inkjet printers if you print a lot of pages.

There Are Some Other Specialist Printing Devices Too

1) **Graph plotters** are commonly used with Computer Aided Design (CAD). They work by an automated arm that disperses ink, moving over the paper. This is often designed to handle large paper sizes and outputs high quality vector graphics (e.g. needed in architectural plans).

2) **Dot matrix printers** used to be used with PCs, but these days they're just used for things like receipt printing. They print a series of dots that appear to form characters at normal reading distance. They can be very useful where carbon copies are to be printed simultaneously.

3) **Thermal printers** are often used in calculators and fax machines. They work by transferring an impression onto paper using heat.

4) **Braille printers**, also known as **embossers**, are used to create sequences of raised dots on paper. This device is intended for the blind and visually impaired.

Hardware — Output Devices

Monitors Are A Pretty Obvious Output Device

Also known as **VDUs** (Visual Display Units) or **display screens**, monitors present a display of text and graphics through arrangements of dots more commonly known as pixels. Monitors can differ in:

1) **Type** — the first decision made on purchasing monitors currently seems to be whether to buy a **CRT** or **Flat Panel** monitor. CRT (Cathode Ray Tube) monitors take up far more space on a desktop as they work on similar technologies to TV sets, with a tube protruding from the rear of the screen. Flat Panel screens (first seen on laptops), on the other hand, are very thin, lightweight and portable. They use **LCD technology**.

2) **Colour capabilities** — most monitors now display millions of colours although some monochrome VDUs (using two colours) are still in use.

3) **Size** — monitors are measured in inches, diagonally from corner-to-corner of the screen.

4) **Display quality** — this is known as resolution and refers to the amount of pixels and how closely packed they are. Measured in dots per inch, common sizes are 1024 x 768 and 800 x 600.

LCD Projectors Get Used More By Organisations And Companies

1) These are commonly used in **presentations**, as they can project video and computer signals.

2) **Display magnification** means output can be provided on large screens.

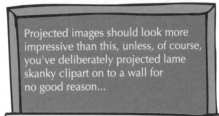

Projected images should look more impressive than this, unless, of course, you've deliberately projected lame skanky clipart on to a wall for no good reason...

Speakers Add Another Dimension...

1) As well as hard copy and visual output, **audio output** can be provided through speakers.

2) This is often required as part of **multimedia systems** where text, graphics, video and sound are integrated.

3) Speakers can be used as the **primary output device** as well though. A good example of this is a speech output for a visually impaired person.

Practice Questions

Q1 What output device would be used for producing hard copy?
Q2 What are two examples of uses of thermal printers?
Q3 Explain what "resolution" means and say what it's measured in.

Exam Questions

Q1 A construction company employs architects to draw up plans for building layouts using specialist software. There is a proposal to upgrade an existing A4 ink jet printer to a more sophisticated output device that can produce precise printed copies of plans in a larger size.

Name a device that would be appropriate for this and say why. (2 marks)

Q2 A school IT room needs a paper output on a network. A laser printer has been installed by the school.

Give two reasons why the school might have decided on a laser printer. (2 marks)

Simon can't hear his lecturer properly — he needs better speakers...

I always forget monitors are output devices. I like having everything on paper you see, so I can dribble tea on it and get jam in between the sheets. I did try that with my computer once, but some of the keys stuck together so that every time I pressed the "b" key, the keyboard would type "swertyuiop". I had to give up after the spellchecker had a breakdown.

Hardware — Backing Storage

Computer systems need to store data so that it can be used again. The data must be kept in such a way that it never gets lost and can always be recovered if necessary. And also, pigs must be reared in such a way so they can always fly.

Backing Storage Devices Are Chosen For Their Speed, Cost Or Capacity

There are **different types** of storage device. Each one stores data in a different way.

1) **Magnetic storage devices** create magnetised areas on magnetic media to represent the data. To read the data they can detect which areas are magnetised and which are not.

   • Magnetic storage media include floppy disks, hard disks and magnetic tape.

2) **Optical storage devices** use lasers to burn spots on optical media and then use light to read the spots and interpret them as data.

   • Optical storage media include CD-ROM, CD-R, CD-RW, DVD-ROM, DVD-R and DVD-RW.

3) **Memory sticks** use semi-conductor memory called flash memory, similar to the memory chips inside the computer, but are able to hold data permanently.

The Speed, Costs And Capacity Can Vary

Media	Typical size	Typical cost	Typical uses, characteristics and limitations
Floppy disk	1.44Mb	around £0.25	Used as a **cheap** back up media for keeping copies of **small files** from the hard disk. Random access, low durability, some systems now don't have floppy disk drives.
Hard disk	up to 200Gb	part of disk drive, or £30-£80	**Main storage media** for most computer systems. Fast, random access. Hard disks consist of a set of stacked disks with a read / write head on each side of each disk.
Magnetic tape	up to 200Gb	a 20Gb tape might be around £10	Generally used for **storing a copy** of all the data on the main hard disk in case it is needed. Data is stored sequentially and is generally all read or written in one go.
CD-ROM	up to 800Mb	included in price of its contents	Used for **sale** copies of program software and high resolution graphic images. Fast, random access on a durable media. Can only be read from, not written to by the computer systems that use them.
CD-R	up to 800Mb	about 18 pence per disk	As CD-ROM, but can be written to once and then **read** as many times as necessary. Useful for permanent backup of data.
CD-RW	up to 800Mb	70 to 80 pence per disk	Can be written to and read from **over and over** again like a hard disk. Data can only be written in one go but can be read randomly.
DVD-ROM	around 4.7Gb	included in the price of its contents	**Fast access.** Especially suitable for video, graphics and sound. Can only be read from, not written to by the computer systems that use them.
DVD-R	around 4.7Gb	around 40 pence per disk	As DVD-ROM, but can be written to once and then **read** as many times as necessary. Useful for a **permanent backup** of data.
DVD-RW	around 4.7Gb	around 40 pence per disk	Can be written to and read from over and over again. Data can only be written in one go but can be **read randomly**.
Memory stick	up to 1Gb	£10 to £60	Useful for **backing up** data files **individually**. Fast, random access. Portable and plugs into any computer's USB port.

Hardware — Backing Storage

Duplicating Data Reduces The Risk Of Losing It

1) The hard disk **stores programs and files of data**. The programs can usually be reinstalled from their original or back up CDs if there's a problem, but data is generally being created and changed all the time.

2) Some systems use **mirrored hard disks** where a second hard disk keeps a mirror copy of the main hard disk. That way, if the main disk fails then the second disk is immediately ready to use. However, this is a very **expensive** option for many systems.

3) To make sure that data is not completely lost on most systems if the hard disk crashes, you should make **regular copies or back ups** of the data onto another storage device.

4) Of course, no storage device is completely safe — there's always the **risk of damage**.

For more on backing up see page 73.

Data can be backed up on:
- Floppy disk
- CD-R
- CD-RW
- DVD-R
- DVD-RW
- Second hard disk
- Memory stick
- Magnetic tape

You Can Save Time By Only Backing Up New Data

1) When you back up data you will often want to copy all your data files to a second backing storage media. This is called a **global back up**. If you do this regularly, it can be quite time consuming.

2) **Incremental back ups** only copy the files that have changed since the last back up. This saves time.

3) If there's a **main hard disk failure** all the backed up data files will have to be copied back onto the system.

4) A global back up can be copied back **quite quickly**, but incremental back ups can take a long time as the latest versions of files must be rebuilt.

5) An **effective method** for backing up is to do a global back up once a week and incremental back ups every day in between. If all data has to be recovered then there will be a maximum of **seven** back ups to recover from.

God's global backup

Practice Questions

Q1 Describe and give examples of magnetic storage media.

Q2 Describe and give examples of optical storage media.

Q3 Explain what an incremental back up is.

Exam Question

Q1 An insurance company uses a variety of software and stores many data files in its computer systems.

a) Suggest some different ways that the company could ensure all the programs and data on their computer system are safely backed up in case of a complete main hard disk failure. (4 marks)

b) Choose two different types of backing storage media and explain how the company might make use of these media. (2 marks)

If the Grand National was sponsored by IKEA — I'd be backing "storage"...

It might seem like that long list of backing storage devices is a bit pointless to learn, but it's information that will be useful to you in the long run. It's always good to keep these things swimming around in the old noggin, cos you never know when they'll come up. And once you have learnt them, you can spend some quality time inventing puns to put into CGP books.

Security of Data

It's been a long trek since section one, hasn't it? But you're doing really well, so don't give up on me now. If you give up then I'll be forced to do something very dramatic. Like, REALLY dramatic... Don't know what, but it'll be good.

Security, Privacy and Integrity — Make Sure You Know the Difference

1)   Data **privacy** is the need for some data only to be accessed by, and disclosed to, authorised persons.

2)   Data **integrity** is the correctness of data both during and after processing.

3)   Data **security** is the use of various methods to ensure data privacy and data integrity as well as preventing the loss or destruction of data.

Data Needs To Be Kept Secure

1)   Computer systems are worth a lot to the companies that use them and the **hardware** needs to be **protected** from theft and damage.

2)   More important than the hardware is the actual data that the computers contain:

- Data is **valuable**, whether showing sales figures or the latest research into new medicines.

- It may be **private** — a lot of data that is stored on computers is personal and, because of the Data Protection Act (see section 4), must not be disclosed to unauthorised people without the person's consent. E.g. details of how much employees are paid, health records, credit card history etc.

- It must be **correct** — if data is not kept secure it may be accidentally or deliberately altered.

3)   So basically, data needs to be **kept secure** so that it is not lost, changed or disclosed to people who should not have it.

- **Accidental loss** can occur due to human error, natural disasters, power failures, and problems with the hardware and software being used.

- **Deliberate loss** can occur due to hacking, cyber crime, viruses and vandalism.

There Are Different Ways of Keeping Data Secure

There are many different ways that companies can keep their data secure.

Keeping Hardware Safe:

1)   Companies can **restrict physical access** to the computers by keeping rooms **locked** when not in use. Many banks and building societies are starting to use fingerprint scanners or iris scanners to ensure that only authorised people can gain access to computers.

2)   **Fire and burglar alarms** can be installed.

3)   An **Uninterruptible Power Supply** (a back up battery) can be installed to prevent loss of data if there's a power failure.

Keeping Software Safe:

1)   Folders can be set as "**Read-Only**" so no one can accidentally delete an important file. After writing files to disk, the disks can be **write-protected** with the same result.

2)   Data that is sent over the Internet can be encoded using **encryption** methods to protect it.

3)   A **firewall** can be used to stop people accessing the computer system by hacking in from outside.

4)   As well as having **user IDs** (user names) and **passwords**, different users can be given different **levels of access** to parts of a system, e.g. they might only be allowed to view and change certain data depending on their job.

5)   User ID and password procedures can also be used to log what each user is doing at any particular time — this is an **audit trail**. Audit trails are useful after data has been compromised, in helping pin-point what happened.

Passwords can be kept secure by following a few standard rules:

1)   Use a **mixture** of numbers and letters.

2)   Don't use a **recognised** word or a word from a dictionary.

3)   Make sure a **record** is kept (somewhere safe) of passwords used, and don't use them again.

4)   **Change** your passwords regularly — every month would be the ideal.

Security of Data

Data Needs To Be Backed Up

1) However good security systems are, it is inevitable that some data will be lost, corrupted or incorrectly altered and so **precautions** need to be taken.

2) This will involve taking back up copies of the data so that it can be restored at some later stage if needed.

3) This may be on high capacity magnetic tapes, zip disks or writeable CDs/DVDs, depending on the amount of data.

"If your name's not down, you're not coming in."

Back Ups Need to be Regular and Kept Secure

1) Data back ups need to be **regular** enough so that if the whole system was lost, and a back up was restored, it would still be directly useful to the users — i.e. taking a back up once a year is pointless.

2) Depending on **how much data** is changed and processed, it may be necessary to back up the data once a week, once or day or even more often (in the case of a booking system for example).

3) **Daily** back ups are usually done **automatically** at the same time each day (often in the middle of the night when there is little network activity), and often just files that have been created or updated are backed up.

4) Companies usually have their own **system** to determine how long back ups are kept, as it's generally not practical to permanently keep every single daily back up. A typical system might involve taking daily incremental back ups which are kept for a week before being overwritten, and also taking weekly or monthly back ups to be stored for longer periods.

5) In case of fire, theft or flood, back ups should be kept in a fireproof safe, and not in the same building as the system they were taken from.

Companies Need To Plan For a Worst Case Scenario

1) As well as ensuring the system is properly backed up, it's vital that data can be **restored quickly** when needed.

2) It's the responsibility of the IT manager to **check regularly** that the back up process is working properly and that data can be easily restored from the back up.

3) Because so many organisations are dependent on computers, it is essential that planning is done in case they **cannot use their systems**. This includes being able to restore the back up data onto **replacement hardware** in a short space of time.

Practice Questions

Q1 Explain the difference between data security, privacy and integrity.
Q2 How can data be kept secure when it is transmitted across the Internet?
Q3 Explain why companies need different types of back up, and what form a typical back up system might take.

Exam Questions

Q1 A local gym keeps details of members and their subscriptions on a computer database. At present the manager takes a back up of the data onto a writeable CD once a month and stores it in a filing cabinet in her office.

a) Give three reasons why this is not a suitable back up strategy. (3 marks)

b) Suggest a suitable alternative back up strategy for the manager to adopt. (3 marks)

Q2 A local Health Centre keeps details of all patients on computer so they can be accessed quickly by the doctors.

a) Why is it important that the data is kept secure? (2 marks)

b) Give four ways in which the data should be kept secure from accidental or deliberate loss or corruption. (4 marks)

Don't back your data up into a cactus — you'll make it cry...

Awwww who's a little bit of data... Awww look at the cute ickle bit of data. Awww diddumms... But seriously: make sure you've got all this info about backing up data down. It's an easy way to pick up marks, and it's also an important lesson. I mean, just imagine what would happen if the ambulance service or the police force lost access to their whole systems.

Networks

Of course it's not all just back ups and roses you know... You have to learn all of this crazy network nonsense as well. Some bits of it get a bit tricky, but read your way through these two pages and you'll get your head around it, no worries.

Computers Can Be Networked or Stand-Alone

1) If you have a home computer, it's probably a single computer not linked to any others, i.e. a **stand-alone** machine.

2) However, most computers nowadays are **linked together in a network**, either to other computers in a building (**LAN**) or to computers around the world (**WAN**).

3) This allows hardware and software to be **shared** and users to **communicate** with each other.

> **Definition of a network: computers linked together allowing resources to be shared and data to be transferred.**

Examples of networks

- People working in an office use computers that are networked in order to be able to **share work**.
- Computers in a school are networked so that **any user can log on** at any machine.
- Computers in branches of a supermarket chain are linked so that **sales and stock data can be shared**.
- Computers in multinational companies can be linked so that data can be shared **internationally**.

Networking Has Advantages and Disadvantages

Advantages of Networking

- Hardware (e.g. printers, hard disks, etc.) can be **shared**.
- Software and data can be easily **shared** and **transferred** between machines.
- A user can access their files **from any computer** on the network (this is called 'hot-desking' — an employee doesn't have a particular desk in the office, but can use any of them).
- **Management of files** (e.g. backing up of data) can be done automatically and access to certain facilities (such as the Internet) can be controlled.

Disadvantages of Networking

- **Extra equipment** (e.g. network cards, cables, servers, etc.) is needed, and more specialised knowledge to oversee it.
- If the network **breaks down**, you won't be able to access your data or run programs if they're centrally stored.
- Users have **less control** over how their computers are set up.
- Networks can be very **slow** if lots of people are using them.
- There's an increased risk of being infected by **viruses** from other people's machines.

Make Sure You Remember the Difference Between LANS and WANS

1) **LAN** — A **Local Area Network** is a collection of computers and peripherals in one building or group of buildings which are connected together using cable or a wireless connection.

2) **WAN** — A **Wide Area Network** connects computers over a large distance to other towns or countries using telephone, cable or satellite connections. There has been a large increase in the number of WANs in recent years, due to the reduced costs of transferring data and the demand for more instant communication.

3) The **Internet** is basically just a big network, of lots and lots and lots of WANs all linked together.

Learn the Right Terms To Talk About Linking Networks

1) A **bridge** can be used to link two similar LANs together.

2) A **gateway/router** is used to link together two different networks — e.g. in the diagram, connecting a LAN to a WAN.

3) A **repeater** is used to boost (amplify) the signal on a LAN which covers a long distance.

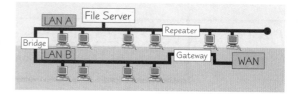

Networks

Networks Need **Particular Hardware** and **Software** To Work

A network requires particular hardware, software and communications rules (protocols) in order to work.

Hardware •	Each computer on the network needs a **network interface card** (**NIC**) and a **connection** (either with a cable or wireless) to the network.
•	There's usually a **main central computer** (**server**) which often stores shared programs and individual files.
•	To connect to a WAN, like the Internet, a **modem** or **gateway/router** will be needed.
Software •	The server itself needs a **network operating system** and software to manage and control the network.
•	Each machine may need a **browser** to view Intranet pages.
•	**E-mail** software will be needed to communicate across the LAN and beyond.
•	If an Internet connection is required then the server will need **connection software** and software to stop unauthorised access from outside the LAN (a **firewall**).
Communication Protocols	For computers to communicate over a network, they need to follow the same **rules** for how data is transmitted and received — sets of rules like these are called communication protocols. E.g. the **protocol TCP/IP** is a set of rules which **allow data to be split into packets**, to be sent across the Internet.

There Are **Different Ways** to **Connect** to Networks

Computers can be linked to a network in various ways depending on the type of network.

1) LANs are usually linked **using cables** such as unshielded twisted pair (e.g. UTP CAT5).
2) **Fibre-optic backbones** (a high-speed line or series of connections in a network) can be used giving very fast links.
3) **WANs** use **long distance** communication technologies, e.g. telephone networks, satellite links or radiowaves. **Mobile phone** networks use **microwave** transmission which works over a short distance.
4) Satellite and radiowave are examples of **wireless communication**. Wireless communication makes mobile computing possible, but data transfer is **slower** than using cables.

Bandwidth Tells Us **How Much Data** Can Be Transferred In a Given Time

1) **Broadband** transmission allows **many signals to be transmitted at once** and is very fast. It's particularly useful for multi-media transmission (sound, video and text simultaneously).
2) The term **bandwidth** refers to the **maximum amount of data** that can travel over a **data transmission channel** in a given time period — i.e. how much data can be sent from one computer to another **in any given time**.
3) Bandwidth is **NOT about the speed** of transmitting the data but about **how much data** can be transmitted. The **more bandwidth** there is available, the **more the data that can be moved**. E.g. video requires a large bandwidth because of the large amount of data which is being transmitted per second.

Practice Questions

Q1 Why has there been an increase in the number of WANs over recent years?
Q2 Explain the following terms when talking about networks: "repeater", "bridge" and "gateway".

Exam Questions

Q1 A small manufacturing company has a number of stand-alone computers and uses them to manage orders, deliveries, invoices and payroll. It has been suggested that the company should invest in a local area network.

a) What hardware would be required in order to install a LAN? (3 marks)
b) Give three advantages to the company of having a LAN. (3 marks)
c) Give two disadvantages to the company of having a LAN. (2 marks)

I know all about bandwidth — I met Pavarotti's backing singers...

There's quite a lot of jargon on this double page. It's important to understand what it all means so you don't get thrown when it appears in an exam. Make sure you've cracked everything on these two pages then go onto the next, where there's a bit more info on different ways of setting up networks. Hip-hip-hooray... It's a networking life for us me hearties, ooh arr.

Networks

Right then — here's the last little chunk on networks. Better make sure you grab a hold of something tight, because this ride's going to go so fast you'll wish you'd never got on to page 72... wheeeEEEEEEEeeeeeeeeeeeeeeeeeeeeeeeeeeeeeeee...

Networks Can Be Arranged In Different Ways

1) Networks can be arranged in various ways, depending on the number and type of computers on the network and how they are going to be used. Each way has its own advantages and disadvantages.

2) The way a network is arranged is called the **topology** of the network.

Bus Networks Are Based on a Single Connecting Cable

1) **Bus** networks (also known as **line** networks) have **one long cable** with the file server usually attached to the middle and the other computers and peripherals (e.g. printers) attached along it.

2) Each connection point is called a **node**.

3) Only **one signal** can travel along the cable **at any one time** so with a lot of **traffic** on the network (i.e. lots of computer activity) it can be **slow**.

4) It's **cheap** as it doesn't use much cabling, but if there's a single **break** in the cable then the whole network will **stop working**.

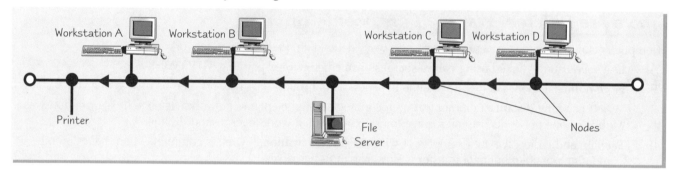

Star Networks Give Each Computer its Own Connection to the Server

1) In a **star** network each computer has its **own separate connection** to the file-server.

2) It's faster than a bus network, but is **more expensive** because more cabling is required.

3) However, if one cable fails, it doesn't affect the other computers, meaning the network is **more fault tolerant**.

4) The topology of a star network also makes it easy to **add extra computers**.

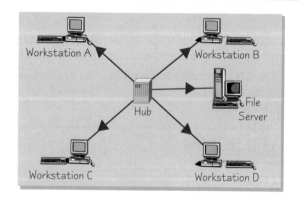

Data Flows Round Ring Networks in One Direction

1) In a **ring** network the computers are linked together by cables into a circle.

2) The data only flows **one way** around the network.

3) It is relatively **cheap** and **fast** although it can become slow if there is a lot of traffic.

4) It's suitable for a **small** number of computers and often doesn't have a file server, with data being stored on the individual computers rather than centrally.

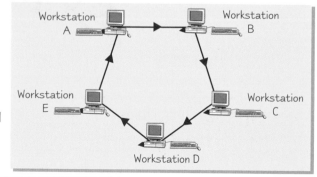

Networks

There Are **Two Types** of **LAN**

There are two types of local area network:

1) **Peer-to-peer** — this is when a small number of computers are linked and can communicate but there is no central file server. It is easy and straightforward to set up and the software to do so is often contained in the operating system.

2) **Client-server** — this is where there is a main server that controls the network. The computers linked to it are called clients, hence the name **client-server network**. It requires specialised software running on the server and is needed when there is a reasonably large number of users (say over 10).

The server controls the following:

- **Storage** of user's files.
- **Printing** over the network.
- **Access** to the network using user-names and passwords.
- Automatic **back up** of data on a regular basis.
- **Storage of some software** such as applications packages (though some may be stored in the client machines).

> In a peer-to-peer network these facilities are the responsibility of individual users.

Mobile Computing Means You Can Use Your Computer *Almost Anywhere*

A **wireless network** means you do not need to have your computer (usually a laptop) **physically connected** to a network. Instead, you can use it **anywhere** within range of the **wireless access point**.

Pros of Mobile Computing

- The computer can be **used anywhere** within range of an 'access point'.
- **No cables** are needed.

Cons of Mobile Computing

- The **speed** of transmission is not as fast as a cable-based network.
- Portable laptop computers are usually more **expensive** than desktop computers.

Practice Questions

Q1   What are the differences between the star, ring and bus network topologies?

Q2   What is a peer-to-peer network?

Q3   What are the advantages and disadvantages of wireless networks?

Exam Questions

Q1   A small publishing company has four computers that are linked together using a peer-to-peer network. The company is expanding and buying a new suite of ten computers which will need to be networked and linked to the existing computers. The manager has been advised that the company should change to a client-server network.

a) Explain the difference between a peer-to-peer network and a client-server network.   (2 marks)

b) Why is a client-server network more suitable for the new situation?   (3 marks)

Q2   A secondary school is installing a new local area network of computers and a decision has to be made whether to use a bus topology or a star topology.

a) Briefly describe in words the difference between these two topologies and draw a diagram of each configuration.   (4 marks)

b) Give ONE advantage of a bus topology compared to a star topology.   (1 mark)

c) Give ONE advantage of a star topology compared to a bus topology.   (1 mark)

(plausible but bloomin' expensive)

LAN LAN LAN your boat gently down the stream, merrily merrily merrily merrily, wireless is a dream...

And that's about all we have time for on section 9. Thanks for tuning in. I hope you all got what you came for and that the interval drinks were to your satisfaction. Remember to retain the knowledge — you have to absorb like a sponge, not reject like a jellyfish on a beach in the morning last Tuesday. Anyway. I think I'm rambling now. On to section ten...

Data Capture

Well it looks like another crazy adventure-filled section is here. I'm not totally sure my stomach or bowels can take it, how about yours? Maybe you should go to the toilet now, before tucking into the tasty world of data capture...

Each Method of Data Capture Has Its Own Advantages

Data capture is the issue of how to **obtain** and **input** data while ensuring it's in a **format** the computer **can understand**.

Manual data capture systems

Data is collected using **paper-based forms** or **questionnaires**, and then has to be entered into a computer. This is sometimes the most cost efficient or practical option, but it is **prone to human error** on keying-in data.

Automatic data capture systems

In these systems, humans don't need to be present to type in data. It is collected through **sensors** or **scanners**. This reduces transcription errors and speeds up the data entry process.

There are three main data capture methods for common office applications.

Typing it in (Direct Data Entry or DDE)
E.g. entering a customer's details onto a computer record.
Devices used — keyboard or keypad.
Advantages — can input text and numbers very quickly with training.
Disadvantages — it's easy to make typing mistakes when entering the data.

Selecting, pointing or positioning
E.g. clicking buttons on a menu in a WIMP environment.
Devices used — mouse, trackerball or joystick.
Advantages — easy to learn and control.
Disadvantages — risk of health problems e.g. RSI (see p.40 for more information).

WIMP stands for Windows, Icons, Menus, Pointers

Optical scanning
E.g. scanning a photograph to include on a web page.
Devices used — flatbed scanner.
Advantages — paper documents can be used electronically.
Disadvantages — the scanning itself can be slow.

Speech Recognition Systems Aren't Perfect

An alternative to entering text with a keyboard is using a **speech recognition system**, known as **voice data entry**.

1)   Speech recognition systems let users **give oral commands** to control software.

2)   This allows **faster entry** of large volumes of data, without having to be a trained typist.

But the **effectiveness** of speech recognition systems is **limited**:

1)   **Software** needs to be **trained** to recognise the user's **pronunciation**.

2)   Only terms which are **in the system's dictionary** will be understood.

3)   **Background noise** can **interfere** with the system's recognition abilities.

Barcodes Give Highly Accurate Data

1)   Barcodes are the **patterns** of thin and thick black and white **stripes** you see on most products.

2)   A barcode represents a number that **uniquely identifies** a product. It contains data about the product.

3)   A scanner **reads** the barcode and feeds it into the computer where the data is displayed (e.g. on a till display).

4)   The use of a **check digit** means the computer can validate the reading is correct (for more on check digits, see p.80

5)   The only real problem with bar codes is that **you can't tell what they say** without scanning them.

More Specialised Data Capture Systems are Worth Knowing About

Here are some **more fancy** data capture devices that are definitely worth knowing about:

1)   **Light pens** and **graphic tablets** are used in specialised **graphics programs** where precise pixel by pixel control is needed on input.

2)   **Touch screens** are handy for navigating through menus, for example on a Tourist Information help screen.

3)   **Portable data loggers** are used to take meter readings (e.g. gas, electric). Each reading is typed into the device where it is stored against a unique reference for that house. This continues until the end of the day when all the readings are downloaded into a central database.

4)   **Traffic counting devices** (such as loop detectors) are used to monitor flows of road traffic. **Loop detectors** are laid under road surfaces and register when metal things pass over them (like a metal detector). In this way they are able to record the amount and frequency of traffic on a particular section of road.

Data Capture

OMR Stands For Optical Mark Recognition

Optical Mark Recognition (OMR) is used as an alternative to keyboard entry.

OMR is a system that **reads marks** that are made in certain positions on a specifically laid-out form, e.g. on National Lottery ticket forms, where an OMR reader reads the marks made below the boxes.

ADVANTAGES

It is a fast data input method, with few errors as long as forms have been completed properly.

DISADVANTAGES

Creases or folds can make forms unreadable. Mistakes made when filling out the form are difficult to correct.

OCR Stands For Optical Character Recognition

Optical character recognition (OCR) is used in conjunction with optical scanners. OCR software is used to **recognise the shape of letters** on paper documents and interpret them as text in word-processed computer files.

ADVANTAGES

With large amounts of text, scanning documents is usually faster than typing data in manually. As the keyboard isn't used, there is a reduction in the development of health problems like RSI.

DISADVANTAGES

The accuracy of OCR is heavily dependant on the software used and on the clarity of the text in the document scanned. Creases or folds can cause problems and the handwriting / font needs to be clear for it to work properly.

Magnetic Ink Character Recognition (MICR) is Hard to Tamper With

1) **MICR** is when magnetic ink characters are **read** by a computer automatically.

2) It's often used to capture data when there are **security issues** because it's difficult to tamper with.

3) A good example are the characters on the bottom of bank cheques.

Plastic Cards are Used Everywhere Now

Banks, credit companies and supermarkets all use plastic cards for data capture.
There's two main types — **magnetic stripe cards** and **smart cards**.

Magnetic Stripe Cards

Stripe cards hold data that can identify the customer and their account on a stripe. Swiping the card through a reader captures the data.

Smart Cards

Instead of a stripe, an embedded processor holds the data. This is used by inserting the card into a reader.

See p.12 for more info on how these cards are used.

Practice Questions

Q1 How is data usually captured in an automatic data capture system?

Q2 What is the main disadvantage of using a keyboard for data entry?

Q3 Give a common use of MICR.

Exam Question

Q1 A PR firm has offices at six different sites, with twenty members of staff employed in each office. The employees already have access to e-mail communication, but the company is thinking of introducing a speech recognition input system to help their busy staff to create e-mails.

   a) State two advantages to the staff of using a speech recognition system. (2 marks)

   b) Give two reasons why the speech recognition system may not be effective. (2 marks)

Shhhh.... be vewy, vewy qwiet — I'm captuwing data...

Well this section looks all right, doesn't it? Just lots of chunks of information to absorb and retain. HA! Just you wait 'til the diagrams on page 87!!! Just kidding guys... This really IS all fairly manageable stuff. Just make sure you know what all the abbreviations stand for. It would be rather embarrassing to lose marks just because you said OCR when you meant OMR...

Verification and Validation

Validation and verification are long words for very easy ideas, so don't be scared off. It's not as if you're being chased around your house by a seven foot big-toothed slobbering monster with bad breath now is it? No. It's not. It's just ICT.

Data Always Needs To Be **Verified And Validated**

A problem with computer systems is that it's very easy to put incorrect data into them. Data **needs to be checked**.

> **VALIDATION means CHECKING THE DATA ENTERED IS REASONABLE**
> **VERIFICATION means CHECKING THE FINAL DATA ENTRY MATCHES THE DATA CAPTURED**

Incorrect Data Can Enter the System at Different Stages

1 At **Data Capture** Stage

Errors are unlikely to enter the system if the data is entered automatically (e.g. barcodes). However the following errors could occur when data is captured manually (e.g. from forms):

- The form could be filled in wrongly, e.g. the wrong product code entered, totals added up wrongly, fields left blank etc.
- A form could get lost before the data has been entered.
- A form could be illegible, e.g. damaged, messy handwriting etc.

An old-fashioned approach to capturing data.

2 At **Transcription** Stage

- When the data is keyed in (transcribed), human error can cause mistakes e.g. misreading a name, adding too many zeroes to a price etc.
- A form could be entered twice by mistake.

3 At **Transmission** Stage

- When data is sent down a transmission medium (e.g. a telephone line) it can become corrupted.

4 At **Processing** Stage

- Problems with hardware or software might lead to data being corrupted.

There Are **Two Different Types of Error**

1) **Invalid data** is data that is either **impossible** or **unreasonable**.

E.g. In 2003, a child's date of birth is entered as 15/4/2008. This date of birth is impossible, so it's **invalid** data.

Invalid data can be spotted with validation checks.

2) **Inaccurate data** is valid data that is **not correct**.

E.g. In 2003, a child's date of birth is entered as 13/8/1994. In fact, the child's actual birthday is 14/8/1994. So, even though this data is valid, it's **inaccurate**.

Inaccurate data resulting from incorrect entering of data from a form can be picked up by verification checks. But this is no good if the data on the form is wrong to start with.

Different **Validation Checks** Test For **Different Things**

We can use computers to check data with a variety of different validation checks:

1) **Presence check**: this makes sure that important information has been entered. For example, a contacts database might require a full postal address. If the postcode field has been left empty, the software will spot this and ask for it to be filled in.

2) **Range check**: this checks that the data is within a specified range. For example, a date of birth entered as 13/13/2000 is impossible. The software will ask for the month to be re-entered.

3) **Check digit**: this checks that numerical data has been entered accurately. The final digit of a number is determined by a formula using all the previous digits. For example, when a barcode is scanned, the software will reject the data if the check digit it calculates is different from the check digit it reads.

Check digit

Verification and Validation

Sometimes *More Sophisticated Checks* Are Used

1) **Cross field checks**

   This checks to see whether the data within a record is consistent.

   E.g. a customer record with 'Bristol' in the town field should have a postcode beginning with BS.

2) **Drop down Lists**

   Users are restricted to a set of pre-defined inputs provided in a drop-down list. These choices are often read from a different part of the spreadsheet a bit like a "look-up" table.

3) **Hash / control totals**

   These check for missing records. A numerical field from each record in a batch is added and the computer checks that the total is correct (by comparing it to the previous recorded total).

	A	B	C	D
1	First Name	Surname	Age group	Addres
2	Megan	Gibbs	15 to 17	
3	Peter	Sweatman		▼
4	Malcolm	Bristow	12 and under	
5	Lucy	Hughes	13 and 14	
6			15 to 17	
7				

   Example of a drop down list

   - **Control total** — this is done where it makes sense to add the numbers (e.g. money owing).
   - **Hash (#) total** — this is done where adding the numbers has no real meaning (e.g. telephone numbers).

Verification Means *Checking For Accurate Input*

Data verification checks to see whether **the data which has been input** is the same as **the original**.

1) Input can be verified by comparing the data in a system with the original. Data that doesn't match up will be re-entered.

2) **Double entry** is when data is entered twice by two different people. The computer compares the two versions and highlights any differences between them, showing where the errors are.

Even *After* Validation and Verification, You *Can't Be 100% Sure*

Problems with <u>validation</u>:

- Error trapping is only as good as the software designed to trap the errors.
- Validation only makes sure the data is reasonable, not that it is correct.

Problems with <u>verification</u>:

- Both double-entry and proof-reading are time consuming and expensive.
- Verification only makes sure that the data entered matches that in the input form, not that it is correct.
- Human error is still possible.

Practice Questions

Q1 Explain the difference between data validation and data verification.

Q2 Explain how a check digit works.

Q3 Describe how three data validation checks work.

Exam Question

Q1 An electricity supply company needs to arrange for householders' meters to be read regularly. Meter readers visit each house and record the current meter reading for each account on a paper data capture document. At the end of the day all the documents are read directly into the computer system to avoid transcription errors.

   a) State two items of data that should be printed on the data capture document before it is given to the meter reader. (2 marks)

   b) Describe two validation checks that should be performed when the data is read into the computer system. (4 marks)

   c) How is it still possible for incorrect data to be stored in the computer system? (2 marks)

I want the TRUTH but I can't handle it — because it's not an object...

I had an awful lot of fun on this page, didn't you? I know data validation and verification might seem a bit confusing at first, but it's only cos they both start with "v". Validation checks make sure the data is of the correct type, range and that type of thing. Verification is about checking the data is actually correct and uses methods like proofreading and double entry.

Databases

Now it's getting really exciting. If there's one ICT topic that's 100% guaranteed to get your pulse racing, surely that subject is... databases. As Dr Johnson said, "A man who is tired of databases is tired of life". Or words to that effect.

Databases are Used to Store Information

1) A database is a collection of **related data**.
2) Databases can **store** vast amounts of data without taking up too much space.
3) Users can **search**, **sort** and **combine** data very quickly.
4) Databases can be used to produce **reports**.

There are Lots of Database Terms You Need to Know

When you're **designing** a database, you have to think about the entities and attributes.

1) An **entity** is a name given to anything that data is stored about. All the data held in an entity refers to that entity. For example, the entity "Customer" will **only** hold data about customers.
2) Every entity has **attributes**. The attributes describe the properties of the entity. For example, the attributes of the entity "Customer" might be: Forename, Surname, Address 1, Town, County, Postcode.
3) When you create a database, the entities become **table names** and the attributes become **fields**.
4) **Tables** contain data about a particular entity, e.g. students, suppliers, customers, etc. The data is organised into rows (records) and columns (fields). The simplest databases consist of a single table and are called **flat-files**. Databases with more than one table are **relational databases**.
5) A **record** is a collection of data about a single item, e.g. a particular supplier, customer, student. Each row in a database table is a separate record. Each record in a table must be **unique**.
6) **Fields** break the records into separate pieces of data. Each field must have a unique name and contain a single data item. Fields can have different data types and have their **own validation**.

A **table** is made up of **records**, records are made up of **fields**.

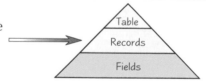

There are Two Main Types of Key

This bit is just for the OCR course.

There are two main types of key that can be used in a relational database — **primary key** and **foreign key**.

The **primary key** is the most important one.

The primary key is a field in a table that allows each record to be uniquely identified.

Every value in the primary key field must be **different**.

The **foreign key** is used to link tables together to form relationships.

A foreign key is a primary key in one table that is linked to a field in another table.

The data types of the fields that are linked must be the **same**.

Forename	Surname
Fred	Stuart
Henry	Brown
Fred	Spencer
Eric	Brown

There is repeating data in both these fields so they cannot be used as a primary key.

ID	Forename	Surname
1	Fred	Stuart
2	Henry	Brown
3	Fred	Spencer
4	Eric	Brown

This field can be used as the primary key as each value is unique.

Use these conventions for describing tables:
Underline the primary key field
Type the foreign key field in *italics* (or <u>double underline</u> it if you're writing by hand)
Write the table name in CAPITAL LETTERS
E.g. the products table shown to the right would be written PRODUCTS (**Item code**, Description, Price, *Supplier*).

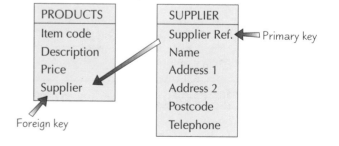

Databases

Tables are Linked by **Relationships**

The tables in a relational database have to be linked through **relationships**.
There are three main relationships that can be used:

One-to-One

One instance of an entity can be associated with **only one** instance of a second entity, e.g. there's one company car for each employee.

It's **unusual** to find a one-to-one relationship in a relational database. If this relationship does happen then the entities would normally be **combined** into one table.

Employee ──── Company Car

One-to-Many

One instance of an entity can be associated with **many** instances of **another entity**. For example, one library member may borrow many books (or many books are borrowed by one library member).

Library member ──< Book

Many-to-Many

Many instances of an entity can be associated with **many instances** of another entity. In reality it's best to avoid many-to-many relationships — you can do this by using a **link entity**.

A **link entity** breaks a many-to-many relationship into two many-to-one relationships:

> **Example** — one customer can buy **many** products and each product can be bought by **many** customers — this is a many-to-many relationship.
>
> Add in the link entity **order** — then it becomes:
> **one customer** can place **many orders** (one-to-many) and **one product** can appear in **many orders** (one-to-many).

Practice Questions

Q1 Explain the meanings of these database terms — entity, attribute, table, field, record.

Q2 Use an example to describe the standard way of writing down the design of a table.

Q3 What are the three types of relationships between tables?

Exam Questions

Q1 Explain the terms primary key and foreign key. (4 marks)

Q2 The entities and attributes in a relational database are:
CUSTOMER (Cust_ID, Surname, Forename, Telephone Number)
ORDER (Order code, Cust_ID, Date, Product_ID, Quantity)
PRODUCT (Product_ID, Description, Price, Supplier_ID)
SUPPLIER (Supplier_ID, Name, Address 1, Address 2, Postcode, Telephone)

a) State the primary keys in the entities PRODUCT and CUSTOMER. (2 marks)
b) State two foreign keys in the database, and say which tables they are in. (2 marks)
c) Give the relationships between:
 i) CUSTOMER and ORDER ii) SUPPLIER and PRODUCT (2 marks)

Just in case that was all too easy, here's an extra complication...

*In addition to normal primary keys, you can also have **composite** primary keys. This is where two (or more) fields work together as the primary key. So you can uniquely identify every record in the table through different combinations of these fields. You'll need to know this for later on where everything gets a wee bit tricky...*

Databases

You really need to concentrate for the rest of this section. Databases are simple at first, but they do get trickier and trickier. And yet fear ye not gentle students! Stick with me and I'll get you through it — TO THE ICTMOBILE!

Flat Files are the Simplest Kind of Database

A **flat file** database consists of a **single table** of data. This table is not connected to anything else. Flat-file databases are often used to store lists and are very easy to create. But they tend to contain a lot of duplicate data.

The example below shows videos owned by a video rental shop.

Primary Key Field — each item is unique | Each column is a different field | Member M0025's details appear twice because she has taken out 2 videos.

Each row is a separate record

Item of data

Code	Name	Type	Certificate	Cost of Hire	Membership No	Member Name	Member Address	Postcode	Telephone	Date
V0001	Gullivers Travels	Drama	U	£1.50	M0001	Heather Palin	The Haven, Skelly Crag	BS4 7RL	0117 4332957	22/11/2003
V0002	The Princess Bride	Drama	PG	£2.50						
V0003	Matrix	Action	15	£2.50	M0025	Barbara Millward	27 Crescent Drive	BS4 6PT	0117 3445817	22/11/2003
D0001	Human Traffic	Drama	18	£2.50						
D0002	American Pie	Comedy	15	£2.00	M0025	Barbara Millward	27 Crescent Drive	BS4 6PT	0117 3445817	22/11/2003

The main **problem with flat-file databases** is the duplicate data which means:

- file sizes are large, storage space is wasted and it's **slow** to retrieve data.
- it's easy to create **errors** or **inconsistencies** when you're entering data or updating it.

Relational Databases Combine Flat Files

Two or more flat files can be combined to create a **relational database**. The different tables are linked using **foreign keys** and **relationships**. Here's a better database for the videoshop example above:

VIDEOS

Code	Name	Type	Certificate	Cost of Hire	Membership number	Date
V0001	Gullivers Travels	Drama	U	£1.50	M0001	22/11/2003
V0002	The Princess Bride	Drama	PG	£2.50		
V0003	Matrix	Action	15	£2.50	M0025	22/11/2003
D0001	Human Traffic	Drama	18	£2.50		
D0002	American Pie	Comedy	15	£2.00	M0025	22/11/2003

MEMBERS

Membership Number	Name	Address	Postcode	Telephone
M0024	John Williamson	35 Priory Avenue	BS4 3AJ	0117 9754412
M0025	Barbara Millward	27 Crescent Drive	BS4 6PT	0117 3445817
M0026	Sanjeev Patel	43 Albert Street	BS4 8UB	0117 9423184

This database uses two tables — VIDEO stores details of all the shop's videos, MEMBERS stores the contact details of all the members. The membership number field links the two tables — it's the **primary key** of the MEMBERS table and appears as a **foreign key** in the VIDEO table.

It's a many-to-one relationship between VIDEOS and MEMBERS because each membership number can appear many times in the VIDEOS table, but only once in the MEMBERS table.

Relational Databases are More Efficient than flat file databases

1) Each data item is stored only once. There's no danger of data being updated in one place and not in another. This is known as **data consistency**.

2) Time is saved on entering data — it's **faster** if the same data doesn't have to be entered repeatedly.

3) No data is unnecessarily duplicated (**data redundancy**) so no storage space is wasted.

4) Relational databases use a database management system (**DBMS**) which can control access to the data, ensuring only authorised users can see certain bits.

5) The DBMS will also have a feature called **referential integrity** — this is a set of rules you can apply to the database that prevents you from entering inconsistent data.

6) Still, it's not all good news. Setting up and maintaining relational databases is **complex** and **time-consuming**, and if the database fails, all applications using the data are affected.

E.g. in a database, if Table A has a foreign key field that links to Table X, referential integrity would make sure that when you change any fields in Table A, the records in Table X that link to it will be updated too.

The main **problems with relational databases** are:

- **complex software** is required to set up and maintain the database
- **expertise** is needed to carry out effective design, creation and maintenance.

Databases

Hierarchical Databases are a Special Kind of Database

1) In a **hierarchical database** the records are linked together in a **tree data structure**. Each record below the top level is a **child**. Each child has only one **parent**, but can be parent to many children of its own. It's a bit like how folders work in Windows Explorer.

2) Users need to know how the tree is **structured** to find data within it (like finding files hidden at the end of a long path of folders in Windows Explorer).

3) Hierarchical databases used to be widely used on mainframe computers, but they're far less common today because of their **restrictive nature**.

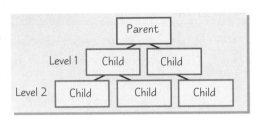

You Can Run Queries to Search Databases

1) You **search** databases by looking for items that meet certain criteria — this is called **querying**.

2) Most modern database programs use a **special language** to query their databases.

3) **SQL** (structured query language) lets you **choose** the data to extract and from what tables.

4) If you know what you're doing, SQL is a very powerful tool for extracting information from complex databases. But it's pretty complicated to learn, so an easier way is to use **QBE** (query by example). With QBE, a **grid** enables you to **select fields** from the tables you wish to query, and **specify search criteria** in a visual manner.

5) Queries can be performed by the DBMS itself or by **other software** which uses the database.

> This query will find all the PG videos which cost more than £1.50 to rent. The name and cost of the video will be displayed.

> E.g. when you do a mail merge, the word processor queries the database to extract the data it needs. Web sites often link to a database to create dynamic content (it is updated as soon as a change is made), e.g. online stores and booking systems.

Reports Make Sense of Queries

1) Query results look just like tables — they're not formatted.

2) **Reports** are used to format the data from queries to make it easier to understand by **grouping** and **summarising** data.

3) **Graphs** are often used because they present results in a very accessible, visual way.

Practice Questions

Q1 What are the problems associated with flat file databases?

Q2 Explain the structure of a hierarchical database.

Q3 What do the following terms stand for: 'DBMS', 'SQL' and 'QBE'?

Exam Questions

Q1	Give four advantages of using a relational database instead of a flat file system.	(4 marks)
Q2	An electricity company has a relational database containing information about all the work it does. Suggest three tables that are likely to be in its database.	(3 marks)
Q3	A school has a table in its database which holds details of all its pupils. The table is named PUPIL. Name 5 fields that this table might contain and state which of them would be the primary key.	(6 marks)

I used to retrieve data from Madonna's rubbish bins — 'til the court order...

Phew, there's quite a lot on these two pages. Some of it's straightforward stuff you just need to memorise, but some of the more involved relational database stuff will need a bit more brain power. I recommend some chocolate, a cup of tea, and a brisk slide down the pole that goes into the batcave, so you can go for a holy-concentration-inducing ride in the ICTMOBILE.

Examples of Databases

Here's a couple of case studies of relational databases. The one on this page is pretty easy, but the next one's a bit trickier. Don't worry though — read it all through carefully and answer the questions, and you'll be laughing... Ho. Ho. Ho.

Example 1 — *a Hardware Shop* Database

- A hardware shop needs a database for the products it sells.
- The **item code**, **description** and **price** are needed for each product.
- When products run out, the manager needs to be able to order more from the **supplier**.
- This means that **contact details** for the supplier are needed. Some suppliers supply more than one product.

The simplest solution for the hardware shop would be a **flat file database**.

Item code	Description	Price	Supplier Ref	Supplier Name	Supplier Address 1	Supplier Address 2	Supplier Postcode	Supplier Telephone
501432	Hanging Solutions	1.99	12	Wallis	Bridgend Business Park	Bridgend	BG21 6EQ	01376 812371
601433	Light bulbs (2 pack)	1.65	34	Kellaway	21 Finsbury Crescent	Gosforth	GF45 6TR	0452 897543
841562	Light bulbs (3 pack)	3.99	34	Kellaway	21 Finsbury Crescent	Gosforth	GF45 6TR	0452 897543
104992	Stanley screwdriver set	6.99	35	Tools Are Us	3 The Buildings	St. Andrews	SA6 6YH	0904 876931

This supplier's details are entered twice.

BUT this is not a very efficient solution because:

- Some of the data is **repeated**, which takes up **more memory**.
- If a supplier **changes**, the new supplier's details will have to be **re-entered** for every single product that will come from them.

It would be **better** to have a **relational database** with two tables:
1) PRODUCTS (<u>Item Code</u>, Description, Price, *Supplier_Ref*)
2) SUPPLIERS (<u>Supplier_Ref</u>, Name, Address 1, Address 2, Postcode, Telephone)

PRODUCTS

Item code	Description	Price	Supplier
501432	Hanging Solutions	1.99	12
601433	Light bulbs (2 pack)	1.65	34
841562	Light bulbs (3 pack)	3.99	34
104992	Stanley screwdriver set	6.99	35

The foreign key in the products table...

SUPPLIERS

Supplier Ref	Name	Address 1	Address 2	Postcode	Telephone
33	Bolton's	33 Carnarvon Road	Lestor	LS1 2AW	0131 9345671
34	Kellaway	21 Finsbury Crescent	Gosforth	GF45 6TR	0452 897543
35	Tools Are Us	3 The Buildings	St. Andrew's	SA6 6YH	0904 876931
36	H&P	121 Johan Street	Gothenbury	GT11 4RF	09871 654382

...is the primary key in the supplier table

This is a **many-to-one** relationship — lots of products can come from one supplier.

Examples of Databases

Example 2 — a Hospital Database

- A hospital is organised into a **number of wards**.
- Each ward has a **number** and a **name** recorded, along with the **number of beds** in that ward.
- Nurses have their **nurse number** and name recorded, and are assigned to **a single ward**.
- Each patient in the hospital has a **patient number** and their name, address and date of birth recorded. Each patient is under the care of a **single consultant** and is assigned to a **single ward**.
- Each consultant has **a number of patients**. Their **consultant number**, name and specialism are recorded.
- When a patient goes to the hospital they always go to the **same ward** and are treated by the **same consultant**.

You couldn't use a flat file database because it's just too complicated. This example calls for another **relational database**. There are four different entities — wards, nurses, patients and consultants. This means there will be four different tables in the relational database:

1) WARD (<u>Ward Number</u>, Name, Beds)
2) NURSES (<u>Nurse Number</u>, First Name, Surname, *Ward Number*)
3) PATIENTS (<u>Patient Number</u>, First name, Surname, Address1, Address2, Postcode, Date of Birth, *Consultant Number, Ward number*)
4) CONSULTANTS (<u>Consultant Number</u>, First Name, Surname, Specialism)

There is more than one foreign key in table 3.

CONSULTANTS

Consultant Number	First name	Surname	Specialism
C001	James	Gibson	Gynaecology
C002	Mary	Somerville	Oncology
C003	David	Clarke	Pediatrics
C004	Malcolm	Hughes	Plastic surgery

Many-to-one / One-to-many relationship.
Many patients have the same consultant / One consultant has many patients.

PATIENTS

Patient Number	First name	Surname	Address1	Address2	Postcode	Date of Birth	Consultant Number	Ward Number
P0001	Charlotte	Ireland	29 Royal Albert Road	Thornbury	BS23 3AD	12/03/1945	C004	W002
P0002	Megan	Gibbs	21 Etloe Road	Frenchay	BS12 7GG	23/05/1939	C004	W010
P0003	Timothy	Long	30 Bayston Road	Little Nailsea	BS10 8HC	30/10/1984	C011	W001
P0004	Robert	Zimmerman	5 Victoria Street	Rosettenville	BS6 8YP	01/04/1943	C020	W001

Many-to-one / One-to-many relationship.
Many patients are on the same ward / One ward has many patients on it.

WARD

Ward Number	Name	Beds
W001	Cotswold	12
W002	Brecon	6
W003	Mendips	9
W004	Chilterns	14

Many-to-one / One-to-many relationship.
Many nurses work on the same ward /
One ward has many nurses on it.

NURSES

Nurse Number	First Name	Surname	Ward Number
N001	Mary	Williamson	W007
N002	Jenny	Sunley	W004
N003	Rosemary	Barnes	W001
N004	Stephen	Simpson	W001

Practice Questions

Q1 Give two reasons why relational databases are better than flat file databases.

Q2 A vet wants to create a relational database of his work. Suggest three tables it would have.

Exam Question

Q1 Cotswold Coaches runs a very comprehensive coach service. Coach routes are divided into different fare stages. All coaches have just 44 passenger seats arranged in two pairs across the bus to a length of 11. The seats are labelled A1, B1, C1, D1 -------- A11, B11, C11, D11. All seats on every coach must be booked in advance. The seat booking system is ICT based and includes the use of spreadsheet and relational database software that can communicate with each other.

Describe THREE tables you would expect to find in the company's booking system. (5 marks)

I relate to databases — but they always give me socks for Christmas...

I know it might take a while to sort out how relational databases work, but here's a tip. If you're struggling to follow the hospital diagram above, try sketching it out for yourself. It will all fall in to place as you start to trace the links between the tables yourself. It's really quite straightforward — just get all the vocab down so that you know what bit is what.

Normalisation

This is where it gets a mite tricky. **Skip these two pages if you're taking AQA.**

Normalisation *Breaks Down Tables into the* **Smallest** *Possible Units*

Normalisation is completed during the **design stage** of a relational database.

1) It creates a **logical structure** of related tables and helps to create a flexible, efficient and easy-to-query database.

2) Normalisation ensures data consistency and integrity and gets rid of repeated data (**data redundancy**).

3) Normalisation is a **staged** process consisting of first (**1NF**), second (**2NF**) and third (**3NF**) normal form.

You've got to know the **rules of normalisation** and be able to identify and explain which normal form data is in.

Before a table gets to 1NF, it is in **unnormalised** form — **0NF**.

A table is in **1NF** if:	A table is in **2NF** if:	A table is in **3NF** if:
• every data value in a field is **atomic** — i.e. the data cannot be broken down any further. • there is a **primary key**. • there are no **repeating fields** within a table.	• the table follows the rules of **1NF**. • each table has a **single** primary or composite key. • there are no **partial key dependencies** — every non-key field must be directly related to the whole primary key (see below for an example).	• the table is in **2NF** (and therefore 1NF) • there are no **non-key** field **dependencies** — there should be no non-key fields dependent upon any other non-key fields (see below for an example).

Note — you only get partial key dependencies if the table uses a composite key.

Here's an **Example**

Each student in a school takes 3 AS level courses. The database is structured like this:

STUDENT (<u>StudentID</u>, Forename, Surname, AS_ID, AS_Title, TeacherID, Teacher_Name, AS_ID, AS_Title, TeacherID, Teacher_Name, AS_ID, AS_Title, TeacherID, Teacher_Name)

Before   After

This is not in 1 NF form because there are **repeating fields** *— AS_ID, AS_Title, Teacher_Name and TeacherID are all repeated 3 times.*

1NF
STUDENT (<u>StudentID</u>, Forename, Surname, *AS_ID*)
COURSE (<u>AS_ID</u>, AS_Title, TeacherID, Teacher_Name)

There are no repeating fields or groups of fields, so it's in 1 NF form now. Each student will have 3 records, 1 for each AS they are taking.

The fields StudentID and AS_ID form a composite primary key for the STUDENT table — each record can be uniquely identified from these two fields combined.

But there are partial key dependencies — forename and surname are dependent on the StudentID field but are not uniquely linked to AS_ID. So they're only dependent on part of the primary key (which is StudentID and AS_ID combined, remember).

2NF
STUDENT (<u>StudentID</u>, Forename, Surname)
COURSE (<u>AS_ID</u>, AS_Title, TeacherID, Teacher_Name)
ENROLLED (*StudentID*, *AS_ID*)

The tables are now in 2NF as there are no partial key dependencies. But there is still a non-key dependency as the Teacher_name field is dependent upon TeacherID (which is "non-key") rather than AS_ID.

3NF
STUDENT (<u>StudentID</u>, Forename, Surname)
COURSE (<u>AS_ID</u>, AS_Title, *TeacherID*)
ENROLLED (*StudentID*, *AS_ID*)
TEACHER (<u>TeacherID</u>, Teacher_Name)

The tables are now in 3NF and provide a logical basis for the database structure.

The database structure can be shown as: Student ⟞⟨ Enrolled ⟩⟞ Course ⟩⟞ Teacher

Data Dictionaries

A *Data Dictionary* Holds Data about a Database

All databases have associated data dictionaries. They're either produced **manually** by the database developer or developed by the database software **automatically** when the database has been created.

1) The main purpose of data dictionaries is to ensure **consistent data usage** within a relational database.

2) If the database needs to be **modified** then the data dictionaries will give all the details about each table and field.

3) Each table contained within the database will have an **associated data dictionary**, so a 3 table relational database would have 3 data dictionaries.

The basic **components** of a data dictionary are:

- **table name** — a unique name for each table in the database.
- **table security** — who has access to write, update, edit or delete values to or from the table.
- **keys** — primary keys are identified.
- **relationships** — the relationships between the tables are identified — one-to-many etc.
- **field name** — each field is identified.
- **field data type** — the data type given to each field — text/string/date/Boolean etc.
- **field length** — the number of characters allocated for the contents of the field.
- **field default value** — if a field has a default value that automatically appears on the creation of a new record.
- **field validation** — any validation applied to the field, i.e. drop down lists, look-ups, presence checks.
- **indexes** — any field that is indexed.

Each data dictionary would give **specific details** about the fields held within the table.

The data dictionary can also be used to identify **different names** used for the **same pieces of data**.

Practice Questions

Q1 Why should a database be in 3NF?

Q2 What are the rules of 2NF?

Q3 Give three items that would be found in a data dictionary that relate to tables.

Q4 Give three items that would be found in a data dictionary that relate to fields.

Exam Questions

Q1 A data dictionary holds information about the data held in a database. Give five items of information that could be held about data in a data dictionary.

(5 marks)

Q2 Explain why the table shown is not normalised.

(4 marks)

Customer Name	Customer Address	Regular Order
Henry Stuart	Fugg House Dog Lane Catshire CT4 4LG	3 pints milk 2 pots cream 5 pints orange juice
George Spencer	The Old House Moggie Court Catshire CT4 3FK	1 pint milk 1 pot cream 3 pints orange juice

Normalisation — it's not big and it's not clever...

Normalisation really is a stinker of a topic. But stick with it and you'll get the hang of it in the end. Make sure you understand how a composite primary key works. Only when you've got that figured will you be able to understand partial key dependencies. And don't forget the reasons for doing it in the first place — you could easily get asked that in an exam.

Entering and Retrieving Data

Do you remember that episode of Star Trek where it turns out Commander Data's got an evil brother? Well that has no relevance at all to these pages — although it is a more entertaining topic.

Data-entry Screens need to be Tailored

Tailored data entry screens are specific screens that have been designed to make it **easier to input data** into a database.

Data-entry screens should be designed through the use of **forms**. If you present the user with the table in a database they will find it difficult to use — providing them with a form with **instructions**, **buttons** and **sensible error messages** helps them. There are **two main factors** to consider when designing and creating data-entry screens:

Consistency	Relevance
1) The **screens** should look as similar as possible.	1) The screen should only ask for **relevant data** — there shouldn't be too much information on the screen.
2) **Buttons** used should be in the same place.	2) The information must be **concise** and **useful**.
3) Data that has to be entered on several screens should have the **same format** on each screen.	3) **Graphics** and **animation** should be kept to a minimum.
4) If the data being entered comes from a paper form the screen must match the **layout**.	

There are Three Main Queries you can do

1) **Parameter queries** are used to search a particular field. The **parameter** is the **value** used to select records. The parameters can be **static**, meaning the parameter is set and cannot be changed, or **dynamic**, where the user inputs the value to be searched for. Dynamic queries are more useful to the user.

A parameter query can also be called a select query.

2) **Complex queries** are parameter queries that search using **more than one** parameter value or field. The parameters or fields are often searched using **logic functions** like AND, OR and NOT.

3) **Cross-tab queries** collate and summarise data together in a **grid**. This makes the data more compact and easier to analyse than parameter queries. To create one, you need to specify which **field's values** you want as **column headings** and which you want as **row headings**.

When **designing queries**, you should ask the following questions:
- "What **information** is needed from the query?" — this affects where the information will come from.
- "How should the query be **run**?" — this could be from a button, shortcut key, icon or menu option.
- "What **error messages** should be displayed?" — these should be helpful and meaningful to the user.

Reports should be Tailored for the User

1) **Reports** are usually printed as the **product of a query**.

2) Reports must be "**fit for purpose**" and **easily understood**. How the information is **presented** should also be considered — this could be through the use of text, graphics, numbers or a combination of these.

3) When you're designing reports, screens and queries you also need to think about:
- **titles** and **colour** to identify the screen, report or query
- **drop down** and **list boxes** to restrict input and provide validation
- **option buttons**
- **default values** for speed of entry
- **buttons**, **icons** and **menu items** that relate to the application only
- useful and user-friendly **help** and **error messages** and context sensitive help
- **dynamic updates**, e.g. selecting "Miss" in the title field automatically updates gender to female
- use of **white space**
- **font**, font size and colour
- the **house-style** of the organisation.

Entering and Retrieving Data

Information Sources can be Static or Dynamic

Static data is usually found on a **CD-ROM**. Static information sources, once created, **do not change**, so the information may become **out-of-date**. The information can be relied on to be **accurate**, as it has usually gone through a checking process, but the amount of information held is **limited**.

Dynamic information is usually found on a **website**. Dynamic information sources are **updated** regularly or can be **changed**. This means it is usually up-to-date and large amounts of information can be held. Dynamic web pages can be **linked** to a database and the user can retrieve information from this by entering details into a form on the webpage. The information may not always be accurate, as **no checking process** may have taken place.

The Internet has Advantages over CD-ROMs

CD-ROMS
1) All **software** needed can be included on the CD-ROM.
2) But if **errors** are found then the changes need to be sent to **everyone** who has bought the CD-ROM.
3) You may need to search **lots** of CD-ROMs to find the information you want.
4) CD-ROMs can be **lost, stolen** or **broken**.

The Internet
1) Lots of information can be found from **different sources** with different opinions.
2) Any errors found can be **changed** quickly and easily.
3) Webpages can contain **hyperlinks** to go to related sites.

Indexes and Keywords help when searching

1) CD-ROMS have a **searchable index** with all the details of the pages contained on it.
2) On the Internet, a **search engine** and **keywords** can be used to find information. To improve search results you can use **logic functions** (AND, OR, NOT) or put in an exact phrase or a company name.

E.g. To find books published by CGP about ICT you would use "CGP AND ICT".

Information on websites can be Filtered

Filtering information means **restricting** the information that is available.
1) Some information is filtered **deliberately**, e.g. ISPs may remove websites from their servers if they are **illegal**.
2) Filtering can also stop people from accessing websites that contain **inappropriate material**, e.g. schools often filter the websites that can be accessed by students.
3) Filtering systems work through looking at **website titles**, searching for any **excluded words** on the website or the use of lists.
4) There are two types of list: an **open list** allows access to everything except what is on the list, a **closed list** allows access to everything on the list but nothing else.

Practice Questions

Q1 What's the difference between parameter and cross-tab queries?
Q2 Explain the terms static information source and dynamic information source.
Q3 Identify two methods that could be used to improve the results of a search on the Internet.

Exam Questions

Q1 Describe four features that should be taken into account when designing a data entry screen. (4 marks)

Q2 Parameter queries and complex queries are used by a publishing company to search a database. Describe and give an example of: a) a parameter query, b) a complex query. (6 marks)

Q3 The books supplied by a publishing company can be viewed on the company website. Explain the advantages of using a website rather than a CD-ROM to show the books. (6 marks)

"Internet" you say? Tell me about this strange new technology...

You're probably all too familiar with the pros and cons of the Internet already, so a lot of this stuff will just be going through what you know that's relevant to the course. The names of the different types of queries might not be familiar, but it's just a question of learning how they work and what they're good for. And that's it for data — gosh, what a roller-coaster ride.

Modelling Software

With a bit of luck, most of the stuff covered in this section will be stuff you've looked at before. The main thing is to learn how to talk about it all though — there's a difference between doing it, and being able to write about it well.

There Are Two **Types Of Modelling** In ICT

A computer model basically consists of a set of **data** about a "thing" and a set of **rules** that control what the data does. There are two main types:

1) Financial Models

These are often done with **spreadsheets**. Spreadsheets have lots of features that make them ideally suited to this type of modelling such as:

- **Formulas** which perform calculations on the data and automatically update when the data is changed — see next page.
- Built-in **functions** to create complex and powerful formulas — see next page.
- **Variables** which hold key data about the model — see next page.
- Logical **arrangement** of data into rows and columns — see page 94.
- Easy **replication** of formulas and functions — see page 95.

These features make it easy to perform "**what-if**" analysis — this is what computer modelling is all about. The user changes certain **parameters** and sees what **effects** this has on the rest of the model. E.g. in a spreadsheet modelling potential revenue from a new product, the user could change the price, the estimated sales and the marketing budget and see how these changes would affect the overall profit.

2) Modelling of Objects

This creates a **virtual representation**. It can be used to model large items like buildings, bridges and aeroplanes — designers can see how different events affect the model.

E.g. a designer can see how an aeroplane will behave when flying in different conditions or how an earthquake affects a building. The model can also be used to **change** and **test** the design, and see how these changes affect the model. Modelling can also be set up to identify all the components that would be used to build the real object. **CAD** is a good example of this type of modelling.

Computer Models are used for **Lots of Reasons...**

1) A computer-based model can be **saved to a storage device** and can be **used by different people** in different locations.

2) **No additional software is needed** (if spreadsheets are used for financial modelling) — spreadsheets are standard business software. Most people are able to use a spreadsheet, so **no specialist training** is needed.

3) The values held in the spreadsheet can be shown in a graph — the graph will **change automatically** as the value of the data is changed. This can be used to **show trends**.

4) Only **one** computer-based object model needs to be built, which can then be **changed**. If the real thing were built, then a new one would be needed for each change made. This takes **time** and can be **very expensive**.

5) They're **safer** than building the real thing. E.g. if a submarine was built and tested and something went wrong, lives could be lost. Obviously this wouldn't happen if a **computer-based model** of a submarine sank.

6) Computer-based models can be **slowed down** or **speeded up** to see effects that are **difficult to see in real life**. E.g. in real life, an explosion in a nuclear power station would happen very quickly. A model can slow the explosion down to see exactly what would happen.

Modelling Software

Learn these key *Modelling Features* of *Spreadsheets...*

Formulas

A formula is an **instruction** to the computer to **process data** held in **specific cells**. They use numbers, cell addresses (cell names such as "Week 1 Sales" or references such as E25) and **mathematical operators**. Formulas can be typed into the formula bar by the user — these are generally **simple calculations**.

> This simple formula adds the contents of cells C3, D3 and E3

SUM	▼	✕ ✓ =	=C3+D3+E3			
	A	B	C	D	E	F
1	Sales Team Performance					
2	First Name	Last name	Week 1 Sales	Week 2 Sales	Week 3 Sales	Total
3	Teresa	Wood	24	15	32	=C3+D3+E3
4	Tanya	Hide	33	30	41	
5	Colin	Moore	27	32	29	
6	Phillip	Farley	18	19	22	
7	Mia	Fernandez	35	33	26	

Mathematical Operators:
* multiply + addition
− subtract / divide

You can also create more **complicated** formulas using the software's built-in functions...

Functions

These are **standard routines** that are built into the spreadsheet. They can perform a variety of common routines and use reserved words. Functions have a help or wizard facility built into the spreadsheet to help the user. They can be nested within other functions in order to create more complicated ones.

Most Common Functions:

SUM: calculates the total of a range of cells.

IF: returns one value if the condition specified is true and a different value if it is false.

AVERAGE: returns the mean or average value from a range of cells.

Variables

A variable is an **identifier** (a cell reference like A3, or a cell name like "Week 1 Sales"). They appear in formulas and are important in "what-if" questions because they let you update many cells in the spreadsheet by just changing one variable. It's the value contained in the variable that is used. So if the variable named "RATE_VAT" contains the value 17.5%, this is the figure that the formulas containing the variable will use.

Practice Questions

Q1 Name a type of software that is used for modelling objects.

Q2 Explain the importance of "what-if" analysis to computer models.

Q3 What do formulas do in modelling?

Q4 Name three common functions.

Q5 What is a variable?

Exam Questions

Q1 Explain three advantages of using a spreadsheet for financial modelling. (6 marks)

Q2 Describe what functions and formulas are, as used in a spreadsheet, giving an example of each. (6 marks)

But more importantly, what-if I actually don't give a monkeys...

... well tough because you still have to learn it. CAD and spreadsheets are good examples of modelling software but you also need to be able to talk about the features of modelling software in a more general way. So remember, you need a set of data, rules that control how the data is used and the capability to do what-if analysis. That's models in a shellnut.

Spreadsheet Basics

Let's get into this spreadsheet thing a bit more seriously, shall we? It's like my old great uncle Bulgaria used to say, "Tobermory" he used to say to me, "Tobermory, stop pretending you're a womble. You don't even live in London."

Spreadsheets Are Made Up Of Various Different Parts

Cell

A cell is a data store that **holds a piece of data**.

They are known by their row and column address, a bit like **coordinates**, e.g. B5 is in column B, row 5.

Every cell in a spreadsheet has a unique address, and they can also be given **names** to identify them, e.g. RATE_VAT.

Each cell can be **formatted individually**. The formatting that can be applied to each cell includes font size and style, borders, alignment, conditional formatting and validation.

Conditional formatting means that the format of the cell is changed if the contents meet certain conditions, e.g. if a number is negative it can be set to turn red.

Cells can also be **protected** through using a password so they can only be changed by users who know the password.

Rows and Columns

A **row** runs horizontally **across** a spreadsheet. A **column** runs vertically **down** a spreadsheet.

Rows are normally identified by **numbers**, e.g. row 5. Columns are normally identified by **letters**, e.g. column B.

If a row or column is inserted or deleted they're renumbered / relettered **automatically**.

The **height** and **width** of rows and columns can be **altered** to ensure that all data and information held is visible.

Rows and columns can be **hidden** from the user, e.g. if rows or columns hold calculations that the user does not need to see.

Range

A range is a **group of cells** that can be identified by the cell references or given a name.

The range is usually given as the **top left cell** to the **bottom right cell**, e.g. B2:D6.

Ranges usually contain similar data and are often used in **formulas** and **functions**.

The same **formatting** can be applied to a range of cells.
This is much easier than applying formatting to the cells one at a time.

Worksheet

A worksheet is basically like a **single page** of a spreadsheet. In MS Excel, worksheets can contain up to 256 columns and 65536 rows. Individual worksheets can be given **meaningful names** to define the data that is held in them.

Workbook

A workbook is a **collection of worksheets** that make up one spreadsheet document.

The workbook contains **all the information**, whilst each worksheet would normally relate to a specific area.

E.g. a business might have 4 sales regions, and each region's sales could be contained within a worksheet (4 in total) with the workbook containing all the information about the business. Data can be **linked** between worksheets, so if data is changed on 1 worksheet, the linked cells in the other worksheets **change automatically**.

Each worksheet held in a workbook can be **given different access rights**, e.g. if each worksheet contained information about a particular shop, it could be set so that only the manager of that shop could see that worksheet.

Spreadsheet Basics

Formulas can have **Absolute** or **Relative Cell References**

It's very easy to **replicate data** in spreadsheets, e.g. by copying and pasting a range of cells from one column to a different column. When **formulas** are replicated like this, the cell references will be affected in one of two ways depending on whether the references are **relative** or **absolute**.

Relative Referencing Means the **Cell References Move**

When a formula is replicated, any relative cell references will change **in relation to the copy**.
If the formula is copied from one column to another, then the **column identifier** will **change automatically**.
If the formula is copied from row to row, then the **row identifier** will **change automatically**.

	A	B	C	D
1				
2	34	97	85	A2+B2+C2 — original
3	78	27	36	A3+B3+C3 — copy
4	A2+A3	B2+B3	C2+C3	

original — copies

Absolute Referencing Means **The Cell Reference Doesn't Change**

An **absolute** cell reference can be used if there is a single value you want to appear **in all the formulas**.
E.g. a delivery charge of £2.50 is added to all orders. This is held in cell B1. The cell references for the total **changes** as it moves down the column, but the absolute reference **does not change**. The spreadsheet knows this cell is absolute because of the $ signs. Cell names can also be used as absolute cell references — you could call cell B1 "delivery charge".

The **main advantage** of using absolute cell referencing is that if that value changes it **only has to be changed once** as all the functions and formulas will automatically use the new value.

	A	B	C	D
1		2.5		
2				
3	Order	Total	Total+Delivery	
4	333	47.2	B4+B$2	
5	334	89.8	B5+B$2	
6	335	56.22	B6+B$2	

Practice Questions

Q1 How are rows and columns identified?
Q2 What is the difference between a worksheet and a workbook?
Q3 What are the two ways cells can be referenced?

Exam Questions

Q1 Explain, giving an example, the purpose of each of the following in a spreadsheet:

a) worksheet   b) workbook   c) cell range. (6 marks)

Q2 Explain each of the following terms, giving an example of each:

a) absolute referencing (3 marks)

b) relative referencing. (3 marks)

Wombles have cell references — they were caught stealing on the common...

Seriously though, wombles were just a bunch of thieving toerags weren't they? "Making good use of the things that we find?" Oh yes Tomsk, that's right. Just take Tobermory and Orinoco up to Wimbledon Common to "find" three wallets, a leather handbag and a confused looking bassett hound called Gerald. They should lock 'em up and throw away the key...

Charts And Graphs

Making charts and graphs is simple. You've probably been making them in class for zillions of years. But that doesn't mean you can skimp on your revision — learn these two pages properly and make sure you don't leave anything out.

Creating A **Chart** Is Dead **Easy**...

Spreadsheets show figures that can sometimes be **difficult to understand**. Graphs and charts show the figures in a **more user-friendly way**. All spreadsheets produce graphs and charts slightly differently, but the basic idea is always the same:

1) Get all the data you want to put into a graph into a single block. It's best if the data is arranged in columns.

2) Highlight the data you want to use — you might need to highlight the column headings as well.

3) Select the type of chart you want — be sensible and make sure it's suitable.

4) Choose a meaningful title for the chart that summarises its contents. Label any axes.

5) Decide if the chart needs a key (also called a legend).

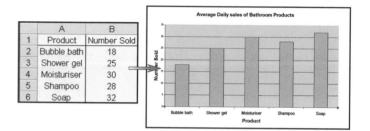

There Are Many **Different Types** Of **Graphs** And **Charts** you can use

1) There are many **different types** of graphs and charts that can be produced by spreadsheets.

2) It's important to choose the **most appropriate graph** for your data.

The most common types of graphs and charts are:

Bar

Bar charts are useful when **comparing** two different sets of data. Each set of data must be **discrete** (separate from the others). The category is shown on the x-axis and the value/s are shown on the y-axis. The bars on the bar chart should be **clearly separated**. If the data is **continuous** then the bar chart is known as a **histogram**.

Bar charts could be used to show things like the number of sales of umbrellas each month, number of school absences for each day in the school week, etc.

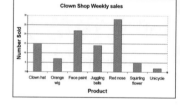

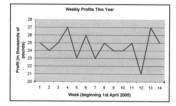

Line

Line graphs are used to show **changes over a given time period**. They're used when the x-axis **isn't in a category**, e.g. time. Line graphs can be used to show things like the amount of rainfall in Blackpool over a 30-day period, the total sales of a company over the period of a year, or the temperature of a room over a 24-hour period.

Scatter

Scatter graphs show the **relationship** (correlation) between two sets of data. One set is plotted along the x-axis with the other set plotted along the y-axis. A **trend line** can be used to show the relationship **more clearly**. Scatter graphs can be used to show things like the sales of umbrellas against the amount of rainfall, or the sales of deckchairs against the temperature.

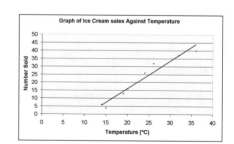

Pie

A pie chart is a circle divided into **segments**. It shows the **proportion** of individual categories of data to the total of all the data categories in a series. It displays the contribution of an individual value to a total. It's best not to have too many categories or the chart gets too cluttered. You can use pie charts to show things like the most popular colour of cars, or how a student spends their school day.

Customising Spreadsheets

Form Controls Can Be Used To Customise A Worksheet

Form controls help the user to **input** the data and let them **add** more features to the spreadsheets.
There are lots of form controls that can be used. The most popular ones are:

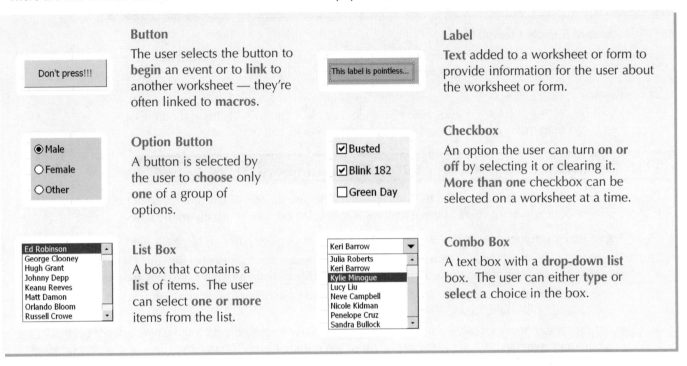

Button

The user selects the button to **begin** an event or to **link** to another worksheet — they're often linked to **macros**.

Label

Text added to a worksheet or form to provide information for the user about the worksheet or form.

Option Button

A button is selected by the user to **choose** only **one** of a group of options.

Checkbox

An option the user can turn **on or off** by selecting it or clearing it. **More than one** checkbox can be selected on a worksheet at a time.

List Box

A box that contains a **list** of items. The user can select **one or more** items from the list.

Combo Box

A text box with a **drop-down list** box. The user can either **type** or **select** a choice in the box.

Macros Can Also Be Used To Customise A Worksheet

1) Macros can be programmed to help users **perform tasks** when they are working on a worksheet.

2) A macro can be **linked to a button** so that when the button is selected by the user a macro is run.

3) Macros can be used to **print** the worksheet, **open** a workbook, **move** to a different workbook or **perform a calculation**. A macro can also be used to **run an event**.

More on macros on p54.

Practice Questions

Q1   What are the four most commonly used charts and graphs?

Q2   Name three form controls that can be used to customise a worksheet.

Q3   Suggest three tasks you could use macros for in a spreadsheet.

Exam Questions

Q1   Say what the most suitable chart would be for displaying the following data about a car dealership.

   a) The number of cars sold each month for a year.   (1 mark)

   b) The relationship between the age and mileage of all the cars.   (1 mark)

Q2   Identify two methods of customising a spreadsheet worksheet and explain their advantages.   (4 marks)

Well, I like bars and I like pies — shame about the rest of it...

Actually, these pages are a big improvement on the rest of the section in my opinion. No horrible formulas, functions or relative referencing — just nice ways to make your spreadsheets look pretty. And, as an added bonus, these are the last pages in this section. You'll like section 12 too, it's got cats' bums in it. My favourite.

Using WP and DTP

Roll up roll up for the software-for-presentation-and-communication circus. It's important to go through all this stuff carefully, not just so you can answer exam questions, but so you can make a darn fine lookin' piece of coursework too. **AQA students won't find the stuff in this chapter in their exams, but will need it for their coursework.**

Word Processing Packages *Have* Some *Helpful Layout Features*

1) **Standard formats / templates**

   Most word processors provide templates for standard documents, such as faxes, memos, letters, etc. These help you create documents with standardised formatting.

2) **Layout**

   Word processors also let you add more visual elements like graphics, tables and numbers. These can help make your document look more professional and readable.

DTP Software *Has* Lots of Features *That Make Layout Easier*

Desktop publishing software has specific features that will **help you design** all kinds of different publications, like leaflets, posters or newspapers. One of these features is that DTP software is usually **frame based**.

1) **Frame based software** means that the text or images are put on the pages in blocks, called **frames**.

2) The frames can be individually **moved** or **re-sized**. This means you can **easily edit** your DTP document by changing the size or position of the frames, as well as easily moving a frame from page to page.

3) Frame based software works a bit like a **noticeboard**. You have different pieces of information which you can move around until you're happy with the overall layout.

4) Word processors aren't usually frame-based, so the position of each object on the page depends on the position of everything else. If you move one thing, **everything else will move too**. This doesn't happen with frame based software (unless you want it to).

DTP packages have lots of **other clever features** too:

1) **Arrange / layers** — frames can be layered. E.g. you may want to put a frame containing text over the top of a frame containing a graphic.

2) **Grids / columns / guides** — these mean that frames can be positioned very accurately on the page.

3) **Rotate / flip** — these features allow frames to be easily manipulated (i.e. rotated or flipped in a certain direction).

4) Pages can be easily **added**, **deleted** or **moved**.

5) **Workspace** — this is the area around the page where images and text can be placed for later use. Nothing in the workspace will appear in the final document — it's a bit like having a notebook open. The workspace gives you the extra room to experiment with ideas and layouts.

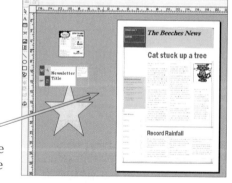

Word Processors *Are More Suited To* Text-Based Documents

1) As the layout can be changed more easily in a DTP package, it's **more suitable** for documents where this is important, e.g. newsletters which use lots of pictures.

2) Word processors are more useful for other documents that are largely **text-based**, like letters, memos, questionnaires, essays and reports.

3) Different users will use software in different ways. The box below shows examples of this for a word processor.

Scientific author —	technical dictionary, thesaurus, automatic section numbering and indexing, specialist clipart, template to automatically format into report style.
Secretary —	wide range of fonts, spelling and grammar check, templates for memos, letters and faxes, ability to create presentations.
Translator —	language specific dictionary, ability to insert specialist characters.

You could create your text in a word processor first, and then **import it** into the DTP package.

Using WP and DTP

You Can Produce **Personalised Documents** Using **Mail Merge**

Mail merge is used to turn **standard letters** into **personalised ones** by "merging" a standard document with personal details from a database or spreadsheet — e.g. a mass-mailed letter about a change of address, a competition, a survey, etc. It can also be used simply to create **address labels** or to print envelopes.

Using Mail Merge

1) Create a spreadsheet / database containing the information to include in the letter (**data source**).

2) Create a standard letter using merge fields that match the fields in the data source. For example, Dear <First_Name> where "First_Name" is a field in the data source.

3) The letter and the data source are then **linked**. The software merges the data by inserting the appropriate fields from the data source into the letter. If there were 500 records in the data source, then the mail merge process would create 500 personalised letters, each greeting the reader by their first name.

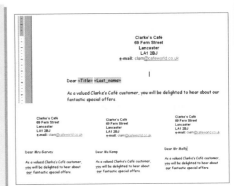

Using mail merge means:

1) You can produce **thousands** of letters **very quickly**.

2) You only need to **proofread** a single letter to know that all the others are correct.

3) You can use **word fields** to select the **exact** group of people to send documents to.

Word fields are extra commands (like Ask, Fill-in, If, and Next/Skip Record) which add extra information to the merged document and allow the user to **control** how the data is merged. Using word fields means data can be taken from other data sources, unwanted data can be filtered out and standard information can be inserted (e.g. date, time, etc).

ASK and FILL-IN	Both these functions prompt the user for information during the mail merge process. This is useful for variable information not available from the data source.
IF... THEN... ELSE	Sets conditions to limit which records are printed. E.g. IF somebody lives in Cumbria, THEN print the document, ELSE (i.e. if they don't), then don't print it, or print something else.
NEXT RECORD	Merges the next data record into the current merged document instead of creating a new document. This is useful if lots of record details are to be included on one document, e.g. names and addresses.
SKIP RECORD IF	Misses (or skips) a record if a given condition is met. Two conditions are compared, and if the comparison is true, SKIP RECORD IF cancels the current merge document, moves to the next data record in the data source, and starts a new merge document. If the comparison is false, the current merge document is continued. This could be used to skip all records of recipients living in Lancashire.

Practice Questions

Q1 Name two features of DTP software that help with layout.

Q2 What is the difference between a word field and a merge field?

Exam Question

Q1 A newsagent uses mail merge to send letters to his customers about the balance on their paper bills.

a) Identify two examples of word fields the newsagent could use. (2 marks)

b) State two benefits to the newsagent of using word fields. (2 marks)

c) Describe two benefits to the newsagent of using mail merge to send letters to customers. (4 marks)

Word fields are where the matrix grows new words for us — like "schtoof"...

You've already gathered this, but keep in mind that it's not about which application is "better" or "worse" overall (we're not computer games journalists here) — examiners always want to know that you've thought carefully about what applications have to offer different kinds of users. The emphasis is on people here, not machines. What do YOU want from your software?

Standard Documents

You should already know most of the stuff on these two pages, but we have to recap it all some time, so make sure you don't skimp on any of the details. It's like sugar — cakes that skimp on sugar taste like cardboard. Be smart. Eat sugary detail.

Standard Documents Are Common, Everyday Documents

1) **Standard documents** are everyday documents like letters, memos, faxes, reports, etc.

2) You don't have to use a **specific application** to produce them. The most appropriate applications are word processors and desktop publishers.

3) Standard documents, whether created using DTP or WP, have lots of basic features **in common**.

Documents Always Have Layout Features You Need To Set Up

There are always basic layout features you'll need to set up when creating a standard document:

Orientation, Margins and Page Size

1) You can choose the **orientation** of your document — this means choosing between landscape and portrait.

Cat's Bum Landscape

2) You can set the **margins** — you can either do this manually, or usually there will be a special dialogue box (like the one pictured here) that will help you to preview what the final page will look like.

Cat's Bum Portrait

3) You can also choose what actual **size** the page itself is.

Paragraphs, Sections and Columns

1) These are all ways of dividing a document into sections, so that the **text can be formatted** either all together, column by column or else separately paragraph by paragraph. For example, you can choose the alignment (left, right, centre, justified), indentation, line spacing, bullets and numbering, and the font and size for each paragraph, section or column of text.

> Jennifer's aunt was a dog-faced woman. There was no polite way around the subject. Jennifer had spent years plucking up the courage to talk to her aunt normally although nature was against it.

> Her dad managed it though. Of course, he had had an extra couple of years to practise. "I wonder what would happen to me if I was a dog-faced woman?" thought Jennifer to herself one day.

> And then, as if by magic Jennifer felt her face being whisked away and replaced by something altogether different. "Are those whiskers?" she said out loud, touching her new face with careful, delicate fingers.

> **"Yes, my dear," said a voice from above. "Those are indeed whiskers. And you are now a dog-faced woman, just as you were thinking. I am the thought fairy — I make all of your thoughts come true."**

> "Ah," thought jennifer. "why exactly did no one ever mention this before? I mean, Thank goodness I wasn't thinking about other things. blimey."

> "Well, not to worry dear," said the thought fairy. "It'll wear off in a while and then you'll have:
> • your own face back
> • a guilty conscience
> So grow up love, and stop daydreaming."

2) **Paragraph styles** can be set up — these are sets of rules for how the paragraphs are formatted (things like spacing, indentations, fonts, etc.). When you apply a paragraph style, all the text in the paragraph will obey the rules.

3) Pressing return ends the paragraph you're in and starts a new one, so this makes a **paragraph break**. You can also insert breaks into documents to start a new **column** or **page**.

Graphics

1) Word processors and DTP packages can both handle **graphics**.

2) You can either select a pre-drawn **AutoShape** (see graphic), use a pre-existing **image**, or **create your own** if what you want isn't available.

3) You can then play with the graphic until you are **satisfied with its appearance** — e.g. by cropping, repositioning, wrapping text around it, etc.

AutoShapes — no bums here

Homemade bum

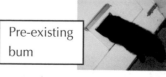

Pre-existing bum

Cropped bum

Standard Documents

Headers and Footers Make Documents More Organised

1) Headers and footers are descriptive **text** or **graphics** that can be added to the top or bottom margins of a document — headers go at the top, footers go at the bottom.

2) They usually contain **information** like page numbers, titles or the date, but could also include graphics.

3) You only have to add a header or footer once and the word processor will **automatically add it** to every page.

4) After adding the standard header or footer, you can also then **change them individually** in different parts of the document. E.g. you could use a unique header or footer on the title page or start the headers / footers on the following page.

Here's the header — the title, which is the same on every page.

Here's the footer — the page number, which changes on every page.

Footnotes and Endnotes Help Explain Bits Of The Document

1) **Footnotes** and **endnotes** are very useful if you want to explain a word or phrase without having to do so in the main body of the text.

2) Instead, you can add a **reference number** to the relevant word or phrase, which will send the reader to the note it's referring to[1].

3) **Footnotes** come at the **foot of the page** the reference number is on. **Endnotes** come at the **very end** of the whole document.

4) You can choose how the notes are **presented**, e.g. whether they're separated from the main body text by a line, and what font and size etc.

Don't Forget To Cater For Your Audience

1) You always have to think about who's going to **read** your document when it's finished.

2) Make sure you've prepared something that is **appropriate** to their needs.

3) For example:
   - young children need clear, uncomplicated documents (e.g. using big fonts).
   - educational documents for older children or adults can have a more sophisticated layout, but still need all the information to be clearly explained.
   - you can use graphs and charts to present figures in a clear and interesting way.

4) Just remember that it's usually better to be clear and cheerful than complicated and confusing. You can do this through careful editing and design in order to make things more **accessible** for your reader.

Practice Questions

Q1   What is a "standard document"?

Q2   Explain what a paragraph style is, and how it can be useful.

Q3   Explain what each of the following are: a) footnotes, b) endnotes, c) headers and d) footers.

Exam Questions

Q1   A company that sells mobility aids for senior citizens produces its own quarterly customer catalogue. Give two formatting techniques they could use to make the newsletter suitable for their customers.   (2 marks)

Q2   Describe how paragraph styles can be helpful when a long document is produced by a team of people.   (3 marks)

This is the funny top tip gag — on a loop[2]

It seems pretty obvious to say that you need to consider who's going to be reading the final document, but it's too easy to get so stuck in to what you're doing that you completely forget your readers will need everything to be clear and well explained in appropriate language. Non in Italiano per esempio... Mi capisci? Forse no. Forse Italiano non e proprio adatto a AS ICT.

[1] Just like this one did.
[2] Go to funny top tip gag.

Clipart and Graphics Tools

Ooh the joy of clipart. Why there's nothing I like better than relaxing on the sofa, sipping my brandy in front of the fire and leafing through my wonderful clipart libraries. My heart swells with pride and love, and occasionally a little trapped wind.

Clipart is Usually Free

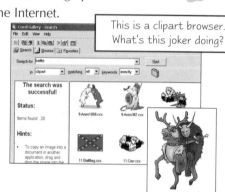

1) Clipart is the name for graphics which have been created by someone and are often freely available to use **under public domain** — this means that anyone can use them without having to pay for a license.

2) The basic idea of clipart is that it's providing **non-artists** with a wide selection of graphics.

3) Clipart often comes **free** with software packages and is available on the Internet.

4) Clipart can also can also be bought in collections on **CD-ROM**. Although you have to pay for these, you normally get an enormous amount for your money (e.g. 120,000 images for a tenner). They'll normally also provide a **browser** so you can browse (surprisingly) the images or search for images using keywords.

This is a clipart browser. What's this joker doing?

5) When you need images on a very **specific** subject (e.g. logos for a newsletter, an essay on WW2 History, etc.) you will normally be able to find an **image library** (also called a graphics library) with the images you need.

6) An image library is simply a **collection** of clipart on the same theme.

7) Some image libraries will be available from **manufacturers** and **organisations** in order for you to use their house style (e.g. freelance designers get sent image libraries from publishers that they need to use).

There Are Pros and Cons To Using Clipart

Good Things About Clipart

- Clipart is either **free** or very cheap.
- It's **quicker** than drawing your own graphics from scratch.
- You don't need to be a skilful **artist** to brighten up your document.
- You don't need special **training**.
- A wide variety of **categories** is available.
- No special **equipment** (e.g. scanners) needs to be bought.

Bad Things About Clipart

- You might not be able to find the image you want because you're **limited** to what clipart is available.
- Because there are so many categories available it can take ages to **search** through them all just to find one image. This is particularly true of looking for clipart on the Internet.
- The **quality** of clipart is very variable. In fact, some of it is just plain pants.
- Images you find may not be **up-to-date**.
- Other users will almost certainly have used that clipart before, so you may end up making your document feel **unoriginal** and **naff**.

You Can Use Software to Tweak Clipart or Create Your Own Graphics

1) You can use graphics software to **edit** clipart images.

2) You can remove certain elements and replace them with others.

3) Of course you can also use **drawing tools** to create completely new components.

4) With the right software, you can even turn clipart graphics into an animation, where images are shown in a sequence with a time delay that gives the appearance of movement.

There, that's a great improvement.

Section Twelve — Software for Presentation and Communication

Clipart and Graphics Tools

Images Are Stored Either As *Bitmap* Or *Vector* Data

Bitmap (or **pixel**-based) images are stored as a series of coloured dots (pixels).
Most clipart, drawings done in 'paint' software, scanned pictures and photos from digital cameras are bitmaps.

- Editing bitmap images basically involves altering each dot **individually**. This means very subtle changes can be made but it can be a long process.
- Luckily there's lots of software packages **specifically designed** for editing bitmap images, e.g. Adobe Photoshop, Corel Photopaint. These packages have tools that let you manipulate the image in different ways.
- Bitmaps cope well with highly detailed and **complex** images like photos.
- The file sizes can be **huge** because each dot is saved individually, but they can be **easily compressed**.
- When the image is **enlarged** by hand in a drawing program, the quality gets worse and the image can become blurry and appear "pixellated".
- Bitmaps are more **consistent** with the general computing environment — i.e. display and printing devices tend to use a series of dots to define images and text.

Vector (or **object**-based) images are saved as a **geometric equation** (e.g. a red circle might be represented by its radius, the coordinates of its centre and a number for its colour).

- Individual objects that make up a vector-based graphic can be **edited** independently, e.g. moved, resized and copied or grouped.
- They're usually **compatible** with drawing programs (e.g. Adobe Illustrator or CorelDraw) and word processing programs, allowing the user to add simple things like squares and lines.
- The file sizes are **smaller** than bitmap graphics of the same proportion, and they **can't be compressed**.
- Vector graphics can be **resized** with no loss of definition.
- You need a high amount of **processing power** to display vector-based graphics.

Practice Questions

Q1 What does it mean to say that clipart is provided "under public domain"?
Q2 Give three advantages to the user of using clipart.
Q3 Explain the difference between a bitmap graphic and a vector graphic.

Exam Questions

Q1 A map-making company uses vector graphics for producing its maps. These show the road, railway and river networks in a particular area.

a) Explain what is meant by the term "vector graphics" and explain why they are used for this application. (2 marks)

b) Give a use for bitmap graphics in this application, stating why they might be suitable. (1 mark)

Q2 Mr Little is the Editor-in-Chief of the medical journal "Knowing Nurses". This monthly publication provides up-to-date information and educational articles for nurses.

Give two advantages to Mr Little's Editorial team of using a graphics library. (2 marks)

My bitmap cuts off everything east of Swindon...

If you've ever messed around with a drawing program, you probably know lots of this stuff already. Remember to revise though, and try the practice questions until you're sure you've got it all down. Especially the difference between bitmaps and vector graphics — watch out for that. By the way, did I tell you that I hate rabbits? I guess the cartoon gave it away, huh?

Clipart and Graphics Tools

Right. This page will at least pretend to be entertaining. And if not, then I'll tell you what — I can't give you your money back, but I can offer you a nice bag of slime from my auntie Maureen's biggest tub of lard. What do you say to that?

Vector Graphic Packages Help You Create and Manipulate Images

Graphics packages have lots of different features that are designed to make creating and manipulating images easier.

Lines
Straight lines and "freehand" lines can be drawn with a variety of brushes.

Shape tools
Regular pre-defined shapes, such as squares, circles and rectangles can be drawn with a special tool.

Fill
Objects can be filled in with a colour. Simply set the outlines and pick a colour, then everything within the outline will be coloured.

Size
You can change the size of the image itself, usually by selecting the graphic and dragging one of the "handles" outwards to make it bigger, and inwards to make it smaller. It's important to keep the proportions the same though, or the image gets distorted. Look at this poor goat.

Shade / Shadow
Some packages let you choose the position of a light source and work out the shadow created by objects, or create shading effects on objects.

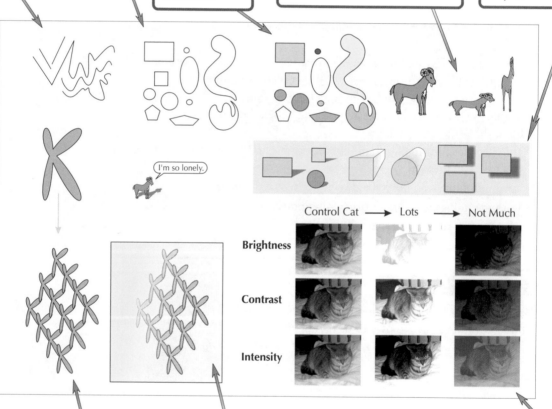

Orientation
You can select a landscape or portrait page set up (i.e. overall the layout of this workspace is landscape).

Layering
One image can be placed on top of another in order to create an overlap.

Transparency
Sections of an image can be made transparent to allow the underlying image to show through.

Brightness, Contrast, Intensity
These three tools deal with the difference between the light and dark areas of an image. A combination of all three can be used to sharpen or blur an image and to make the colours appear more saturated. They can also be used to make specified areas of an image stand out. Normally you'll be able to access all three tools via the same menu, and lots of programs will have a "preview" function that lets you see exactly how each tool is affecting the image.

Clipart and Graphics Tools

Sophisticated Graphics Packages *Have Some* Quite Fancy Effects

There are all sorts of crazy tools and effects you can apply if you have a sophisticated enough graphics package.
These are just a few examples:

Control Cat

Interactive Fill Tool

Colour Balance

Interactive Editing Tool

Pattern Fill

Perspective Tool

Emboss Effect

Swirl Effect

Sphere Effect

Blur Effect

Stained Glass Effect
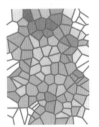

Fog Effect

Practice Questions

Q1   Describe how Fill and Shade can be used to enhance a graphic.

Q2   A graphics package has the features Brightness, Contrast and Intensity. Describe these features.

Q3   Describe 2 tools you could use to draw a plan of your ICT classroom.

Exam Question

Q1   Get16 is a popular culture magazine aimed at young teenagers. The publication's designers aim to engage their readers through imaginative graphics images and layout. The pages include photos and vector graphic images.

   a) Describe three ways that the publication's designers could use graphics software tools
      to create and manipulate vector graphics.   (3 marks)

   b) Describe three ways that the publication's designers could use graphics software tools
      to manipulate photographs to make them more visually appealing.   (3 marks)

I have an interactive cat tool — it turns everything into cats which bite me...

Hard to say "learn all this" really... Just bear in mind that these tools exist, and that they're always really useful for livening up an image or even a whole page. And you don't have to use cats. I hear dogs are "in" this year. Or fish. Just don't use my friend Amanda's fish. They died. Horribly. In smelly water. But other than that, use whatever animals you like...

Multimedia Presentations

Ah. A page with lots of text on it. I remember these. These are like the things your parents used to learn from. I'll bet they haven't got a clue what applications like PowerPoint are though. "PowerPoint? Yes dear, it's where I plug the telly in."

OHPs *Used To Be Used All The Time In* Presentations

1) **Overhead projectors** (OHPs) used to be used to give presentations all the time (and often still are). They project information printed on transparent sheets (OHP slides) onto a wall or screen.

2) The OHP slides can be printed in black and white or in colour, and the person giving the presentation uses them one by one to illustrate important points.

3) You need to have a photocopier or printer linked to a computer in order to create OHPs, but the actual presentations themselves use an **overhead projector**. This means you don't need to buy any fancy software or expensive multimedia projectors in order to use them.

4) However, they can look a bit **naff** and **old-fashioned** — there are lots of disadvantages to using them:

Disadvantages of Using OHPs

1) The speaker has to change each slide **by hand**.

2) Transparencies can be **easily damaged**, e.g. by fingerprints, making them look unprofessional.

3) You can skip between slides with little trouble, but it's easy to muddle up the **order** of the slides.

4) The speaker may have to **cover** with their hands any information they don't want the audience to see yet.

5) Animation, sound and video can't be used, making the presentation potentially quite **boring**.

Multimedia Presentations Combine Text, Graphics, Video and Sound

You can use a software package to create a multimedia presentation. Multimedia presentations use a **combination** of **different media** elements — e.g. graphics, animations, videos and sound which all help to keep the audience **interested**.

They work by displaying electronic slides in a sequence, and you click buttons to get from one slide to the next.

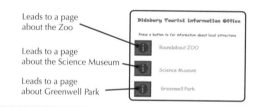

Different features of presentation software:

1) **Sound** can be used to liven up a presentation. It's much more effective to give audiences an audio element than just plodding on with boring silent visual images. The sound can be specially recorded or it could be an existing sound file, e.g. a company advertising jingle. The sound can be set to tie in with certain functions (e.g. skipping to the next section of a presentation) or it can play in the background or as part of a video.

2) **Video clips** can be inserted into the presentation, either specially recorded or from an existing file. Using a video can help break up the presentation and really emphasise certain parts that you want to get across. They can be set to play on a specified user action, usually a mouse click.

3) **Animation** effects are special sound or visual effects that are added to text or objects, e.g. charts, graphics. They can be used to change how items are displayed on a slide. For example, a bulleted list can be animated so that each bullet point will fly onto the slide separately. Or, you could set up an animation to compare different bar charts, so that you can watch the bars getting shorter or taller as you move to the next chart.

4) **Slide transition** sets how you move from one slide (or page) to another. Different effects can be applied so that you move to the next slide in an interesting way (e.g. one fading into another, one sweeping in from the side, etc.). You can set the speed of the transition effect, and can choose if you want to apply the effect to just one slide or to a whole presentation.

5) **Hyperlinks** can be inserted. When you click on them, they take you on to a different bit of the presentation.

6) **Hotspots** can be added to graphics — this is where different parts of the graphic act as hyperlinks. You usually need to get back to the page you started on through another hyperlink, so it's best not to use too many hotspots or the presentation gets too complicated.

This image has 3 hotspots, each taking you to a different slide or page. The hotspots are usually invisible, and the image gives the cues about where it should be clicked.

Multimedia Presentations

Presentations Should Have a Consistent Design

1) All the slides in a presentation should follow a similar kind of **design** and **colour scheme**. The software will have templates you can use, but making your own template will make your presentation look more original.

2) The software will also have some **auto-layouts** (a choice of pre-designed individual slide layouts). These suggest where the different elements of a slide could be positioned (i.e. the text, images, hotspots, etc).

3) A **master slide** could also be used. This is a bit like a style sheet in a desktop publisher, or a set of paragraph styles in a word processor (see page 100). It lets a team of people work on the presentation separately, and when their work is collated it's all in the same style. If any changes are then made on the master slide, then all the other slides will be changed automatically.

4) Fancy effects should be used carefully so they don't get distracting for the audience. The presentation needs to have a **consistent look** overall if you want it to feel professional.

You Don't Even Need a Speaker for Multimedia Presentations

1) Presentations are often given by a **speaker** who introduces the slides as they are projected on to a large screen.

2) Using presentation software, you can also create **self-running presentations**. One slide automatically moves to the next after a specified period of time, and the whole presentation can be set to re-start as soon as it has finished.

3) You can use these while a speaker gives the presentation, though it's **not really ideal** for verbal presentations because the speaker can easily be delayed and get out of time with the slides. Self-running presentations are more appropriate where **no speaker is involved**, e.g. a museum might want a self-running presentation to run constantly in the background of an exhibition, showing useful images and data about the exhibit.

4) Of course, whenever a presentation is left to run on its own, there's always the danger that something will **go wrong** with the program or the display hardware and no one will be on hand to fix it.

Advantages of Using Presentation Software

1) It produces professional looking presentations.

2) Using multimedia helps hold people's attention.

3) Presentations can be saved and used again, with or without a speaker being present.

4) It's easy to edit presentations and adapt them for different audiences.

Disadvantages of Using Presentation Software

1) It's very easy to get carried away by the technology and produce badly designed slides.

2) The software needs expensive hardware to run the presentation.

Practice Questions

Q1 What is an OHP presentation?

Q2 Explain the following features of multimedia presentations: i) hyperlinks, ii) hotspots and iii) animation.

Q3 Give one advantage and one disadvantage of a speaker using a self-running presentation.

Exam Questions

Q1 Mr Sharpe is a training consultant who frequently needs to give presentations to large groups from different companies. He currently uses OHP slides and an overhead projector but is considering switching to multimedia.

Give 2 advantages and 2 disadvantages to Mr Sharpe of continuing to use OHPs. (4 marks)

Q2 Mrs Jenkins is using a software package to design a multimedia slideshow presentation for use in work. Describe how she can use each of the following features to make an effective presentation:

a) slide transition   b) buttons   c) sound   (6 marks)

I thought multimedia meant having more than one telly...

Okay, there's quite a lot on this double page. Although you need to learn it all for the exam, remember that most of it's really useful for when you're creating your own presentations. If I've said it once I've said it a hundred thousand million billion trillion quadrillion quintillion sextillion septillion octillion nonillion decillion times — think about your audience.

Creating Web Pages

Of course the other way to present something to people is to stick it up on the old Internet. That way it's always there and people can look at it at their own leisure. Or else they'll ignore it entirely and go looking for more interesting sites...

You Can Build A Web Site **Without Learning HTML**

Web pages are written in a language called **hypertext mark-up language** (HTML). However, you don't have to actually learn it yourself in order to build a web site. There are two main methods of creating web pages:

1)   Use a dedicated **web-authoring package** (e.g. Microsoft FrontPage or Macromedia Dreamweaver).

2)   Use a standard **word processing** or **DTP** package. Most of these can convert documents into HTML format.

Web-Authoring Software Has Lots Of Helpful Features...

1)   Web-authoring packages will have **WYSIWYG** (What You See Is What You Get) capability, which means that the layout on the screen is exactly what will appear on the web page.

2)   Most packages will have in-built **wizards** to help, e.g. one wizard might help a user create a site map.

3)   Some packages include web site **management tools**, e.g. tools to help the user upload and check pages.

4)   Some packages will automatically check any **links** and alert users if they need updating.

5)   Impressive **effects** like animations or nifty graphics need the use of other applications — you'll need to integrate code samples written in a scripting language (e.g. Java), and you'll need a companion program to the web-authoring package that lets you do this. This kind of thing is more advanced and **specialist training** is needed.

6)   With most authoring packages you can choose to **edit** your webpage either by what appears on the final screen (WYSIWYG) or by editing the HTML directly. This means they're suitable for novice and experienced users.

...But Also A Few Downsides...

1)   Even though web-authoring packages have nice user interfaces, users still need **training** before they can use the software, especially the more **complex functions**.

2)   In a company or organisation, the additional staff training would obviously have **time** and **cost** implications.

3)   The web-authoring packages and other associated applications can also be very **expensive**.

You Can Make Really **Naff** Web Pages Using **Standard Applications Software**

1)   You can create a web page using just standard applications like a **word processor** or **desktop publisher**.

2)   It doesn't require any major **technical ability**, and (as you've probably already got the applications and the Internet connection), it's not going to **cost** you anything.

3)   You simply design your page, select the "**save as web page**" option, then view the page in a browser.

4)   Even a really inexperienced user could build a web page in this fashion, but there are disadvantages:

       1)   It's really difficult to get the page to **look exactly how you want it**, as it's not WYSIWYG. All sorts of graphics and other elements will **jump around** as the standard application converts your page to HTML.

       2)   Because the standard application you'll use was primarily designed with other uses in mind, the code it creates is very **messy**. It's often a bit rubbish and might not be compatible with all browsers.

       3)   The code produced is often **longer** than it should be, so the page can take a long time to download.

       4)   Only **limited wizards** and **tools** are available to write the script and manage and upload the site.

       5)   **Uploading** your page to the Internet is fairly straightforward — you can buy some web space from your ISP, or maybe get some free through a web site, e.g. Yahoo.

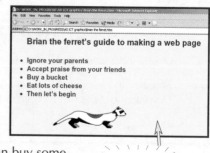

Look at this. It's rubbish.

Creating Web Pages

You Can *View* Your Final Web Pages With An *Internet Browser*

A browser like Netscape Navigator or Internet Explorer displays HTML pages in a way that people can easily understand. Browsers have standard features that help you to navigate the Internet:

1) Websites are connected by **hyperlinks**. When you click on a hyperlink, the browser will automatically take you to the linked web page. You can choose whether it does this within the **same browser window**, or whether you want it to open the link in a **new window**.

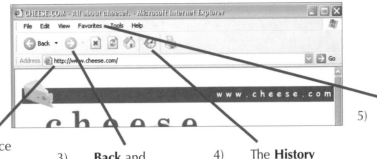

2) The Uniform Resource Locator or **URL** is the **address** of the web page. To go to a particular web site, you simply type the URL into the address bar of your browser. (See page 22 for more on URLs.)

3) **Back** and **forward buttons** help you to find pages you've visited recently by retracing your steps.

4) The **History** button displays links for all the web sites you've visited in one big alphabetical list.

5) **Bookmarks** (or "favourites") store URLs of web sites you want the browser to remember. You can then select web sites from your bookmarks list and the browser will take you straight there. You can organise your bookmarks into folders, e.g. a music folder for all your music sites, a cheese folder for all your cheese sites, etc.

If you don't know the URL of a website, or you're not sure where to find the information you're looking for, you can find web sites using a **search** instead. (See page 23 for more.)

Practice Questions

Q1 What are the two main methods of creating web pages?

Q2 What is a URL?

Exam Questions

Q1 A school wants to develop a web site. This can be done using web authoring software or standard applications software and converting to HTML.

   a) Explain the advantages of each of these methods. (6 marks)

   b) Explain, with reasons, why the school should keep a similar layout on each of the web pages within the site. (4 marks)

Q2 Browsers and search engines are both associated with the Internet. Explain what is meant by:

   a) browser (1 mark)

   b) search engine. (1 mark)

Web pages are to presentations, as the London Underground is to Jam...

So, that rounds off our section on doing presentations then. I admit that creating a web site is an excessive solution if you're a nervous speaker, but if you can find some web space to practise on, it's all useful stuff to know, not least for the exams. Web design scares me though. Once you've seen it for yourself — bah. Maybe I've watched the Matrix too many times.

Planning — Choosing a Project

Take a deep breath for this section, it's a monster. Still, this section WILL get you better marks in your coursework. Okay? And watch out for the big hairy smelly foul-breath blowing ICT beastie behind you. It's even worse than coursework.

This section is based around AQA module 3 — "The Use of Generic Application Software for Task Solution".
If you're doing OCR, you should find it helpful for "Structured Practical ICT tasks" module (2513).

It's **Down To You** To Get The Work Done

1) Right. First things first. Your coursework is going to be worth **40%** of your final grade. This means it's a really REALLY **important piece of work**, in case you hadn't gathered. The project proves you can apply the theoretical knowledge and skills you've learnt to a **real life situation**.

2) This section will give you plenty of advice on how to tackle your coursework, and your ICT teacher will be there to help you out and set you deadlines. But remember that at the end of the day **it's down to you** to choose a suitable project and to plan enough time to be able to complete it successfully.

3) Your tutors need to have your work marked, internally moderated and assessed by mid-April. If you can **complete your project before the hand-in date** then there will be time for you to get some feedback and make corrections. This is very important and could make all the difference to your grade.

Make Sure You Pick a **Suitable Situation**

Some situations are suitable for ICT projects and some aren't. Pick a situation which **needs improving** — if it's already working well then you won't have anything to talk about. Here are some examples of **suitable situations**:

- **boring** or **repetitive** tasks
- jobs which have to be done **quickly**
- jobs where **data** needs to be **better organised**
- jobs that need **more security** (e.g. passwords)
- jobs where there is a **shortage of labour**
- jobs where **more information is needed** in order to **make decisions**
- jobs where there needs to be **better presentation** (e.g. a newsletter, not a dog)
- jobs that need to be **accessed remotely**

Bears:
not suitable for
ICT projects

You Should Pick a **Task Related Project**

1) A **task related project** is related to **one specific problem** — it's not meant to be about an entire system.

2) Don't **invent** the problem yourself. The moderator will be able to tell, and you won't get any marks.

3) It's also **not a good idea** for your **tutor** to set the problem for you to solve, unless it's a **real** one.

Pick An **Appropriate End User**

1) **Don't be your own end user**. These projects tend to get low marks.

2) Your project will also probably be more effective if your end user **isn't your ICT tutor** — having a "real" end user will make your project more realistic. Besides, teachers are often pretty busy, so it would be better to pick someone you can pin down more regularly.

3) An obvious one to pick would be your **parents**, relatives, or someone else you live with.

4) Another one could be through your **part-time job**, especially if you work for a small business / company / shop (probably best not to try and fix the shop's problems if you work somewhere big like Tesco though).

5) **Other ideas** for end users could be your parents' friends, clubs or societies you belong to, small local businesses (e.g. plumbers, electricians, accountants, computer hardware builders, dress and cake makers, quilt makers have all been used successfully in the past).

6) Whoever your end user is, make sure they realise the **importance** of their position. You might be able to get your tutor to write a letter to your intended end user spelling out what will be expected of them.

7) Above all, make sure you choose an end user you can **keep in regular contact with**.

Planning — Choosing a Project

There Are Good Topics and Bad Topics

Here are some topics you should avoid when picking what to do your project on:

- **payroll** — this gets too complicated because of tax, national insurance and lots of other tricky deductions.
- **stock control** — although this might be okay in smaller companies, it's a nightmare in a large one.
- **word-processing projects** — i.e. projects that only involve basic mail merging. There's not enough to do.
- **anything really obvious** — most of the generalised examples you'll have read about in a text book (e.g. newspaper delivery, video rentals, driving schools, etc.) **unless** you personalise them well enough.

Here are some good topics:

- **booking systems** — e.g. doctors, dentists, hairdressers, beauticians.
- **invoicing systems** — e.g. for small companies.
- **timetabling of facilities** — e.g. computer rooms in a school, tennis courts, sports and fitness trainers.
- **record keeping** — e.g. collections, hire equipment.
- **web sites** — e.g. for clubs, hotels, plumbers, chemists, accountants, electricians, security device fitters, sportswear manufacturers, fitness trainers, recording studios.
- **scheduling systems for events** — e.g. meetings, lessons.

Make Sure You Pick The Right Software

1) **Spreadsheet** or **database packages** are often the best choice, as they let you show off your data fairly easily.

2) You could use a DTP or web-based package instead, but you'll need some help from your ICT tutors with the **advanced features** and ways to process data.

3) Remember — moderators are always on the look out for projects that show some **originality** in a range of applications. It makes all our lives more interesting.

Application	Brand names	Suitable for	Not suitable for
Word/Text Processing	MS Word Star Office	Presentation projects Document processing	Data storage Projects involving calculations on data
Spreadsheet	MS Excel Star Office	Data handling Data calculations Flat file databases	Presentation Relational databases
Database	MS Access Filemaker Pro MySQL	Data handling Relational databases Web-based database systems	Presentations Projects involving complicated calculations
Slideshow Presentation	MS PowerPoint Star Office	Presentations Multimedia use of sound and graphics	Data handling
Website Projects	Netscape/Mozilla Composer Dreamweaver MS FrontPage Star Office	Web sites Presentations	Data handling except for form submissions — online databases would be appropriate

Practice Questions

1) Describe three features of a task in which ICT could be used to improve efficiency.
2) Make a list of people who could help you with the project.
3) List three characteristics that you would look for in a good end user.
4) Name three project scenarios you should avoid.
5) Write down three different problems that could be solved using a database.

Use ICT to predict the lottery numbers — now there's a good project...

It really is important that you think carefully about what kind of project you want to do. I know it sounds pretty obvious — I mean, everything sounds pretty obvious when you say it out loud. Things like "bottles don't go in the washing machine" or "don't put cats in the toaster they don't like it". But sometimes we need to be told the obvious to stop us doing silly things.

Planning — Developing an Idea

Planning and research, planning and research, wherefore art thou? I recall, my bonny sweet planning-and-research love, how thou didst forsake me in my hour of need, and left me stranded in a field selling lipstick to farm animals...

Example Project — Ticknall Cricket Club

Ticknall village has a thriving cricket club with over 100 members. It has a new pavilion and an attached social club. It has three teams, including a junior one, which each play 20 games a year. Fixtures are played all over South Derbyshire.

You could base a project on this cricket club quite easily. It's ideal for a computer-based solution because:

- the events that require organisation are **mainly repetitive**,
- they need to be done **speedily**,
- they require a **professional output** that is easily produced using ICT.

It's probably best to stick to using **one** application other than your word processor.
The table below shows possible uses of databases and spreadsheets that you could put in this project.

Application	Possible uses
Database	Database of members and / or players Database of fixtures Database of equipment Booking system for facilities e.g. hiring out the social club Mail merges to members / players Generation of membership cards Database of fixtures linked to website
Spreadsheet	Members lists and subs payments Trading accounts League tables and statistics Player performance analysis e.g. batting average / wickets Match analysis

1) Think about how much **detail** you need to make a decent project — just producing a project on one of the things mentioned in this table **won't give you enough to write about**.

2) By adding players' fixtures, squad training times and team membership to a basic database of team members, you could develop a piece of work with enough **scope** and depth to get a decent mark.

Once You've Chosen, You Need To Start Researching

Here are the main research tasks you'll need to carry out for the business / end user you've chosen:

1) **Collecting documentation** used by the business — invoices, bills, price lists, photographs.
   - How were they produced?
   - Do they need updating?
   - Could their use be automated?

   You can get lots of points by including **relevant** examples of real documentation you've thought about.

2) Carrying out a **structured interview**.
   - Produce the questions beforehand and check them with your ICT tutor.
   - Make sure the questions are not all "closed" questions (i.e. questions that can only be answered by one word answers). You need the end user to tell you what their requirements are.

3) **Using questionnaires**.
   - Produce questionnaires for other end users you will not be interviewing (e.g. cricket team members, or other employees if using a small company as your end user).
   - Think how you can prompt and focus useful responses.

4) **Observing the processes** undertaken by end users. This is rarely done or documented in projects, so doing so is likely to get you a few extra marks.
   - Arrange to visit your end user and sit back and observe the various stages and processes that the task you are studying involves.
   - E.g. how does the cricket club secretary manage the subs, mail merging, team selection sheets, keeping the league table up to date?

5) **Researching similar businesses / situations** to see what similarities there are and what ideas they have to offer.
   - Use the Yellow Pages or Internet search engines to find similar firms or organisations.
   - Thompson's Local Directory or trade journals at the local library are other good sources.

Planning — Developing an Idea

Think about how **Data Moves** through the System

1) When you're researching, remember to think about how data you collect will be **processed into information**.

2) It's important to find out as much as possible about the way that **data moves round the system** you're studying.

3) It's helpful to **use a diagram** to illustrate how data moves through the system, where data and information is stored and what processes take place to transform data into information or change the format of information (i.e. inputs into the task, the processing that takes place and the output generated by the task).

4) The **symbols** you use in your diagram are not important but you must be consistent and show a key.

5) The diagram below is a model **dataflow context diagram** — it puts the task into its context.

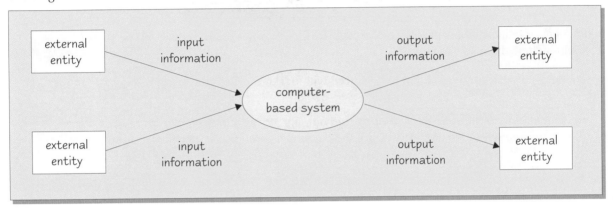

- This is a "**level zero**" diagram because it just shows the main **inputs**, **outputs** and **external entities**.
- There's not much about processing. **Processes** are shown in detail in **level one** dataflow diagrams (see p117).

A **level zero** dataflow (context) diagram for Ticknall Cricket Club might look like this:

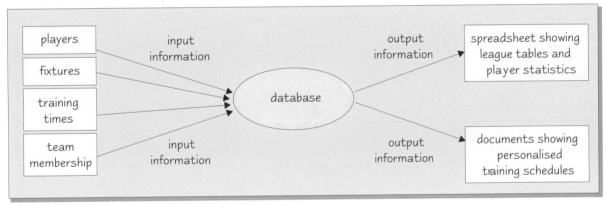

Practice Questions

1) Which software application would be best suited to record cricketers' scores and batting and bowling averages?

2) With reference to the cricket club example above, who would be the best person to interview?

3) Write down five questions you might ask him/her.

4) List four ways of finding out about the processes involved in the task you're undertaking.

5) What is a dataflow context diagram?

6) Draw a context diagram for a web site project using the model above.
Think carefully about the inputs, outputs and processes.

Milk is a process too you know — at least from the cow's point of view...

I love cows. Big hairy cows with their lovely long eyelashes and their funny big faces. They're just like ICT moderators really. You know, they're sweet and cute from a distance, they're a bit simple, and then we kill them inhumanely and eat them with chips for dinner. Actually, from that point of view, I guess cows are more like pigs, chickens and geese then.

Design — Requirements Specification

You need to produce a decent requirements specification. I made one once that just said "car is broken. Fix car."
It didn't really go down very well. I ended up selling the car to some sucker on eBay. Is that wrong? Oops...

You Need A **Top Notch Requirements Specification**

1) The **requirements specification** should give a clear and thorough picture of what the system is required to do.

2) This means thinking about the whole **systems life cycle** and explaining everything clearly from beginning to end.

Your **Requirements Specification** Should Include...

A requirements specification needs to **state the problem** clearly and **explain how it will be solved**
— it should include these key items:

1) a **clear statement of the problem to be solved** with **background** to the problem.

2) **documentation of the research you've carried out**, e.g. observations, results of interviews and questionnaires, analysis of the documents used by the business.

3) a **clear statement of the end user's requirements**.

4) a list of **aims**, **objectives** and **performance indicators**. See below...

5) a list of the **inputs**, **processing** and **outputs** required. See page 116...

6) an analysis of the **hardware and software constraints**. See page 118...

7) a **test strategy**. See page 128 for more about this...

You Need To Identify Clear **Aims and Objectives**

1) **Aims** are **general** points, while **objectives** are **specific** ones.
Your **objectives** should explain **how** you intend to **achieve your aims**.

> <u>Example</u> **Aim:** to increase the number of mail order customers for the Melbourne Net and Tackle Co.
>
> **Objective:** to make their products available 24/7 on the World Wide Web by mail order so the number of customers will increase.

2) Objectives can be **quantitative** or **qualitative**. **Quantitative** means they are objective, and therefore can be easily measured. **Qualitative** means they are subjective — i.e. open to personal opinion and not easily measurable. **Quantitative** objectives are best.

3) Remember to **number your objectives** so that you can track them through the project and refer to them easily.

> **Examples of objectives for a web design project:**
> 1) To ensure the Home Page downloads within 10 seconds (quantitative).
> 2) To ensure that navigation is intuitive and consistent (qualitative).
> 3) To ensure that the pages can be read in the 4 most commonly used browsers (quantitative).
> 4) To ensure that forms submit all their contents in full (quantitative).

Design — Requirements Specification

Indicators Help You Measure Your Success

Performance indicators say how you're going to fulfil the performance criteria — so they tell you if your objectives have been met. Here are some examples to match the web site objectives from the previous page:

1) The Home Page should be no more than 50 Kilobytes in size with graphics which are in a compressed format such as gifs or jpegs.

2) Navigation buttons on each page must be in the same area of the page. Buttons must be consistent in shape, have consistent lettering and have consistent actions.

3) The pages must be correctly coded with opening and closing tabs for each element. They are then viewed in four browsers, Internet Explorer 5.5, Netscape 4.7, Mozilla Firebird and Opera to check that they can be read properly.

4) Data input into forms should reach the intended recipient in the expected format. I shall input some names and addresses into the form then post it to myself in order to check the truth of the contents.

Practice Questions

1) Explain what the requirements specification is for, and what it should contain.

2) Why are quantitative objectives preferable to qualitative ones?

3) Say which of the following are quantitative objectives and which are qualitative objectives for a website.

   a) The page download speed.

   b) The look of the colour scheme.

   c) Ease of navigation.

   d) All links on the pages work.

   e) The Home Page has no scrolling vertically and horizontally.

   f) All graphics load in the correct place.

   g) The site has a professional look and feel.

4) Read through the following example and answer the questions below:

> Simsbury Arboretum needs more paying visitors to provide funds for the upkeep of its trees. It's hoped that a web site will boost attendance. Newspaper and magazine advertising have proven to be very expensive. The Arboretum owners are computer literate but have no expertise in producing a web site.
>
> The owners need a web site that's easy for them to update, allows visitors to buy tickets through a web page, tells visitors what they can see at different times of year, sells products made at the Arboretum and other garden products, contains directions to the Arboretum, and logs the number of visitors to the site.
>
> **The web site designer sets out the following performance criteria objectives:**
> The site will be based around templates.
> The site will have a link to an on-line booking system (e.g. Ticketmaster).
> The site will have a link to a webcam.
> The site will use an online shopping database.
> The site must have a map of some sort to help visitors find the Arboretum.
> The site will have a visitor counter on its front page.

   a) Turn the Arboretum web designer's performance criteria objectives into performance indicators.

   b) How would the web site consultant find out about the present advertising methods used by the Arboretum?

You don't need a requirements specification for life — just chocolate...

Going into detail really is the key, as always. It's important not to skimp on any information. The moderator isn't going to realise what you've done unless you tell them. Of course I'm going to have to remind you again that you need to use detail WITHOUT WAFFLE because waffling is bad and sort of annoying and tum-de-tum blah blah oh I'm sorry. Was I waffling?

Design — Inputs, Processes, Outputs

Noooooooooo... When are the words "input", "output" and "process" ever going to go away? I can't bear it for much longer, I can't. It's enough to make a perfectly sane person go crazy!!! In other news, ICT is good for the soul. Really.

You Need To List Your **Inputs**, **Processes** and **Outputs**

1) The functioning of all ICT systems involves three basic elements — **input**, **processing** and **output**.

2) It's vital that you can describe them in **detail** in the AS Project. You have to state the input, processing, and output needed to **match** the **requirements specification**.

3) If you're stuck on the meanings of these, go right back to the start of this revision guide and start all over again.˙

4) In order to discover what the inputs, processes and outputs relating to your project are, you should use **observation**, **documentation**, **questionnaires** and **interviews**. All of these relate to your **end user**.

Typical **Inputs**

1) With inputs you need to consider **what** is to be input and **how** it is to be input.

> E.g. in a database you'd need to document the type of data that can be put into each field (number, text, date) and perhaps the length of that data (i.e. the number of characters allowed).

2) **Typical inputs include**: text, sound, graphics, end user skills and knowledge, hardware, research and development.

Processing **Changes Data Into Information**

1) The concept of **processing** in certain applications is obvious — e.g. in databases and spreadsheets it's things like searching or querying, sorting and totalling.

2) It can be trickier to grasp the concept of processing in **other applications packages** (e.g. DTP or Presentation). In this case the processing means things like manipulating the graphics or formatting text.

3) **Typical processes include**: calculating (add, divide, subtract, multiply, etc.), coding, sorting, merging, editing, updating, submitting data, deleting, manipulating (e.g. graphics — rotate, crop, skew, recolour, etc.), searching, formatting, appending.

The **Output** is **What Comes Out At The End**

1) This is fairly self-explanatory. The outputs are basically the **end result** of the project.

2) **Typical outputs include**: paperwork, printed material, material on screen, video, photographic material, sound.

You Need To **Break Tasks Into Parts**

It's important to break your tasks down into manageable parts, so you can see exactly what all the inputs, processes and outputs are. This way you won't miss any of them out. The example below deals with a skiing holiday **insurance calculator** for a travel company:

The stages involved in getting holiday insurance:

1) A customer / client goes to a travel company to book a holiday and **requests** a quote for insurance.

2) The member of staff **opens** the software that calculates quotes for insurance.

3) She creates a file for him, **entering** his personal details.

4) She enters the **specifications** of his holiday, e.g. what type of skiing, what equipment, etc.

5) She enters **other information** that relates to the insurance cost, e.g. customer's medical history.

6) Once she's finished entering data, she instructs the software to **calculate** a quote for the cost of the insurance.

7) She **checks** the quote on-screen with the client, who confirms or rejects it.

8) Once confirmed, she instructs the software to **process** the booking and store the details in the main database.

9) She **prints** off a copy to give / send to the customer.

Design — Inputs, Processes, Outputs

Separate Your Inputs, Processes and Outputs Clearly

Once you've identified all the different stages that your product will be involved in, you need to separate them into clear lists showing your inputs, processes and outputs. Here's what they'd be for the insurance calculator:

Inputs

- client's **personal details**, e.g: forename, surname, address, sex, age.
- **length of holiday** e.g. 7, 14 days.
- **area of holiday** e.g. Europe, USA.
- skiing **risk assessment** by type: e.g. on piste, off piste, cross country, extreme, snowboarding.
- **equipment cover** e.g. for skis, poles, boots.
- **personal belongings cover** e.g. for baggage/credit cards.
- **piste closure cover**.
- **medical history** of client.

Processes

- **Multiplying** factors such as age and medical condition. These will increase the cost of insurance.
- Quote **calculated**.
- Quote **confirmed** and **transferred** into the main database to be stored.
- Quote **formatted** for printer.

Outputs

- **Quote** on computer screen.
- Quote output in **PDF** file format.
- Professional **quote printed off** with ski insurance company logo and sent to customer.

An Alternative Is To Use a Flow Diagram

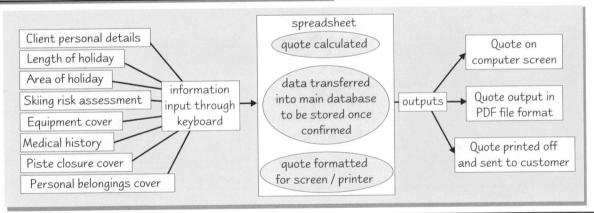

Practice Questions

1) How would you input sound into a multimedia project?

2) What processes could be applied to graphics when preparing them for placement in a web page or DTP brochure?

3) Complete the table with 3 inputs, processes and outputs for each of these scenarios:
   a) A school lending library system.
   b) A school attendance system using swipe cards to register students in every lesson.
   c) A booking system for an ICT room to be used by non ICT examination classes.

Inputs	Processes	Outputs

Number One, the Flow Diagram — Number Two, the Larch...

'E's not pinin'! 'E's passed on! This parrot is no more! He has ceased to be! ' E's expired and gone to meet 'is maker! 'E's a stiff! Bereft of life, 'e rests in peace! If you hadn't nailed 'im to the perch 'e'd be pushing up the daisies! 'E's kicked the bucket, 'e's shuffled off 'is mortal coil, run down the curtain and joined the choir invisible!! This... is an ex-parrot.

Design — Hardware and Software

Wow, this requirements specification is going to be one helluva read. So what's next... oh yes, here we are — "analysing the hardware and software constraints".

Give **Details** About The **Hardware**

Make sure you do **more** than just write a list of what hardware you're using — go into detail. Most computers built over the past two years are capable of running most generic software packages. You need to think about more **specific details**:

1) **the screen** — size, resolution and quality (the larger the screen, the better for DTP projects).

2) **printers** — type, quality of print and paper, the size of paper they can print to (A3 might be useful with spreadsheets), whether they support colour or not, and the cost of cartridges, special papers and labels.

3) **peripherals** — including scanners, digital cameras, CD-ROMS, CD-rewriters, DVD players and writers, speakers and plotters.

Comment on the suitability of each of these to solving your problem.
The table below describes some of the main hardware elements you might use in an AS project.

Hardware Element	Example	Comment
Processor make	Intel Pentium4 or AMD 2000XP	Makes little difference to the performance of software but the Pentium attracts a premium price.
Processor speed	Measured in Gigahertz	The faster the better, especially for graphics programs and multimedia projects.
RAM available	512Mb	The more RAM the better, especially for multimedia.
Monitor/VDU	Standard 17 CRT or TFT flat screen	Again, the larger the better. With a DTP project a screen that can show an A4 sheet in full is best. Use a TFT where there is limited space available for your end user.
Printer	Laser or Inkjet, black and white or colour	Lasers are great for text but colour lasers are still quite expensive. Inkjets are cheap to buy but expensive to maintain. Also consider the cost of special papers to print colour photos from an inkjet.
Scanner	Most scan up to 1200*2400 dots per inch and can scan in 48 bit colour	Resolution, colour depth and speed are important.
Digital camera	A 3 megapixel is really the minimum specification for a usable digital camera	3 megapixel is needed to print a page up to A4 in any real quality.

Other hardware elements you could include are CD and DVD players and writers and speakers.

Make **Full** And **Effective Use** Of Your **Software**

1) As well as describing the major applications packages you are going to use, you should also describe **other packages** you might use to solve the problem.

For example — in a web site based project you might use a WYSIWYG editor like Dreamweaver, but you'd probably also use an HTML editor, like Arachnophilia or Notepad, scanning software, a photo editor (such as Photoshop), a word-processor, several Internet browsers and, of course, Operating System software. In this case, you'd need to give full details of all the additional bits of software you're using.

2) You also need to show the moderator that you've thought about the **constraints** imposed by having different versions of the same program running on different machines (e.g. Access 97 at school, Access 2000 at the end user and Access 2002/XP at home). There's more about this on the next page...

3) Where a database seems to be the only solution, you should discuss the pros and cons of using **different database packages**, e.g. you could compare the key features of MS Access with those of Filemaker Pro.

Design — Hardware and Software

Example — Constraints On The Hardware and Software

Here is an example of how you could **discuss hardware constraints**:

1) This section deals with the **hardware** that I have at school and that owned by my end user, Mr Jones, who is secretary of the Swarkestone Tennis Club.

← Introduce the subject.

2) He uses a desktop computer with a 17″ monitor, which is a decent size and easy on the eye. It shows more of the spreadsheet than a standard monitor, which cuts down on the amount of scrolling he has to do. As the spreadsheet is not viewed for long periods of time, a **screen filter** will not be necessary.

*← Even though this screen filter is **not** being used, it's good to mention as it shows you're thinking about what is needed.*

3) The desktop computer has a high specification and includes a hard disk that holds 40 gigabytes of data which is more than adequate. It has **a Pentium 4 processor and 512 MB of RAM** which is enough to run the spreadsheet and other applications he might need to use. The computer is also equipped with a floppy drive which is useful for back up of small files. Mr Jones also has an A3 inkjet colour printer which is great for printing out large spreadsheets. He has an **ADSL modem** and **internet account** which allows him to link quickly to the internet. This facility also allows him to easily transfer files amongst Tennis Club officials.

← Good to give specific details like this.

← Oh goody more detail.

4) Mr Jones also owns a **laptop** which has 128Mb of RAM, an AMD 475 MHz processor and a 20Gb hard drive. This is sufficient to run a program such as Excel. The 14″ laptop screen is useful as it gives him a wide view of each worksheet. The main improvement he could make to his laptop would be to add an internal modem.

← Be sure to mention all available bits of hardware, even if he does most of his work on his desktop computer.

5) At school the equipment is rather old. Students use Intel Celerons made by Research Machines. These have slow processors (333 MHz) and have only 64Mb of RAM. The storage space allocated to my files is limited to 15Mb on the network so I have a constant battle keeping inside my space limits.

← Don't forget to talk about your own hardware constraints, and not just the end user's.

Here is an example of how you could **discuss software constraints**:

1) The software available to Mr Jones both at home and on his laptop is Microsoft Excel. Unfortunately they are different versions of Excel and there is some incompatibility due to different macro languages being used. Mr Jones will have to be very careful that he saves his files in a format that allows him to transfer data easily.

← Make sure you explain exactly what the problems are.

2) His two machines run different operating systems; the laptop has WindowsXP and the desktop has Windows98 SE. The machines I am using at school run Windows95 which causes problems as it doesn't support the latest versions of the Microsoft Office suite.

← Don't forget that in the objectives section you'll have to say how you plan to overcome these problems.

Practice Questions

1) Name five common "peripherals".
2) What type of project benefits the most from having a large monitor?
3) What features are important in a scanner?
4) Describe the hardware and software you would need to produce a multimedia web site project.
5) What problems might you have using different versions of the same software on several different machines?

My personal hardware is constrained by time, space, gravity and burgers...

It's a good idea for you to talk about constraints, because it can help the moderator see why you've done things a certain way. It's not admitting failure — it's about being realistic and making the best of what's available to you. Other than that, all I have left to say is mmmmmMMMMMmmmMMMmMMMMMMMmMMMMMMMMmMMMMmmmMMMmm. Tasty burgers.

Design — Working With Data

Data data data — there's no just no escaping it in ICT. And oh look — here's a couple of pages of useful advice for handling data capture, validation and presentation. Just get stuck in, my long-suffering friend...

Decide how to **Capture** your Data

1) Data capture can be **manual** or **electronic**.

2) **Electronic** data capture systems include OMR, OCR, bar codes, MICR, magnetic stripe cards, keyboards, sensors and graphics tablets.

3) To select the most appropriate method of data capture you need to think about:

- **speed** of input and processing required
- **quantity** of data being processed
- **ease** of entry and processing
- **environmental conditions** under which the entry and processing takes place

4) It's more than likely that all your data capture will be done **manually**, with a paper and pen. But you should at least think about the alternatives.

5) Whether manual or electronic, you need to **think carefully** about the design of your entry forms and screens, spreadsheet worksheets, web pages and any paper based documentation for data collection.

You'll have to set up **Validation Checks**

1) Validation makes sure that data input is of the **correct type** and is within the **correct range**.

2) It prevents the end user from letting incorrect data into the system, which would result in nonsense coming out the other end.

Spreadsheet validation methods:

Validation of spreadsheets involves checking data as it is input into individual cells.
There's various different types of check you can set up...

Validation	Explanation
Text length	Only accepts text up to a set max. no. of characters.
Whole number	Only accepts whole numbers within a given range.
Decimal	Only accepts decimal numbers within a given range.
List	Restricts input to a list which the user selects from.
LookUp	"Looks up" values from a data table in the spreadsheet.

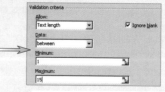

Setting up data validation in a spreadsheet — this will only accept text of up to 15 characters.

Database validation methods:

Database validation should be at table and form level, e.g. your forms can have check boxes, drop downs and "combo boxes", offering limited choices and preventing the input of "incorrect" data.

Validation	Explanation
Presence check	Checks data has been entered when it is required e.g. date of birth or credit card expiry date.
Format check	Data entered must fit a preset format such as class being named after its teacher using a three character code.
Range check	Checks data entered is within a range e.g. "date of birth" is between 1986 and 1991.
Look up check	Data is checked against an acceptable list of values.
Check digit	An extra digit on a data code (e.g. ISBN number). The data code is checked on input by performing a standard calculation which should give the check digit.

The format property controls how fields are displayed. In this example, DOB is formatted to "long date".

Design — Working With Data

Web page validation methods:
If you do a web project you'll need to include some data submission forms.
Here are the main validation checks you'd use on these...

Validation	Explanation
Presence check	Checks that all required fields have data entered.
Format check	Checks the correct type of data is input into a field.
Drop down lists	Restricts the user to choosing from a list of preset choices, e.g. Title (Mr/Mrs/Ms) or Gender (M/F).

Data validation in a web-based form. The "destination" field has not been completed and an error message has been generated — "please fill in the following fields".

DTP program validation methods:
It's hard to validate data in a DTP package, because DTP packages are more concerned with manipulating things you bring into them (e.g. graphics). You'll have to work on validating things in other applications before importing them in to your document.

Think about how you're going to **Organise Data**...

1) Look at the **methods** of organising data that are **currently used** — how can you adapt these for your system?
2) Does the company have other procedures that **rely on** their current system?
    Will these procedures need changing or can you make your system fit around them?
3) If they already have an IT system, will your system require data in a **different format**?

...and how Data is **Presented** to your User

Your system will almost certainly need to produce both **screen** and **paper** outputs.
The format of these is important...

1) They should **only** contain information the user actually needs — no extra information.
2) Information should be **organised sensibly**, e.g. would the user prefer the data in a table or chart?
3) All your outputs should have a **consistent** layout and feel. This looks more **professional** and is better for the **user**.

The **user interfaces** you design and implement need to be appropriate for the **end user** — don't have lots of features that'll confuse them or use language they won't understand.

Practice Questions

1) Name five electronic data capture systems.
2) Name three things that will affect which means of data capture you choose for your project.
3) Give three specific examples of spreadsheet validation methods.
4) Give three specific examples of database validation methods.
5) Give three specific examples of web page validation methods.
6) What systems exist in your school or college to enter data into a computer system?

I find Data very easy to work with — when he's sober...

Wouldn't it be funny if Data off Star Trek Next Generation had been played by a different actor — say, Hugh Grant? What a bumbling idiot he'd be. I just can't imagine Hugh Grant being able to pull that off. Oh well... Idle thoughts... No time for them now. Now is the time for getting on with ICT. Be careful with the data you use — make sure you validate all of it.

Design — General Advice

Ooh designs eh? Remember that designs don't automatically mean diagrams. You could use a spreadsheet, or a listy type thing, or a goat, or maybe a cow with brown spots and a big long tail instead. Huh. How did I get onto farms, suddenly?

The **Designs** must explain how to **Implement** your Solution

1) Whatever the project, your designs will show the moderator how you're going **to solve the problem**.

2) The moderator needs to know how you've **produced** your designs and needs to be able to **follow them easily**.

3) The designs need to be good enough for a **third party** to be able to pick them up and **implement** your solution.

4) This means you need to use a lot of **detail**, and you need to present it in a very **straightforward** way.

5) Remember — you can always make some very minor tweaks **at the end**. BUT if you do the whole design at the end it'll be really obvious (because there won't be any mistakes to correct and learn from) and you'll lose all your marks.

Things you need designs for:

inputs, processes, outputs

testing

back up / security systems

validation (spreadsheet / databases / web pages)

user interface (help screens and user guide)

the flow of data through the task

Your **Designs** Need To **Avoid Certain Things**

There are certain things you need to avoid like the plague when doing your designs:

- **a poor level of detail** — e.g. too little or no annotation.
- **poor presentation** — e.g. scruffy diagrams, diagrams in poor quality pen (use colouring pencils).
- **processes that aren't designed** — e.g. macros in spreadsheets, queries in databases, back up systems, password systems, form submissions in web design projects, the scanning and manipulation of graphics for DTP, presentation and web projects.
- **poor design of outputs** — e.g. database reports, mail merged documents.
- **lots of pages of input designs** — e.g. spreadsheet forms or database tables and nothing else.
- designs produced **very obviously during the implementation stage** of the project.
- **not amending your designs** after making changes in the implementation section.

Designs Should Be **Easy To Understand**

1) Don't make your designs too **complicated** for the end user.

> Think carefully about how to make the designs user-friendly — e.g. navigation around database and spreadsheet forms and web pages, careful use of colour, consistency in the use of objects such as buttons on switchboards and other menus, etc.

2) Make sure you have catered for the end user's **needs and abilities**.

> Use templates that the end user can amend as much as possible and make it clear where the data goes by a set of instructions on the template. In database projects the end user should input the data into the tables through a clearly labelled form. With spreadsheets you should provide the end user with forms to input data. With presentation projects you need to "shield" the end user from typing directly into a text frame. With web site projects, don't expect the end user to update their web pages using HTML.

3) Projects change as you work through them so it's OK to change the designs as you go along. Just make sure that you hand in designs that reflect the solution that was implemented, and whatever you do **DON'T** just do all the designs at the end. That will be obvious to the moderator and you will do badly.

4) Above all, remember it's got to be **easy** enough for a **random third party to follow them**.

Design — General Advice

You Should Include **Diagrams** To Show How your System Will Work

1) It's a good idea to produce a **diagram** (or diagrams) that give an overview of your design — it can make it easier for the moderator to follow.

2) If you find you don't have enough elements to your diagram, your project probably isn't complicated enough. In this case you'll need to think of **more elements** to add.

3) It doesn't matter what **symbols** you use in your diagrams, as long as you're **consistent** and you provide a **key**.

Example — Design For A **Database Project**

1) The following grid is an example of a popular and **effective** way to design a **data table** for a **database**.

2) You would need to produce a grid like this for each table.

Fieldname	Field Type	Field length (if text)	Example data	Validation
Last name	Text	15	Smith	
First name	Text	15	Jacob	
Age	Number		56	< 120
Start date	Date	N/A	01/01/96	> 02/02/1992

Example — Design For A **Graphics Project**

1) The design process does get a mite **trickier** when you're talking about graphics, as the processes aren't always so obvious.

2) The table below shows an **example** of how you might **design the processes** involved in scanning a photograph for a web page and then manipulating it.

Process description	Scanning and preparing a photograph for a web page
Stage1	Select graphic and place on scanner
Stage2	Select area to be scanned
Stage3	Select output
Stage4	Save as jpg or GIF
Stage5	Import into MGI Photosuite and adjust size
Stage6	Crop back to the area needed
Stage7	Resize image to x by x pixels
Stage8	etc.
Stage9	etc.

Practice Questions

1) What is meant by the term "third party implementation"?

2) At what point in a project should you do your designs?

3) Name five general things you should avoid when creating your designs.

4) What elements need to be taken into consideration when designing screens that appear on computer monitors?

5) What symbols should you use if presenting your design as a diagram?

6) Produce a table to design the process of making a macro that closes your spreadsheet when you click on a button on the front worksheet.

What's brown and comes out of cows — the Isle of Wight ferry...

Hm. That joke doesn't really work on paper, does it? Because you'd need to write "Cowes" the place, not "cows" the beast. Oh well. Scratch that one up to experience I suppose. Always got to admit your failures. Also, I'm a bit sorry about making that crack in general. I didn't mean to compare the ferry to cow pats. I'm sure it's really nice. Sorry, Isle of Wight ferry.

Implementation — General Advice

Implementation is where you actually make the system you've spent all this time designing — also known as the fun bit. But remember — you must document everything that you do — that's where you actually get the marks...

It's *Easy* To *Avoid Losing Marks*

Here are a few basic "don'ts" for starters...

See the advanced features on p126-127

1) Don't think you'll be able to get high marks using just the **basic functions** of the software — you won't.
2) Don't expect the evidence in the user guide and testing section to **count as implementation** — you need more.
3) Don't **undersell** what you've done — you need to show off every little detail so you can get marks for it.
4) Don't use **built-in features** (e.g. MS Access documenter) to provide evidence of what you have done.

You need to *Provide Evidence* of *Everything you do*

The easiest way to document your implementation is to produce a **project log**.
You can do it as a list of dated entries or a list of sessions.

The two main things it should include are:

1) **Technical descriptions** of what you did.
2) **Screenshots** that show the result of the work you've described.

Here's a sample of what it might look like:

Date	What I did	Problems encountered/solved
29th December 2003	Set up a template for the sites pages	
30th December 2003	Started work on the Home Page based on the template	Had problems resizing the logo to fit the page.
2nd January 2004	Worked on hotspots on logo.	Couldn't get this to work initially need to check how this works in Dreamweaver.

1) You should take **regular screenshots** by using the PrintScreen button on your keyboard or by using screenshot software that gives you more control over the image you're capturing.
2) Make them **big enough to see easily**. Place no more than two screenshots per A4 page and don't "over crop" them (e.g. on a spreadsheet you shouldn't remove the column or row labels).
3) **Annotate** all your screenshots in your word-processing package or by hand
   – point out the key features of the documents you've made.
   – add brief comments explaining why you've done things a certain way.
   And don't forget to give each screenshot a **title**.
4) Ensure that printouts are **relevant to the solution** and not there just to fill up space in the project.
5) And don't put all your screenshots into one document or the file could become massive and cause problems when saving it. Break the work down into **smaller documents**.

Here's a couple of examples of the kind of screenshots you'll need to include for different projects...

Spreadsheet
For each worksheet, you'll need:
1) A **user view** screenshot (showing how it will appear to the end user).
2) A **design view** screenshot (showing how it looks to the designer, i.e. you).
3) A screenshot showing all the **formulae**.

Database
1) **Table designs** — showing data types, validation, etc.
2) **Relationships**
3) **Forms** — show how you've changed default values, calculated fields, etc. Do separate screenshots for design and user view.
4) **Queries** — either of the query grid or the SQL code.
5) **Reports** — separate screenshots for design and user view.

> The key thing to remember is that your implementation evidence has got to be **detailed enough** so that someone could use it **to reproduce your work**.

Implementation — General Advice

Using **Wizards** And **Templates** Is **OK** As Long As You **Change The Defaults**

1) It's fine to use built-in wizards or templates to start off the production of your forms, tables in database projects or pages in web site projects. **But** you are expected to take the initiative and **change the defaults**.

2) For example, after making a form with a wizard in a **database package**, you'd be expected to change the size, colour, font size and type, add a graphic, add buttons, re-arrange the order of fields etc. In a **web site** project you'd have to change text, colours, font, the link colours and logo graphics on a page cloned from a template.

Keep your Files **Well-Organised**

1) Use a **logical system** for labelling files and objects (e.g. forms, tables etc.) — **don't** use default names like table1 or query1 and query2. Give everything meaningful and consistent names, e.g. qryVacanciesAugust for August vacancies in a lettings database for holiday cottages.

2) Keep a **separate folder** in your user area at school and at home for your coursework project. Create sub-folders inside this folder so that you have some order to your work. Everything's easier if you do this at the start.

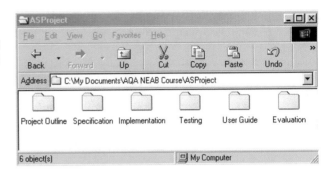

3) Be aware of **how much space** you have in your user area, especially if you are working on a school network. You don't want to run out of space and be unable to save your work if you can't find the network manager.

4) Constantly **back up** your work on to CD/R, Zip drive, Yahoo! Briefcase or whatever you can. Save your work regularly with a different file name e.g.: AnalysisVer1, AnalysisVer2, AnalysisVer3 etc. when you have made some significant changes to it. This will make it easier to keep track of your progress.

Gantt Charts Help You to **Plan Your Time**

1) **Gantt charts** are a good way to **schedule** your time throughout your project.

2) You should create a Gantt chart to break each main stage of your project into **separate tasks**.

3) Include the Gantt charts in your **implementation evidence**.

4) Don't forget that tasks will **overlap** and that sometimes things will not go according to plan. It's a good idea to **annotate** your Gantt charts to show this.

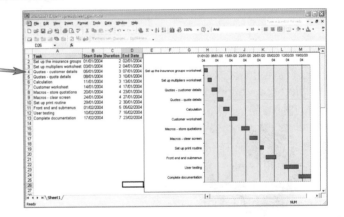

Practice Questions

1) Give four implementation don'ts.

2) What are the two main things to include in your project log?

3) What should you do if you use built-in software wizards or templates?

4) List three good pieces of advice for keeping your files well-organised.

5) How can Gantt charts be useful in your project?

I find time keeping so hard, I don't know why — I just gantt do it...

Organisation, people. That's the dish of the day. Organisation, organisation, organisation. A well-organised project just feels different. The moderator will know it, and you'll know it too. If you're well-organised it means that you'll be more confident with your work. Everything will be methodical and in its place, and there's less room for things to go wrong.

Implementation — Advanced Skills

Okay so, it's not just about which software you use, it's about making sure you use it appropriately. It's no use opening up a spreadsheet and shading all the boxes pink you know. You need to use all the funky tools — fun-keh, fun-keh...

Find The **Most Appropriate Tools** For The **Task**

1) You need to focus on finding the most **appropriate software tools** for your task — you can use more than one package if it's the best way to solve the problem.

2) But remember, you're meant to be displaying a high level of **generic** and **package specific** skills in these packages. If your time is limited, you're best advised to stick to **one** package **other than your text processor**.

> **Generic Process Skills** = general skills you can apply to all the packages you use for your project.
> **Package Specific Skills** = skills used for special features found in different types of applications package.

You Need **Good Generic Process Skills**

1) Efficient **navigation** of packages using **menus** and other relevant **features**.

2) Showing you know how to use **help files** and **on-line tutorials** to use the program effectively.

3) Effective use of **predefined elements** like templates, styles, glossaries, etc.

4) Use of **wizards** as starting points for your work (but showing you've put your own thought into it too).

5) Effective use of **macros** — macros found in libraries as well as ones you've produced yourself.

6) Appreciation of the benefits of **OLE** (Object Linking and Embedding — allowing an object in one document to become part of another).

7) Selection of **suitable formats** for the presentation of output.

You Need To Know **Advanced Features** Well Too

You need to know lots of the **advanced features** of the software you use in your project. Just using them to show off isn't enough though — you need to show that you're using them because they fit in with your own analysis, design and implementation. Here's some checklists for the main ones:

Database Projects Advanced Features

They must be fully relational (2 or more tables) and include as many as possible of the following:

- Action queries — to append (add), archive (remove), and delete data from tables.
- Parameter queries involving user input (queries which produce a prompt box).
- Customised reports and forms with logo, headers and footers.
- Forms with sub-forms.
- Summary reports based on queries with calculated totals and grouped data.
- Data entry screens with list or combo boxes, and command buttons for navigation.
- Validation of input data or use of simple input masks (these specify the format of the data input).
- Referential integrity enforced (i.e. if you enter A as a spouse of B, it will only let you enter B as a spouse of A).
- Calculated fields.
- Macros to automate commonly used features.
- Security features especially for multi-users.
- "Cleaning down" facilities (deleting old data from the system).
- Creating a run-time application (i.e. the application can run independently from your database software).

Spreadsheets Projects Advanced Features

These must contain linked multi-sheets and include as many as possible of the following:

- Basic formulae.
- Charts and graphs.
- Filters.
- Macros to automate common processes such as sorting and printing set areas.
- User forms, combo boxes, dialogue boxes and drop-down lists.
- Pivot tables and multiple scenarios.
- Named ranges.
- Lookups and IF functions.
- Customised and automated solution hiding normal features of the software from the end user.
- Use of Visual Basic is optional, and you won't get extra credit for using it. Any coding must be fully explained and annotated.

Implementation — Advanced Skills

Web Site Projects Advanced Features

Some advanced features would include:

- Use of tables to position text and graphics.
- Ability to alter HTML code.
- Use of templates.
- Use of CSS — cascaded style sheets.
- Use of Metatags — these are keywords and descriptions that are used by search engines.
- Graphics manipulation (in a package such as Adobe Photoshop).
- Navigation — ensure you are consistent.
- Installation of a bulletin board, form or guestbook using CGI, PHP or ASP (try Hotscripts.com).
- Installation of visitor counters.
- Use of Javascript, e.g. for a menu system.
- Browser recognition feature (load alternative pages for different browsers as they display pages differently).
- Testing of pages viewed in different browsers.
- Posting documents on the site in PDF format.
- Awareness of HCI (Human Computer Interface) and usability.
- Buttons with "rollovers", hotspots, anchors, forms.
- Mail merging from a web-based database.
- Multimedia elements on some pages (e.g. an mp3 message from a managing director or a one minute video on a karate club).

DTP Projects Advanced Features

Should include:

- Master templates.
- Columns.
- Text wrapped around images.
- Image manipulation — colouring, cropping, resizing, skewing, flipping, rotating.
- Use of frames, frames with shadows.
- Watermarking.
- Consideration of margins, gutters, white space, text, leading, kerning, tracking.
- Advanced graphics — splicing, extrusion, fitting text to complex paths, colour washes, separation, gradient fills, neon styles.
- Long document support — indexing, tables of contents, printer set up, links.
- Consideration of how the end user will input data into documents.

Practice Questions

1) Describe the differences between generic and package specific skills.
2) Which of the following are generic skills and which are package specific?
   a) producing columns in a DTP package
   b) use of wizards
   c) effective use of macros
   d) use of scripting in a multimedia package
   e) effective use of templates
   f) understanding of the use of OLE.
3) Which advanced package skills might you expect to use in a spreadsheet?
4) Explain why no brand names have been mentioned in this two page spread.

Well apart from Adobe Photoshop, but just ignore that, OK...

My generic process skills include sighing and rolling my eyes...

Well these checklists are about as much fun as a delayed train sitting outside Swindon for three and a half hours with no air conditioning. But, unlike a delayed train sitting outside Swindon for three and a half hours with no air conditioning, they are actually useful. It pays to be pedantic in this game. Forgotten features could mean fewer marks — use as many as you can.

Testing

Testing, testing... one, two, one, two... testing? Check, check, one, two, one, two, one, one, one, one, one... Is anyone out there? You're reading this so you must be there. So why can't I hear anything? Hm... testing, testing... is this thing on?

You need to make a **Test Strategy** during the **Design Stage**

You need to start thinking about testing during the design stage and put together a **test strategy**.
This gives an overview of:

> - **what** you're going to test and **how** you'll test it
> - **when** and in what **order** you'll do the tests
> - the **expected outcomes** (i.e. what you expect to happen)

1) The order of your tests needs some thinking about.
   - In a database, data validation should be tested while you're **entering** the main data. And you can't do the queries until all the data's been entered. So data validation has to be tested **before** queries.
   - In a web site project, you might test how the pages look in different web browsers before testing the links between pages.

2) Make cross-references back to the **performance indicators** in the analysis section
   — you have to make sure your test strategy checks the system does exactly what it's **supposed to do**.

3) Testing **must not be static** — just like your designs may have to change as a result of developments in your implementation, you may also have to produce new tests along the way.

4) Your test strategy should cover unit, integrated, system and user testing:

> **Unit testing** — where individual elements are tested, e.g. validation of an item of data input.
>
> **Integrated testing** — where several aspects are tested at once, to see if changes made to either one affect the other, e.g. testing if data from a database merges correctly into a form letter in a word-processing package, or testing if a form on a web page submits data correctly.
>
> **System testing** — where the whole system is tested from the input of data to the final output.
>
> **User testing** — where the end user tries out the system to see if it works like they wanted.
> The end user should be critical, supportive and honest about how good the solution is.

Remember, testing needs to happen **throughout** implementation — you can't just do it all at the end.
Your test strategy doesn't have to be very detailed, but it needs to let the moderator know that you've **thought about** the process of testing.

You Have To **Design A Test Plan**

For each type of test you'll also need to make a test plan — these are usually done as **tables**.

Test no	Purpose of test	Test data used	Expected outcome	Actual outcome	Evidence
1	Test password	Soll Niederau Pamporovo	All fail except Pamporovo		
2	Test Main Menu Options		Correct sub menus open each time. Application closes when Exit button pressed		
3	Test Option button (sex)	Click on male/female	Returns 1 or 2 in E15		
4	Test Combo box (age)	70+	Returns 10 in E22		

Example test plan for a web site project
(to go in the design section)

You should also produce screenshots to go with your tests and annotate these, e.g. with details of how you've corrected any mistakes.

Test no	Purpose of test	Test data used	Expected outcome	Actual outcome	Evidence
1	Test password	Soll Niederau Pamporovo	All fail except Pamporovo	Only Pamporovo succeeds	See printout 1 on p67
2	Test Main Menu Options		Correct sub menus open each time. Application closes when Exit button pressed	All buttons when clicked opened submenus except Exit macro which failed. Corrective action required.	See printouts 2 to 6 on pp67-68 for successful opening of submenus. See page 69 for alterations of VB code. Retest Test 31.
3	Test Option button (sex)	Click on male/female	Returns 1 or 2 in E15	Returns 1 or 2 in E15	See printout 7 p69
4	Test Combo box (age)	70+	Returns 10 in E22	Returns 10 in E22	See printout 8 p69

Completed test plan (to go in the testing section)

Testing

Choose Your Test Data Carefully

It's a good idea to declare your sets of test data in the **design section** of your specification.
You should use a **good range** of test data which includes **normal**, **extreme** and **out of range** data.

Normal data	**Extreme data**	**Out of range (erroneous) data**
This is data **your system should cope with**. This type of data is usually provided by your end user.	This is data **at the boundary of acceptance**, e.g. a file allows a maximum of 20 characters to be input — the extreme data you'd test it with would be a phrase with exactly 20 characters.	This is data **outside of the acceptable range**, e.g. where a file allowed a maximum of 20 characters, a phrase of 50 characters would be out of range.

The easiest way to display the test data you're going to use is usually in a **table**.

This table shows a set of data to be used for testing a database.

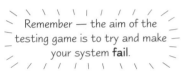
Remember — the aim of the testing game is to try and make your system **fail**.

Field	Comment	Normal data	Extreme data	Out of range
Membership ID	Integer — not negative and less than 1000	54	999	1003
First name	Text (max 10)	James	James Troy	James Troyes
Surname	Text (max 10)	Green	Greenhough	Greenhough-Smythe
Subscription	Currency (max £50.00)	£10.00	£50.00	£100.00
Address 1	Text (15 max)	8 Field Road	8 Fielding Road	8 Field Road, Ticknall Derby
Postcode	Text — format check	DE1 2LF	DE217FE	DEE731ZZZ
DOB	Date > 01/01/82	01/01/90	02/01/82	20/03/55

And finally — some testing Dos and Don'ts

DO
- Do your testing as you go along.
- Re-use any screenshots you made in the implementation section.
- Reprint the table you produced in the design section showing the extra columns filled in.
- Show a range of tests and test data.
- Provide evidence that your end user has tested your system and user guide.

DON'T
- Produce a test plan with ticks or phrases such as "OK", "failed", or "as expected".
- Have identical tests.
- Provide no end user involvement.
- Produce printouts without annotations, titles or cross-referencing to the test plan.
- Make anything up...

Practice Questions

1) Write a sentence to define each of the following:
   a) unit testing, b) integrated testing, c) system testing and d) user testing.
2) What's the difference between a test strategy and a test plan?
3) When designing a test plan table what column headings could you use?
4) What are the three main categories of test data?
5) Write down three project testing 'do's and three 'dont's'.

It doesn't work, the USELESS bloomin' — oh I see, there's an "on" switch...

Don't get confused with all the similar sounding terms on this page — the test strategy gives an overview of the testing and needs to be included in the design part of your coursework... so do the test plans which are tables describing the individual tests you'll do... and so should your test data tables which just show the range of data you're going to test with.

Evaluation

Evaluation already? How can we have reached the evaluation stage already?! Is it going as quickly for you as it is for me? Why I feel just delightful... like cherry blossom dancing over the hills on a warm spring day. Or maybe a small pile of mud.

Evaluation *Is* Ludicrously Important

1) Evaluation is a very important part of the project, but unfortunately it often gets left too late and is rushed. Try to give yourself **enough time** to do your project justice.

2) Lots of evaluations are only a couple of pages long. If you can make yours **longer** than this, you'll be off to a good start. And I mean properly longer, not just increasing the font size by a few points...

3) The moderator will be looking at your evaluation section for evidence that you've **understood** what the solution was meant to do and **assessed** it effectively, and also that you know what **mistakes** you made and have made efforts to **correct** them.

There Are **Four Key Elements** To A Successful Evaluation

A **successful evaluation** of the project hinges on having four things:

- a suitable **end user**
- a good list of **end user requirements**
- a good list of **performance indicators**
- a rigorous and efficient **testing strategy**

There Are **Some Things** You **Have** To **Comment On**...

To give an effective evaluation, you need to talk about these things in detail:

- How successful you were at hitting the end user's requirements.
- How successful you were at hitting the performance indicators.
- What shortcomings there were with your solution.

...and **Some Things** You **Have** To **Avoid Mentioning**

In order to make your evaluation direct and professional, it's a good idea to avoid mentioning these:

- Your package specific skills — you've already discussed this earlier in the project.
- Your time management skills — you've already discussed this.
- The amount of help you have received from your ICT tutor — well, duh...
- What you have learned from the six months project writing exercise — this is not relevant.

Write Your Evaluation Up Carefully

1) Go back to your original **objectives** and **performance indicators / criteria**.
   Handy hint — cut and paste them into your evaluation document then add your comments under each one.

2) **Consider** each of the criteria in turn and **discuss** how successful you were in meeting them.

3) Show **evidence** from the testing to **support** your statements. This could take the form of a screenshot of a test or a photocopy of a comment from the end user.

4) **Discuss** the **limitations** and **failures of your solution**.

5) Describe what **improvements** you'd like to make to meet the performance indicators if you had the opportunity to do the project again (or had more time to develop it).

Evaluation

Example 1 — *Evaluating Your Objectives*

1) You need to evaluate your objectives **one by one**.
2) The example below shows what you might put for a web site project.
   (The text in italics has been copied and pasted from the analysis section of the project.)

> *Objective 1: To ensure that the Home Page downloads rapidly (within 5 seconds of the command).*
> *Performance criteria: The Home Page should be no more than 50Kb in size and needs to contain graphics which are in a compressed format such as gifs or jpegs.*
>
> I managed to fulfil this. I kept the main graphics on the Home Page to 30Kb. The original files were much bigger but I compressed them to a smaller size by using the 'save to the web' option in Adobe Photoshop. The proof of the file size can be seen in Test 16 of my project on p.96. My end user was impressed by the fact that the graphics, though tiny in kilobytes, were still sharp. I did this by using the "sharpen" filter. Other objects such as buttons were also compressed to minimise download times.
>
> *Objective 2: To ensure that navigation is intuitive and consistent.*
> *Performance criteria: Navigation buttons on each page must be in the same areas of each page. Buttons should be consistent in shape, have consistent lettering and have consistent actions.*
>
> I based all pages on a template with the buttons in the non-editable area of the template. All buttons worked on each page and were tested by my end user. However, initially some of them didn't find the correct page. I sorted this out by altering the html code, see p.104 of my project. The buttons to external links opened pages in a new window as I wanted them to do.

Example 2 — *Evaluating Your Limitations*

> The Guestbook was hosted on some web space that was beyond my control. I would prefer to have the script running from my own web site.
>
> I didn't manage to get the JavaScript code working for the visitor counter and had to link to one supplied by a company called Nedstat which unfortunately included some advertising on the Home page.
>
> The end user wants to update the web site herself. I haven't completely worked out how to do this easily for her.

Example 3 — *Evaluating Possible Improvements*

> My end user, after working through my solution, asked if she could have an online database of products which could be updated daily if required.
>
> I will investigate how to use the program Macromedia Contribute so that my end user can update parts of the site easily.
>
> My end user would like me to investigate how to install an online booking system for visitors. Initially this might be through e-mail or a form. Eventually I hope that this could run in almost real time on the web site.

Practice Questions

1) What's the absolute minimum length you should aim to make your evaluation section?
2) What are the four key elements to writing a successful evaluation?
3) Should you mention any shortcomings in your project?
4) How would you involve your end user in the evaluation of your project?

Objective: turn cheese into gold — evaluation: didn't work for some reason...

Evaluation is really where it all comes together. You need to be clear, precise and honest. Admit your mistakes, and explain exactly what happened. Remember — the moderator isn't looking for the perfect golden project. The moderator wants to know that you understand exactly what went on, and that you are a methodical and logical person who tried to sort it out.

User Guides

I've always thought user guides were lovely little critters. So cute and furry, with those big ears and the big thumping feet... What's that you say? Those aren't user guides? Huh. What are they then? What? Who is this Bugs Bunny you speak of?

User Guides Are There To Help Your End User

1) The aim of the user guide is to help **steer your end user** through the **solution** you've produced.
2) It's **not** a guide to the application program you have used to solve the problem.
3) The end user should make written comments and suggestions on a hard copy of the guide.

> **Very Important! It's worth noting that moderators will often turn to your user guide FIRST in order to gain an overview of your solution. So make sure you make a good 'un!**

Your User Guide Must Be Comprehensive

1) You should start the guide with a description of the **purpose of the system** — i.e. describe what your solution actually does.
2) The next section should run through the minimum **hardware requirements** for the solution.
3) You must keep your written language **jargon-free** and **appropriate** to your end user.
4) The guide must be **well-illustrated**, so include a good range of screenshots taken from the implementation and testing sections. However, it isn't necessary for the user guide to be produced in colour.
5) You should include a set of **instructions** showing your end user how to install the software on their machines. You must ensure that the installation procedures are **appropriate** to the end user's situation. It is pointless referring to an installation of the solution on your school network.
6) You need to give an overview of **how the system works** under normal working conditions.
7) It is also a good idea to show how the solution works **from start to finish** — i.e. from input of data at the start of the process to the production of the final output.
8) You need to include a section that shows what **error messages** might occur during normal operation, followed by descriptions that show how to fix them.
9) You should have a section that describes **saving** and **backing up** routines.
10) You could produce a **glossary** of terms or unusual words used in the project.
11) Lastly, you need to think about the **environment** the solution is going to be used in. Is a normal user guide going to be enough, or would it be appropriate to produce a prompt / quick-reference sheet as well?

It Needs To Feel Like A Professional Publication

The guide needs to be **well-organised** with:

1) a contents page at the front
2) numbered pages throughout
3) an index at the back.

Don't Worry About On-line Help

1) Producing an on-line help resource is **incredibly time consuming**.
2) It also **uses up lots of resources** on small and humble computer systems.
3) Although a successful on-line help system could get you a few extra marks, it's almost certainly **not worth doing**. You'd be better off spending your time on other parts of the project.

Special Formats Aren't Necessary

1) Don't worry about producing your user guide in a special format — it's **what's inside that counts**.
2) An A4 document of about 10-15 pages should be more than adequate.

User Guides

Warning — One Thing To Avoid Like The Plague

Whatever you do, **don't include big chunks of other user guides** (i.e. commercial user guides) or the "online help" provided in the packages you're using. The user guide needs to be **all your own work**.

Make A **Checklist** To Make Sure **Nothing Gets Forgotten**

Use this list to ensure that all key points have been covered in your user guide.

What Is Needed	Tick ( )
Table of contents and index.	
Pages numbered.	
Introduction to system and guide.	
System requirements stated (hardware & software).	
Advice on installation of software.	
Main features (step by step) explained.	
Language is jargon-free and concise.	
Screenshots of main features.	
Advice given on back up procedures.	
Help — telephone support / web address / e-mail.	
Error messages explained.	
Error recovery, e.g. What happens if you have made a wrong data entry?	
End user comments on user guide.	

If In Doubt, **Read The Manual**...

The AskTog web site (URL - http://www.asktog.com) contains a brilliant article called "How to Publish a Great User Manual". It suggests some basic principles which need to be considered when writing commercial User Manuals, many of which are still poorly written. It's worth a look as a point of comparison. Briefly, the points it makes are:

1) Supply a **real manual** — one that you can hold, not a web based one or PDF format one.
2) **Explain the problem** being solved.
3) Make sure that **all levels of your audience** are catered for — from novice to expert.
4) Make it **easy** and **enjoyable** to read.

Practice Questions

1) Who is the target audience for your user guide?
2) Why is the user guide a useful starting point for the coursework moderator?
3) List five things that should definitely be included in a user guide.
4) Do you need to produce your user guide in colour?
5) Kieron is copying and pasting bits from a commercial user guide into his coursework. Explain whether you think this is a good idea or not.
6) List 6 points you could include on a checklist to help you complete your user guide.

User Guide to fun — employ your time in a profitless and non-practical way...

This is a chance for you to really shine. Now, while it's true that the moderator isn't going to be impressed with a flashy looking user guide if the content is rubbish, it's also true to say that the moderator will be impressed if the content is awesome and the presentation is attractive and well-planned. Show off a bit, why not? No one else is going to do it for you.

Final Tips For Your Project

Okay team, are you ready? Yeah! Go team! Go gettem champ! Yeah! Okay that's enough American rubbish for now I believe. Read through the notes on these pages, then bally well scurry off and do your coursework, you little pixie.

Read Through These Final Tips Then Get Cracking

Right. Here's the final countdown of hints and tips for your coursework — so read them all then get a move on:

1) **Present your project smartly**, hole-punched and secured with string or treasury tags.
2) Put your name, candidate number and centre number in the **footer** of every word-processed page.
3) Make sure you complete any **Exam Board documentation** and declarations for the project before going on exam leave. I'm sure the last thing you want is your ICT tutor phoning your house...
4) Get a copy of the marking grid and **marking criteria**.
5) Use the **spelling** and **grammar checking** facilities in your word-processor (but take some of the grammar warnings with "a pinch of salt" as they might not understand some of the technical phrases you use).
6) Keep a **back up** of the project (e.g. on a CD-R).
7) Take **photocopies** of any handwritten diagrams, flow diagrams etc.
8) **Don't expect** to do the project in one weekend — doing a thorough bit of work will take you time.
9) Don't leave in any work that contains **teachers' comments** you've failed to act on.
10) Bind the whole piece of work into **one complete document**. Moderators hate projects in pieces.
11) Take **screenshots** as you go along. Drop them into a word-processed document, along with the date and the purpose.
12) You don't need 100 pages of unit and button testing. The production of around **30 well-designed tests** based on the user's requirements is more than adequate.
13) Use a **common design** for database and spreadsheet forms and web page templates to keep it consistent.
14) Try and do a little bit of work on your coursework **every day** (or at least every few days).
15) Don't wait for inspiration to come and grab you — it won't. You just have to **get on with it**.
16) Try not to exceed **6000 words** — this doesn't include text on diagrams, in cells or screen dumps.
17) **Don't** hand in a **digital version** (e.g. on floppy, CD-ROM or Zip).
18) Make sure you **get to know** your applications software well — this will take longer than you're expecting.
19) Investigate **Internet help sites** like "Mr Excel" or "UtterAccess" for helpful tips. Google groups can also be very helpful (e.g. news.microsoft.access.beginners or news.macromedia.dreamweaver).
20) Stick to the deadlines set by your teacher — always **let them know** if you run into any problems.

A Framework for your Project

You can use the following points to help you structure your project.

Use it as a checklist and try to get ticks in as many boxes as possible.

Analysis Requirements	
Your end user has been identified (photograph or statement).	
The nature and context of the problem has been described.	
A substantial solution has been proposed.	
End user requirements recognised, specified and documented.	
End user signs off list of requirements.	
Aims and suitable objectives (quantitative/qualitative) documented.	
Real end user paperwork provided (e.g. bills, invoices, flyers).	
Analysis techniques used (interviewing, observation and questionnaires).	
Full potential of the appropriate / available hardware facilities discussed.	
Full potential of the appropriate / available software facilities discussed.	
End user's current ICT skills identified.	

Final Tips For Your Project

Design Requirements	
Alternative solutions to problem have been discussed.	
Reasons given for choice of application program used.	
Designs neatly drawn in pencil and annotated where appropriate.	
Inputs specified and designed.	
Processes designed.	
Outputs designed.	
Test strategy described.	
Test plan present and linked to objectives in Analysis by cross-referencing.	
Test data present with examples of normal/extreme/erroneous data.	
Time management schedule included (e.g. GANTT chart).	
End user involvement in design evident, i.e. signed off with a suitable and relevant comment.	

Implementation Requirements	
Sub tasks outlined in the design have been followed closely.	
Solution fully implemented, relatively unaided.	
Documentation is clear with appropriate screen dumps and annotations.	
There is a project log with descriptions of corrections.	
Advanced features of software can be seen.	
There is a description of data collection methods employed.	
Data validation methods are described.	
There are printouts of all forms, code, web pages etc. with annotation.	
End user involvement in the Implementation is evident, i.e. signed off with a suitable and relevant comment.	

Testing Requirements	
All testing stages are cross-referenced to objectives / criteria.	
Test plan present.	
Expected test outcomes shown.	
Actual test outcomes documented.	
Normal, extreme and erroneous data seen.	
Questionnaire for end user included.	
End user involvement in testing is evident, i.e. signed off by end user with a suitable and relevant comment.	

Evaluation Requirements	
Objectives / criteria copied and pasted from analysis section.	
Comment on whether you met each of these objectives.	
Cross-reference to testing to prove objectives met (use numbering).	
Discuss limitations and difficulties, especially where you have hit a problem and solved it.	
Point out where your implementation is significantly different from the design section.	
Screenshots of objectives met (2 or 3 will do).	
Enhancements, e.g. what extra features you might add or what you might change if you tackled this again.	
End user comment on success or otherwise.	
Letter of acceptance from end user.	

For the user guide checklist see p.133.

I just saw Carol Vorderman crying — she said it was the final countdown...

*But Carol Vorderman can't cry — she's a robot. Robots don't cry. Robots don't get lonely. *sniff sniff* Anyway, as they say in all the most respectable establishments, "That's all folks". From here on in you're on your own. You'll be fine though. As long as you take the time to plan and prepare things properly, you'll be okay. Well, so long. Don't forget to write, okay?*

Answers

Section 1 — Information

Page 3 — Data, Information and Knowledge

1 a) It consists of a set of characters (in this case 8) **[1 mark]** and has no context to give it meaning **[1 mark]**.

b) It could be a date (e.g. 21st Sept 2002) or it could be some form of ID or reference number. **[1 mark for any reasonable answer.]**

c) Information is converted into knowledge by applying a rule. E.g. if the data refers to the date of birth, the age of the person can be found (the knowledge) by applying a simple calculation (the rule) that compares the data to the current date.
[2 marks available — 1 for explanation, 1 for a suitable example]
The important thing to remember here is that you need to talk about using <u>rules</u> to convert information into knowledge.

2 a) Any of the following: data must be accurate, up-to-date, reasonable, complete and correct. **[3 marks available — 1 for each quality]**

b) Possible answers:
- To ensure data is <u>accurate</u>, the company must ensure that clear and unambiguous questions are used.
- To ensure data is <u>up-to-date</u>, the company must find current facts and opinions, and must avoid using data collected in the past.
- To ensure data is <u>correct</u>, the company must use reliable sources — they must ask only young people and parents in order to ensure accurate results.
- To ensure data is <u>reasonable</u>, the company could give the person being asked a choice of possible answers.
[3 marks available — 1 for each sensible example]
Remember — don't write your answers in note-form unless you're <u>drastically</u> running out of time. Notes won't get you full marks, but full and reasonable explanations will.

Page 5 — Data, Information and Knowledge (cont.)

1 a) Possible answers:
- Data may be coded in order to save space.
- Data may be coded so that it can be easily validated/checked.
- Data may be coded so it can be processed more easily.
[3 marks available — 1 for each point]

b) Possible answers:
- The gender of a person can be stored as M or F rather than the longer "Male" or "Female".
- Dates should be coded in numerical format. The computer can be instructed with rules informing it which dates have been entered incorrectly e.g. 09/04/19788 is wrong because "year > 2010".
- The questionnaire could give people options to say what country they were born in. e.g. England 01, Ireland 02, Scotland 03, Wales 04, Other 05. Coding this data as numbers will make it quicker to process.
[3 marks available — 1 for each example]
You can use any decent examples for this sort of question — it's good to keep it as straightforward as possible. I've used gender, dates and birthplace because they're pretty easy to explain. Just because they're basic doesn't make them bad — they cut straight to the chase.

2 a) The questionnaire results are input using an appropriate input device, e.g. a keyboard, scanner, Optical Character Reader etc.
[1 mark]

b) Data is then processed (manipulated) using the computer system to group the data together and analyse it — e.g. the different responses may be added up and percentages calculated (to show what proportion of the sample gave each response). **[1 mark]**

c) The results are displayed in an appropriate way, e.g. as a table of results or graph, either displayed on screen or printed. **[1 mark]**

Page 7 — Value and Importance of Information

1 a) Possible answers:
- Tastes / fashion in skiing and ski resorts may have changed in 4 years, and the 2001 data will not reflect this.
- The facilities at the resorts may have changed and the data might not now be relevant.
- Data from 2001 would not reflect any resort closures / openings.
- Using data from a single year makes it hard to predict a trend — it would be better if they could compare figures over different years.
[2 marks available — 1 for each point]

Hey hey, this looks like a simple 2 marks here, but don't blow it by forgetting to put enough detail in. Basic rule here: just writing "it'll be out of date" won't score you any marks at all...

b) Possible answers:
- Staff would be needed to conduct surveys or survey results would need to be bought from an external source.
- Data would need to be validated and verified to ensure its accuracy. This would mean paying out more to staff for the work.
- Added storage space would probably be needed to cope with volumes of data.
- If the company wants to produce new information from the database, it will need to invest in appropriate software for processing it.
[2 marks available — 1 for each point]

2 Possible answers:
- It's faster, as it will save time when collecting customer information over the telephone, meaning that more customers can be dealt with.
- It's more accurate (unless there were mistakes in the original database) because the road and town names will not have to be physically keyed in.
- Customers' details will be more complete because of the data stored in the database.
- It will ensure that only customers who live in areas the company delivers to will be able to set up an account, thereby cutting down on cancellation and enquiry paperwork.
[3 marks available — 1 for each advantage]

Page 9 — Capabilities and Limitations of ICT

1 Possible answers:
- They can manipulate / process data to produce information.
- They can transfer data from one place to another.
- They can search for and retrieve data.
- They can store vast amounts of data.
- They can deal with different types of data (textual, graphical, audio, video)
- They can carry out repetitive tasks.
[3 marks available — 1 for each appropriate example]
Easy money on this question — there are squillions of possible answers to this one. Anything sensible and properly explained will do.

2 Possible answers:
- Communication Technology is the transferring of data from one point to another via links between computers, such as broadband cables, telephone lines, modems and satellites.
- Communication Technology means the transfer of data between computer systems, mobile telephone communications or fax.
- Communication Technology in this context refers to the transfer of data between different computer systems, using electronic links and devices (e.g. modems, routers, broadband cables, telephone lines, etc).
[2 marks available — 1 for a definition and 1 for appropriate examples]
There's 2 marks here — you'll need to say more than "the transfer of data" in order to get both marks, don't forget.

Section 2 — ICT in the Real World

Page 11 — ICT in Industry and Manufacturing

1 Any reasonable examples accepted — for example:
- The use of robotic arms to weld and paint car bodies in the automobile industry has eliminated many jobs because the entire manual job is taken over by the robotic arms.
- The use of CAD systems has transformed the jobs of draughtsmen and designers. Instead of working with pencil and paper they now work with computers. They can design a product and then make small changes until they are happy with the result. This requires completely different skills.
- An example of a new job is the maintenance and upkeep of robotic arms to handle delicate objects. The machines need sensors to be checked and grip and release need to be monitored to be kept in perfect working order so the goods are not damaged.
[6 marks available — 1 for each of 3 examples. An additional 1

Answers

for each explanation]
The trick to these types of question is to remember that you're looking for 6 marks, so break the question into 3 chunks. In this case, it's eliminating jobs, transforming jobs and creating jobs. Then make sure you give a sensible, thorough example and explanation for each one.

Any reasonable answers accepted — for example:
* Robots can be used to assemble goods instead of humans. This results in greater output because robots can work day and night.
* CAD can be used to design products. The designers are able to see the designs in 3 dimensions and rotate designs so that they can be seen from all angles.
* Robots can be used to inspect and clean chemical tanks, which would otherwise need to be emptied, resulting in lengthy downtime. When robots are used to perform the task, the downtime is significantly reduced.
* In car plants, CAD can simulate car crashes in safety tests. This is safer and less costly than tests which use real cars.
[4 marks available — 1 mark for each of 2 examples of a use of ICT, and 1 additional mark each for stating the benefit.]

Page 13 — ICT in Commerce
a) Possible advantages:
* There will be an increase in retail possibilities without needing to increase the shop floor or employ more shop staff.
* There will be an increased customer base.
* There will be increased sales and profits.
* They will be in a stronger position to keep up with the competition.
* There will be cost savings due to a decrease in shoplifting.
[2 marks available — 1 for each reasonable advantage]

b) Possible advantages:
* It saves time, rather than having to travel to a retail outlet.
* It saves the cost of travelling to a retail outlet.
* It allows people with limited movement to shop from home.
* It is more convenient as it can be done 24 hours a day.
[2 marks available — 1 for each reasonable advantage]

c) Possible answers:
* Customers cannot handle the goods or try on the clothes.
* There is a possibility of credit card fraud over the Internet if the security of the site is compromised.
* The social interaction with sales personnel is lost.
* There is a time delay between purchase and receipt of goods.
[1 mark available for a suitable disadvantage]

a) Any one of the following is acceptable:
* Reduces strain on staff as certain things can be carried out by ATM e.g. giving a statement, paying in cash etc.
* It allows new services which might encourage new customers e.g. quick print of statements, changing pin numbers etc.
* It increases the building society's potential market.
* It encourages customers to stay with the building society.
* It allows the building society to compete with other banks.
[1 mark available for any of the answers above]

b) Possible answers:
* It allows cash to be obtained 24 hours per day, 7 days a week, whenever the user requires it.
* There is no need to queue at branches, therefore it saves time.
* It can reduce the amount of paperwork for the customer, as customers can decide whether to obtain receipts from the ATM or not.
[2 marks available — 1 for each reasonable advantage]

a) Possible answers:
* The ordering of stock is made faster.
* The store can be kept fully stocked / not overstocked more efficiently.
* Less time and money is spent on stock ordering.
* There is less risk of human error, apart from the initial inputting of data.
* Statistics can be easily produced so the shop is able to analyse seasonal trends and predict sales more efficiently.
[2 marks available — 1 for each reasonable advantage.]
This is a standard question that is very popular. Don't answer using vague things like "quicker", "easier to use", and "prevents unsold stock".

The other thing that you need to think about is the generality of the question; it is a simple stock ordering question — it does not refer to the automated warehouse where robots are used.

b) Possible answers:
The customer always finds the goods they require in stock if the levels are maintained automatically. The customer finds prices may be lower if less staff are used, or if there is less wastage of stock, or if less space is needed for stock.
[2 marks available — 1 mark for stating an advantage and an additional mark for a reasonable explanation]
Be careful in this kind of question — you won't get two marks for just giving two advantages — the second mark is only for the explanation.

Page 15 — ICT in the Home
1 Possible answers include:
The friend probably thinks ICT means "computers". ICT is not limited to meaning "computers". Anything with a microchip in it uses ICT. Examples of very common devices with microchips include digital watches, or any digital timing device such as a clock on a cooker, and video machines. Central heating systems are almost always controlled by programmable timing devices which use microchip technology. Other examples include washing machines, burglar alarms, video cameras etc. Most households would include at least one of these, so could not be said to be free of ICT.
[5 marks available — 1 for saying ICT refers to more than just computers, 1 for saying that anything with a microchip uses ICT, 3 each for any 3 suitable examples]

2 a) Possible answers (for children):
* Example: finding information for homework.
  Benefit: there is more information available on the Internet than in any library.
  Drawback: the children may accidentally see unsuitable material such as pornographic sites.
* Example: using instant messaging systems to chat to friends.
  Benefit: they can keep in touch with people who may live far away without running up large telephone bills.
  Drawback: Most children use texting language so they get into bad habits for writing English.
[6 marks available in total for two suitable examples — give 1 mark for each example, 1 mark for a benefit and 1 mark for a drawback]

b) Possible answers (for adults):
* Example: home banking.
  Benefit: they can do much of their banking from home at any time of the day or night.
  Drawback: banking is becoming less personal and many people never meet their bank manager.
* Example: on-line grocery shopping.
  Benefit: they do not have to lift heavy goods into the trolley and out again, or to pack the goods into bags.
  Drawback: if the product they order is not available, they do not get a chance to choose an alternative.
[6 marks available in total for two suitable examples — give 1 mark for each example, 1 mark for a benefit and 1 mark for a drawback.]
Other possible examples for adults or children are downloading music, playing on-line games, using e-mail. As long as you're clear you'll be fine. Remember — 1 mark for a use, 1 for a benefit and 1 for a drawback. ALWAYS READ THE QUESTION to avoid silly slip-ups.

3 Possible answers:
* One use is to monitor and control home security systems. This results in more sophisticated systems which can detect intruders and activate alarms.
* Another example of ICT in the home is a games console, which provides entertainment for children and adults by playing films, music and games.
[4 marks available in total — 1 for each of two uses, and an additional 1 each for stating the benefit]

Page 17 — ICT in Education and the Police Force
1 a) Possible answers:
Teachers, head of year, careers staff, pupils themselves.
[3 marks — 1 for each sensible user.]

Answers

b) Possible answers:
* <u>Teachers</u> obtain standard reports, such as class lists together with grades. They can also obtain more complex information using the sort and search functions, such as which pupils attained an A grade in maths and in science.
* The <u>head of year</u> will be able to produce reports looking at the grades attained for the whole year, looking at a comparison between classes and groups and identifying any problem areas.
* <u>Careers staff</u> can find lists of pupils with particular interests and abilities in case of a special event. They can look at pupils' profiles to see what careers advice is needed.
* <u>Pupils</u> can track their own progress, identify their own problem areas, and monitor their progress in relation to the average performance of the year.

[6 marks available — 1 mark each for brief descriptions, OR 2 marks each for fuller descriptions]
Because 6 marks are awarded for this question, you know you need to give some pretty meaty examples of how each user will use the package.

2 a) Possible answers:
* <u>Teaching programs</u> provide students with content and questions. Students answer the questions and are given automatic feedback. This means that students do not have to wait for the teacher to grade their answers to find out if they are right or wrong.
* ICT provides efficient ways of <u>organising and storing data</u>. Schools can use databases to store information about students which can be used by staff to produce things like class lists, grade sheets, absence lists.

[4 marks available — 1 for each of two examples, and an additional 1 each for stating the benefit]

b) Possible answers:
* Computerised police databases (e.g. fingerprints and DNA databases) allow detectives to search for matches on samples found. This speeds up the detection of criminals.
* Systems such as HOLMES2 allow police to enter the details of crimes onto a database and management system and then search through all the data for similar cases, anomalies in the evidence and other useful information which will help them solve the crime.

[4 marks available — 1 for each of two examples, and an additional 1 each for stating the benefit]

Page 19 — ICT in Medicine

1 a) An expert system combines artificial intelligence with a database of specialist knowledge. It is programmed with a set of rules that tell it how to analyse the information in its database and form conclusions.
[2 marks available — 1 mark for explaining the database aspect, 1 mark for explaining how it uses rules to turn the data into knowledge]

b) Possible answer:
The doctor would input relevant details into the system, e.g. the symptoms, patient's past medical history, family history of illnesses. The expert system will search its database and produce the most likely diagnosis based on the data entered by the doctor.
[2 marks available — 1 for a basic description, 2 for a more detailed answer]

2 Possible advantages:
* Patients have easy access to large stores of specialist knowledge without having to visit their GP.
* These systems can help people recognise symptoms that point to serious problems which they would otherwise have ignored.
* Less patients visit GPs with minor ailments as they can now diagnose these themselves — this give GPs more time to deal with more serious cases.
* Expert systems should contain very reliable, up-to-date information as they are compiled and reviewed by medical specialists.

Possible disadvantages:
* There is a risk of patient's misdiagnosing conditions as they don't have the specialist knowledge to correctly identify their symptoms.
* They are lessening human interaction with patients unable to benefit from one-on-one discussion of their problems.
* Many people may take legal action if their misdiagnosis results in a serious illness not being picked up.

[6 marks available — 1 each for up to 3 suitable advantages and 1

each for up to 3 suitable disadvantages.]
In questions like this, you need to give an equal number of points for and against to be sure of picking up all the marks.

Page 21 — Information and the Professional

1) Possible answers:
* New workers should be willing to work flexible hours, as user support may require working at times when the users don't need their equipment, e.g. installing new software or fault correction out of office hours or at lunchtimes.
* New workers should be able to communicate well orally to enable efficient and effective communication with users and colleagues, e.g. questioning effectively to obtain user requirements and details of problems.
* New workers will need good written communication skills to record faults clearly and document solutions and actions.
* They will need to be able to work as part of a team, which means being able to exchange views and share information.
* They will need the ability to work under pressure as large problems can occur suddenly.
* They will also need good organisational skills and the ability to multi-task, having several different jobs running concurrently as many users will need attention at the same time.

[8 marks available in total — 1 for each of 4 qualities, and an additional 1 for each suitable reason to accompany them.]
Examiners would also accept other answers like ability / willingness to learn new skills as ICT moves forward so quickly. If you only state the qualities and do not give reasons then the maximum mark you can get is 4. Make sure the reasons are relevant to the job and not ones you just made up.

2 Possible answers:
* <u>Good communication skills</u> will be needed in order to explain to users exactly what the problems and their solutions are, as well as to advise clearly on future use of ICT to avoid further problems.
* They should be <u>approachable</u> so that users feel comfortable and able to go to them with all their ICT problems, even the ones they consider to be small and insignificant.
* They need to have <u>good written skills</u> so that they can, for example advise the whole company at once via e-mail about any forthcoming changes to their system.

[4 marks available — 1 for each of 2 qualities, and 2 further marks for explanations of why each quality would be needed]

Section 3 — Communication Systems

Page 23 — The Internet

1 Any two of the following:
WAP phones, e-mail telephones / new telephone boxes, digital television **[2 marks available, 1 for each]**
The trick to this question is remembering to give full answers. E.g. "WAP phone" will get one mark, but just saying "phone" won't. Similarly, referring to a company name such as "SKY tv" will not. PADS / Palm tops / PDA / Play Station 2 are not acceptable as you cannot access full Internet services through them.

2 a) Possible answers:
* a browser is used to display / view / navigate web pages **[1 mark]** in a readable form **[1 mark]**.
* a browser is used to display HTML pages **[1 mark]** in a viewable format **[1 mark]**.
* a browser is a piece of software / a program **[1 mark]** that enables the viewing of web pages **[1 mark]**.

b) Possible answers:
* A search engine is used to find specific pieces of information / web pages / websites / URLs **[1 mark]** using key words **[1 mark]**.
* a search engine is a piece of software / an application / a web site / a web page **[1 mark]** used to find websites / words / topics **[1 mark]**.

Be careful not to refer to the browser or the search engine by trade names (e.g. Google, Lycos, Netscape). You won't get any marks for stating trade names without a full explanation. Also, 4 marks are available here, so for each part you need to make 2 decent points.

Answers

Page 25 — The Internet (cont.)

Possible answers:
- It costs less to send an e-mail than a letter (provided the friend has Internet access).
- E-mails arrive much more quickly than regular mail.
- You can send the same letters / information to many people at once.
- You can attach other files and documents to the e-mail and send them at no extra cost.

[2 marks available — 1 for each sensible reason]

2 Possible answers:
- Companies can use the Internet to advertise themselves widely *[1 mark]* which will increase their customer base *[1 mark]*.
- Companies can set up an on-line store to sell their goods *[1 mark]* which will save money on staff / amount of retail space needed *[1 mark]*.
- Companies can use the Internet to communicate with their suppliers more quickly *[1 mark]* which will increase efficiency *[1 mark]*.
- As the Internet is available 24 hours a day, customers can browse their site at any time they like *[1 mark]* which is likely to lead to a sales increase *[1 mark]*.

[4 marks available — 1 for each of 2 sensible reasons. An additional 1 mark for each accompanying explanation]

Page 27 — Other Communication Systems

1 Possible answers:
- It increases road safety *[1 mark]* as it forewarns drivers of problems ahead *[1 mark]*.
- It prevents cars from being delayed *[1 mark]* because it alerts drivers to potential traffic problems in advance, allowing them to find an alternative route *[1 mark]*.
- It allows better route planning *[1 mark]* because up-to-date information about roads and traffic is available *[1 mark]*.

[4 marks available — 1 for each of 2 reasons. An additional 1 for each accompanying explanation.]

Remember there are 4 marks available here. You need to back your reasons up properly to get them all.

2 Possible answers:
- Digital TV produces a better quality picture than analogue sets.
- Digital TV provides viewers with more choice.
- Digital TV allows the viewer to use the television as a communication device.

[3 marks available — 1 for each reasonable benefit]

Page 29 — Other Communication Systems (cont.)

1 Possible answers:
- She could use her laptop (if connected to the Internet via a wireless connection) *[1 mark]* to send a report by e-mail *[1 mark]*.
- She could use a mobile or video phone *[1 mark]* to send messages / images in to the office / relay her report verbally *[1 mark]*.
- She could use a fax machine *[1 mark]* in order to send documents *[1 mark]*.

[4 marks available — 1 for each of 2 acceptable ways. An additional 1 each for a more extended explanation]

Make sure that you read any question on teleconferencing properly. Video conferencing includes moving images but teleconferencing may not include this. Okay. Now take a deep breath and check out the answers...

2 a) Sample answer:
Videoconferencing is when people at different locations are able to have an interactive discussion *[1 mark]* in which they are able to see each other *[1 mark]*. The discussion will have been enabled by the use of telecommunications *[1 mark]*. Specialised video link equipment and / or sophisticated studios are needed for this *[1 mark]*.

Watch out — there's 4 marks for this question, so you need to give plenty of detail in your answer. Basically it breaks down like this: 1 mark for saying it's a real time system (i.e. that it's interactive), 1 to say they can see each other, 1 to say that it's enabled by ICT, and the other 1 for saying you need special equipment in order to do it.

b) Possible advantages:
- It saves the cost of travel.

- It saves time travelling to a common meeting place.
- It's useful when a quick response is needed.

Beware of answering this question by saying "you don't have to travel". People don't have to travel to a common meeting place but they may have to travel to the videoconferencing unit — be sure to make this clear.

Possible disadvantages:
- The quality of the video image can be poor.
- There can be annoying minor time delays.
- The equipment is expensive to buy.
- Training in use of the equipment is needed.
- There is a loss of social interaction.
- There may be difficulties agreeing on a suitable time due to the time difference between the UK and US.
- It can be harder to control or keep track of the meeting.

[4 marks available — 1 for each of 2 reasonable advantages, 1 for each of 2 reasonable disadvantages]

Section 4 — Legal Stuff

Page 31 — Malpractice and Crime

1 Possible answers:
- They might not log off correctly, leaving data accessible to others.
- They might disclose their password, allowing others to access the data.
- They might visit unsafe websites and download viruses.
- They might use illegal /downloaded software and download viruses.
- They might open email virus attachments.
- They might deliberately access data they shouldn't.

[3 marks available — 1 for each of 3 correct answers]

2 Possible answers:
- They could implement an Internet usage policy for staff.
- They could use filters to block particular sites.
- They could create levels of access through passwords so that users can only access software and data at a particular level.
- They could develop policies to reduce and control e-mail use.

[3 marks available — 1 for each of 3 correct answers]

3 Possible answers:
- Power failure — the company can use UPS to prevent loss of data.
- Hacking — the company can install firewalls to check access before allowing it.
- Cracking — the company can encrypt data during transfer.
- Physical theft or access — the company can use guards, locks and CCTV to protect hardware.

[2 marks available — 1 for an appropriate threat, 1 for an appropriate measure the company could take]

Page 33 — Legal and Ethical Issues

1 Possible answers:
- Hacking — you could set up firewalls to block access to computer systems.
- Stalking — chat rooms can be monitored, Internet filters can be used to disallow access to chat rooms, public awareness of the dangers of making contacts through chat rooms and e-mail can be increased.
- Credit card fraud — firewalls can be set up to block access to computer systems.
- Copyright infringement — download sites can be monitored, Internet filters can prevent access to download sites.
- Paedophilia — access to selected sites can be monitored, Internet filters can stop access to high risk sites by children, public awareness of the dangers of making contacts through chat rooms and e-mail can be increased.

[4 marks available, 1 mark for each of 2 crimes, an additional mark each for a suitable preventative measure]

Remember guys, there's 4 marks available here, and there's oodles of answers to pick from. Just make sure you pick a crime that's fairly straightforward, and whose prevention you can explain pretty easily.

2 Possible answers:
- Children might access inappropriate material by accident as some are listed by unrelated keywords.

Answers

- *Children might use the Internet to download files illegally.*
- *Children might deliberately access inappropriate material.*
- *Children might use the Internet extensively and cause high bills to be incurred.*
- *They might download software and introduce viruses.*
- *They might put themselves at risk by contacting people they don't know.*

[3 marks available, 1 for each of 3 valid concerns]

Page 35 — Software and Data Misuse

1   Possible answers:
- *Using a piece of software without the proper licence (e.g. installing and using software on several computers with only a single-user licence).*
- *Software piracy (e.g. professional criminals mass-producing illegal copies of software and selling them through illegal outlets).*
- *Downloading files (MP3, video) from illegal websites to avoid paying for them.*
- *Copying text or images from the Internet and using them (e.g. in a publication) without obtaining the copyright owner's permission.*

[3 marks available, 1 for each of up to 3 appropriate answers]

2 a) *Any of these are acceptable:*
- *It is an agreement between the user and the producer of a piece of software on how that software may be used [1 mark].*
- *It is a legal document which specifies how a purchased piece of software may be used [1 mark].*
- *It is a contract from the producer of software which is purchased at the same time as the software. It sets out the terms of use [1 mark].*

The trick here is to make sure you pad your answer out in order to get both marks. In other words, don't just write "it's a legal document" — make sure you explain it properly.

b) *No, it would not be breaking the agreement. The agreement does not actually prohibit them from installing the software on more than 5 machines. It will only be broken if the software is used on more than 5 machines at the same time.*

[2 marks available — 1 for saying "no", 1 for an appropriate explanation]

Page 37 — Data Protection Legislation

1   Possible answers:
- *Consent is not required for the storing of the data, as it must be stored for legal purposes.*
- *Consent is needed for the processing of details for direct marketing, as this is not required by law, and it does identify an individual.*
- *There is a legal requirement for charities to process this sort of data to produce accounts, so data subject consent is not needed for this.*
- *Management analysis will often look at general trends and will not identify individuals so, again, consent is not needed.*

[4 marks available — 1 for each appropriate point]

2   Possible answers:
- *The eighth principle states that data cannot be transferred to a country or territory without adequate data protection. As long as data is transferred within the EU there is no problem.*
- *The second principle states that data must be used only for the purposes stated in the register. If data is being transferred to a third party, it can only be transferred if this was stated in the register.*
- *The seventh principle states that appropriate measures must be taken against unlawful processing and against accidental loss of, destruction of, or damage to, personal data.*

[2 marks available — 1 for each of 2 correctly described principles]

Okay, only 2 marks here, which means you're going to have to fight for them. Just identifying the principle by number isn't going to get you anything — you need to give a proper description in order to get your marks here. Bit of a scummy question really, such a long intro and it's only worth 2 marks. Oh well...

Page 39 — Data Protection Legislation (cont.)

1   Any two of the following are acceptable:
- *Data held by an individual about themselves or their family is exempt from the need to register. This is because data is personal to the collector and they own their own data.*
- *Data collected by journalists for producing an article (as long as it*

is in the public interest) is exempt from the need to register. This is because the use of the data is in the public domain (although it must be accurate and up to date).
- *Data collected by writers / artists for inclusion in their work (as long as it is in the public interest) is exempt from the need to register. This is specified by the DPA, because data collected by writers / artists for inclusion in their work is not exploitative and can have public interest.*
- *Data collected for research purposes is exempt from the need to register. This is because the data doesn't generally identify individuals.*
- *Data collected for producing statistics is exempt from the need to register. This is because the data doesn't generally identify individuals.*

[4 marks available — 1 for each of 2 examples, a further 1 each for an accompanying reason]

b) *Any two of the following are acceptable:*
- *Police records held during an investigation are exempt from subject access. This is because access to these records might interfere with the investigation.*
- *Legal records held about a court case are exempt from subject access. This is because access to these records might interfere with the outcome of the case.*
- *Tax records for tax assessment purposes are exempt from subject access. This is because access to this data might help someone commit tax fraud.*
- *Any data that relates to a number of people so that access by one person will identify another is exempt from subject access. This is because access to data about another individual is not permitted unless that person has given their consent.*

[4 marks available — 1 for each of 2 examples, a further 1 each for an accompanying reason]

Well, question 2 is fairly straightforward, and you can't go far wrong as long as you've got some decent examples up your sleeve. The thing to watch out for here is the wording of the question — make sure you've put in **two** examples plus **two** reasons for each part... Bloomin' examiners...

Page 41 — Health and safety

1   Possible answers:
- *There should be a smooth changeover from the old system to the new one to minimise stress.*
- *The new system must be an improvement on the old system.*
- *The system should be easy to use, with provision for training if necessary.*
- *The new system must not be unnecessarily slow.*
- *There should be the facility for the user to use shortcuts.*
- *New hardware must be appropriate for the software so as not to cause too much stress.*
- *New hardware must operate within acceptable time limits.*

[3 marks available — 1 for each correctly identified point]

Ooh this is a bit tricky — don't get thrown off by the fact that it's asking about experienced users. Almost all of the same points apply to experienced and less experienced users.

2   Possible answers:
- *They can take regular breaks from looking at the screen.*
- *They can use an ergonomic mouse and keyboard or wrist guards.*
- *They should avoid sitting still for too long and should move around during breaks.*
- *They should sit up straight and sit in a chair with back support.*
- *They should make sure that the chair and keyboard are at the correct height.*
- *They should sit with their eyes at least one metre from the screen.*
- *They should make sure that there is adequate lighting and no glare on the screen.*

[3 marks available — 1 for each correctly identified point]

Section 5 — Systems Software

Page 43 — Software Drivers

1   Possible answers:
- *A printer driver is a piece of systems software that allows the printer to be configured by the operating system to work as intended.*

ANSWERS

Answers

- A printer driver is a program which allows communication between the DTP program and the printer.
  [2 marks available — 2 for a full answer, 1 for a partial answer]

2 Any two of the following possible answers is acceptable:
  - Compression — A utility program converts data into a format that takes up far less memory space, enabling faster communication.
  - File conversion — A utility program enables applications to open files with different file extensions.
  - Configuration files — A file which provides information on system parameters that applications should adapt to.
  [4 marks available — 2 for each of two full answers, 1 for each of two partial answers]

Page 45 — Operating Systems

1 a) Possible answers:
  - It manages all applications installed on the computer.
  - It monitors the systems input and output devices.
  - It allocates memory on request.
  - It schedules programs and resources.
  - It provides an interface between user, hardware and software.
  - It logs errors.
  [3 marks available — 1 for each of 3 appropriate tasks]
  b) Possible answers:
  - An operating system with a Graphical User Interface, as this provides easy-to-use mouse-driven systems.
  - A single user system, as there is likely to be access from one user at a time.
  Be careful not use trade names (e.g. Microsoft Windows). You won't get any marks for stating trade names without a full explanation.
  [2 marks available — 2 for naming an appropriate system and providing an explanation, 1 for the name or explanation only]

Page 47 — Human / Computer Interface

1 Possible answers:
  - When the user is prompted to do something it must be clear how they do it.
  - There must be on-line help that appears at the right time.
  - All inputs must be validated or must use a method that makes it easy for the user to enter data (e.g. drop-down lists, validation of text input).
  - It must not require the user to remember sequences of commands.
  - It should have all required items on screen at once (the user shouldn't have to scroll up and down to find things).
  - It should conform to general practice for user interfaces on that platform (e.g. work like a Windows application).
  - It should be consistent in its approach so that new users can begin to understand it intuitively.
  [3 marks available — 1 for each of up to 3 suitable features]

2 Possible answers:
  Advantages:
  - They are easy to use.
  - Most controls are fairly intuitive — we know to click on a button, select from a drop-down list, etc.
  - They don't depend on the user remembering long lists of commands.
  Disadvantages:
  - They require more processing power and can cause software to be slow.
  - They can be limited in their function and some of the more useful functions can be hidden.
  - Some users would prefer to enter all data in one way (e.g. type it all) and can become frustrated by some of the graphical controls.
  [4 marks available — 1 for each of 2 suitable pros, 1 for each of 2 suitable cons]

Page 49 — Software Upgrade and Reliability

1 a) Possible answers:
  - They could upgrade their hardware output devices, e.g. with a faster printer / more printers.
  - They could upgrade their processing hardware, e.g. with a faster processor / parallel processors.
  [2 marks available — 1 mark for each of 2 correct answers]

b) Possible answers:
  - Staff would need to learn to use the new version of the software.
  - The new version may have lost some familiar features which staff will have to re-learn.
  - Time may be needed to transfer the data to the new system.
  - The changeover can cause stress.
  [2 marks available — 1 mark for each of 2 correct answers]
c) Possible answers:
  - There should be a test plan covering every testing possibility.
  - There should be functional testing to ensure that everything works correctly.
  - There should be performance testing to ensure that the new database does perform better than the old one.
  - There should be recovery testing to ensure that data is not lost if there is a system failure.
  - The plan should cover all types of test data — typical, erroneous and extreme (valid, invalid, boundary).
  - Alpha testing should be carried out by users within the software development company.
  [3 marks available — 1 mark for each of 3 correct answers]

Section 6 — Generic, Specific and Bespoke Software

Page 51 — Generic Software

1 Generic — possible answers:
  - Generic software means software that is appropriate to many areas.
  - Generic software is software that can be used for a variety of day to day tasks.
  Possible examples are: word processors, desktop publishers, spreadsheet programs, database management systems, integrated packages, presentation software.
  Task specific — possible answers:
  - Task specific software is software that serves a particular function for users who have technical knowledge of the subject area.
  - Task specific software is software that supports a specialist application.
  Possible examples are: payroll programs, CAD/CAM programs, project management software, music software.
  Bespoke — possible answers:
  - Bespoke software is software that has been specially written for a specific user.
  - Bespoke software is software that has been specially commissioned by a particular company, organisation or even individual.
  Possible examples are: database for a hospital, timetabling programs for a bus company, booking system for a travel agency or tourism organisation, etc.
  [9 marks available — 1 each for suitable explanations of "generic", "task-specific" and "bespoke" software, an additional 1 for each of 2 supporting examples]
  You could get away with giving "e-mail application" or "web browser" as an example of either generic or task-specific software here, but not both...

Page 53 — Capabilities of Software

1 Possible advantages:
  - It's readily available for purchase.
  - It has been widely tried and tested.
  - There is lots of support available on-line and from books.
  Possible disadvantages:
  - The software won't be specific to the newsagent, so may not be quite appropriate for his needs.
  - The newsagent may waste money buying software with features that he doesn't need.
  - It has a larger memory footprint.
  [4 marks available — 1 for each of two suitable advantages, 1 for each of two suitable disadvantages]

Page 55 — Customising Applications

1 Possible answers:
  - Buttons could be added to the interface. Different buttons could take the user to another document, run the selected action or sort data.
  - Menus could be added to the interface. They give users all the options to choose from in a single list, and limit and direct the user to selected options.

Answers

- Forms can be added to the interface. Drop down boxes can be used for data selection, and boxes that fill in automatically can be used, depending on what other data is entered.
- Macros can be added to the interface. They save time by letting you add information at the click of a single button. For example, you can record a macro to add a header containing the filename, date and page number into all your documents.

[6 marks available — 1 for each of 3 customising features, an additional 1 each for a description of how they would work]

2 a) Possible answers:
- A spreadsheet with macro capabilities has the ability to record and store a sequence of instructions that can be used to carry out repetitive tasks for a user.
- If a spreadsheet has macro capabilities, it means it is able to use macros to carry out certain repetitive tasks so the user doesn't have to. Macros do this by recording a series of commands and then carrying them out when prompted.

[2 marks available — 2 marks for a full explanation, 1 mark for a partial explanation]

This is a bit of a tricky question. They've allowed 2 marks for it because it's quite a tricky definition to come up with, but there's no obvious way to break it down into what you get the separate marks for. The main thing is to write an explanation in detail — i.e. whatever you do don't just write: "a spreadsheet with macro capabilities is a spreadsheet that can use macros".

b) Possible answers:
- They could be used in a word-processor to change the details in the header.
- They could be used in a spreadsheet program to format cells in a particular way.
- They could be used in a presentation program to add particular buttons to slides.

[2 marks available — 1 for each appropriate example]

This is an easy question to pick up marks on — there are LOADS of examples of things you could use macros for.

Page 57 — Templates, Style Sheets and Wizards

1 Possible advantages:
- Documents can be created more quickly.
- The application is more user-friendly for inexperienced users.
- Documents can be kept in a house style.

Possible disadvantages:
- All documents will look similar, which may mean they become boring and difficult to distinguish from each other.
- The wizard's templates may not match the user's needs precisely.
- Users are limited to the choices offered by the wizard, so it's harder to make adjustments.

[4 marks available — 1 for each of 2 appropriate advantages, 1 for each of 2 appropriate disadvantages]

2 Possible answers:
- Templates could be used to govern layout and ensure that all company documents have a consistent style and "look." The template ensures that everyone is working to the same document format.
- Style Sheets can be used in other programs to make sure that different users follow the same stylistic guidelines.
- Wizards can be used to create documents — as they have their own pre-set templates, users could agree to use the same one in order to keep their documents looking consistent.

[2 marks available — 1 for each appropriate example]

Remember, only 2 marks available here, so no need to go off on one...

Section 7 — Information Manipulation and Processing

Page 59 — Types of Processing

1 a) Transaction processing system OR Interactive processing system
Possible reasons:
- It is important that a booking is completed before allowing another booking to be made.
- The system must prevent two users from booking the same seats on a flight.
- Details of seat availability must be available on request.

[2 marks available — 1 for naming a suitable processing system, 1 for a reasonable explanation]

b) Batch processing system
Possible reasons:
- Changes to the output are not needed immediately.
- All processing can take place at once.
- Processing can take place out of normal working hours so as not to disrupt the system.

[2 marks available — 1 for naming a suitable processing system, 1 for a reasonable explanation]

c) Real-time system
Possible reasons:
- It must be able to react immediately to any situation.
- It needs to update regularly enough to be able to control the reactor.

[2 marks available — 1 for naming a suitable processing system, 1 for a reasonable explanation]

Page 61 — Processing Different Data Types

1 a) Possible answers:
- It could be stored using the ASCII standard, as sets of bits.
- It could be stored using the ASCII standard, with 8 bits per character.
- It could be stored using the ASCII standard, where each separate keyboard character has a specific code.

[2 marks available — 2 for a full answer, 1 for a partial one]

b) Possible answers:
- It could be stored using the MIDI standard, as sets of bits where each group of bits represents a particular pitch or amplitude.
- It could be stored using the MP3 standard, as sets of bits where each group of bits represents a particular pitch or amplitude.
- It could be stored using the WAV standard, as sets of bits where each group of bits represents a particular pitch or amplitude.

[2 marks available — 2 for a full answer, 1 for a partial one]

c) Possible answers:
- They could be stored as vector graphics / object-based graphics, as a set of data stored about the shape or line.
- They could be stored as vector graphics / object-based graphics, as positional data.
- They could be stored as vector graphics / object-based graphics, as a set of properties for the shape or line.

[2 marks available — 2 for a full answer, 1 for a partial one]

2 Possible answers:
- It might store the picture data as a bitmap, which is a series of bits for colour, shade and brightness. The more colours used, the more bits there are.
- It might store the picture data as a JPEG, which is a compressed bitmap.
- It might store the picture data as a GIF file, which is a compressed bitmap.

[2 marks available — 2 for a full answer, 1 for a partial one]

Page 63 — Formatting Data for the End User

1 Possible answers:
- Accounts could be presented to the tax office as a complete set of numbers in a table / spreadsheet for complete reference.
- Accounts could be presented to the company directors as information in graphical form for an easier overview.
- Accounts could be presented to the shareholders as a slide show / report containing graphs of sales figures.
- Accounts could be presented to potential new customers as a video / animation to make a more appealing and engaging presentation.

[4 marks available — 1 for each appropriate presentation method]

2 Possible answers:
- There is likely to be text on the web page.
- There might be bitmap graphics.
- Graphical icons might be used.
- Animations could be used on the page.

[3 marks available — 1 for each suitable output format]

This is a really easy question — just make sure you understand the question exactly, and don't think it's asking you how you could format

Answers

text differently, or anything stupid like that.

Section 8 — Hardware

Page 65 — Hardware — Input Devices
1 Possible answers:
- A mouse could be used to navigate a web page on a home PC. They are designed to fit in your hand and be easy to use. However, the mouse can be slower than using keyboard commands and shortcuts. Mice can be prone to picking up dirt, which may affect their performance.
- A trackball or trackpad could be used to navigate a web page on a laptop. These can be integrated into the machine, so there is no need to plug in a mouse or provide an extra surface space for one. However, users can find both of these difficult to adapt to if they are used to a mouse.
- A numeric keypad can be used to navigate a web page on a mobile telephone. Special keys are assigned to navigate and click on buttons. They are small and convenient to use. However, the keypad itself can be quite slow and offers limited access options for more complicated sites.
- Touch screens can be used to navigate web pages on public Internet terminals. These are integrated into the system, so there is no need for detachable devices which could be damaged or stolen. However, it is difficult to pinpoint particular areas and they are quite clumsy compared with more precise devices.

[6 marks available — 1 for each of two suitable examples, then a further 1 mark for a suitable positive and negative point to accompany each one]

Hmm... This is a bit of a stinker. The trick is to look back at the question and work out what it's asking you — it's asking for two examples, and says you need to evaluate them. This is very tricky, as it can feel a little unstructured, but the easy way to think about it is that for each example you'll get 1 mark for an appropriate example, 1 mark for a full and appropriate pro, and 1 mark for a full and appropriate con. Once you've broken it down like that it should be pretty easy to just reel off the facts, one by one...

Page 67 — Hardware — Input Devices (cont.)
1 Possible answers:
- A scanner could be used to input existing photographs.
- A digital camera could be used to input new photographs.
- A keyboard could be used to input textual slogans.
- A pointing device (e.g. mouse / trackball / trackpad) could be used to position photographs and text.

[3 marks available — 1 for each of three full answers]

2 Possible answers:
Benefits:
- Limited keys make it simpler to use than a conventional keyboard.
- They can have larger functional areas for people with limited hand movement.
- They have a sealed surface that is less likely to be affected by dirt and liquid than a conventional keyboard.

Limitations:
- They are limited to the specific system they were designed for.
- All applications must be designed especially for the keyboard.

[2 marks available — 1 for an appropriate benefit, 1 for an appropriate limitation]

Page 69 — Hardware — Output Devices
1 Possible answers:
- A graph plotter would be appropriate because it can output high quality vector graphics.
- A graph plotter would be appropriate because they usually print on paper larger than A4 size.
- An A3 laser printer would be appropriate because it is able to output high quality vector graphics.

[2 marks available — 2 for a full answer, 1 for a partial answer]

2 Possible answers:
- Lots of students will want to print at once, and the laser printer is very fast, so it means less waiting around for output.
- Laser printers print at a very high quality, which is useful for school

projects and presentations.
- Laser printers are relatively quiet so it is less likely to disturb other working pupils while it prints.

[2 marks available — 1 for each suitable reason]

Page 71 — Hardware — Backing Storage
1 a) Possible answers:
- They should keep the original disks with program software on them.
- They should make copies of the original disks in case the originals get damaged.
- They should copy the whole of the main hard disk to different backing storage regularly, e.g. once a week.
- They should copy all data files that have changed each day.
- They could use a mirrored hard disk system to keep a constant copy of the data.

[4 marks available — 1 for each suitable suggestion]

I know it says "some", but look at how many marks are available. You need to make four solid points here.

b) Possible answers:
- They could use magnetic tape for backing up data (global or incremental).
- They could use CD-R / DVD-Rs for keeping copies of program software.
- They could use CD-RW / DVD-RWs for keeping copies of individual data files.
- They could use a second hard disk for back up data.
- They could use a second hard disk for mirroring the main hard disk.

[2 marks available — 1 for each suitable answer]

Here's the main thing to remember here — there's only two marks, so don't mention floppy disks or memory sticks. They're too small for a useful back up in this situation.

Section 9 — Networks and Security

Page 73 — Security of Data
1 a) Possible answers:
- Backing up is not done regularly enough. The system could be restored to a back up that is 30 days old, and an entire month's work could potentially be lost.
- If her back up disk gets corrupted, the CD from the previous month may need to be used, resulting in a 60 day old out-of-date system being restored.
- She needs to store the back up disks away from the office in case the building itself is compromised.
- The system depends on the manager remembering to take a back up rather than it being done automatically, so it is less reliable.

[3 marks available — 1 mark for each suitable reason]

b) Possible answers:
- Data should be backed up on a daily basis.
- Back ups should be done automatically by the system.
- Data should be backed up to magnetic tape instead of CDs which can become easily corrupted.
- Back ups should be stored in a different location to the computer.

[3 marks available — 1 mark for each reasonable answer]

Pretty much any question you get on backing up is going to require these sorts of answers. The trick is to have all the information ready to go in your head, so you can answer it without a moment's pause.

2 a) Possible answers:
- The data is private and sensitive and so should not be available for others to see.
- It is important that the data is correct, and is not tampered with, so that doctors can make an appropriate diagnosis of a patient's illness.

[2 marks available — 1 mark for each reasonable answer]

b) Possible answers:
- By physically restricting access to the computers.
- By having a password system.
- By having different levels of access for different medical staff.
- By having a UPS in case of power failure.
- By taking regular back ups.

[4 marks available — 1 for each reasonable way]

Answers

Page 75 — Networks

1 a) Possible answers:
- A file server would be needed to control the network.
- Each computer on the network must have a network interface card.
- Each computer must have cabling (or a wireless link) in order to be connected.

[3 marks available — 1 for each reasonable answer]

b) Possible answers:
- Hardware (e.g. printers) can be shared.
- Data (e.g. showing orders or sales) can be easily made accessible to all employees.
- Data can be stored centrally and is more secure.
- Data can be backed up automatically.
- Users can access their work from any computer terminal.

[3 marks available — 1 for each reasonable answer]

c) Possible answers:
- Expensive hardware (e.g. a file server) and software is needed to run it.
- If the server breaks down then no one can use the network until it's fixed.
- More specialised knowledge is needed to maintain the network.
- Users have less control over the way their computers are set up and who is able to access their work.

[2 marks available — 1 for each reasonable answer]

These questions aren't too complicated — they're just testing that you've memorised all the good and bad things about networks. Not too tricky at all...

Page 77 — Networks (cont.)

1 a) In a peer-to-peer network the computers are linked together but there is no file-server. In a client-server network, one central computer (the file-server) controls the flow of data in the network and stores the data and usually the software on its hard disk.

[2 marks available — 1 for a reasonable description of a peer-to-peer network, 1 for a reasonable description of a client-server network]

b) Possible answers:
- As there is an increase in the number of computers, a client-server system will be needed to help with the increase in traffic.
- A client-server system allows central storage of data which will free up space on individual machines, making them run better.
- A client-server system allows automatic back up of data which means an increased level of protection against data being corrupted or destroyed.

[3 marks available — 1 for each reasonable answer]

2 a) In a bus topology all the computers are linked in a line to one cable with the file-server in the middle. In a star topology there is an individual cable from the hub to each workstation.
Bus network:

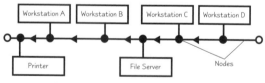

Star network:

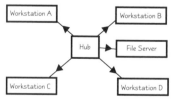

[4 marks available — 1 for a reasonable description of a bus network, 1 for a reasonable description of a star network, a further 1 for each of two supporting diagrams]

Don't get scared if you don't like drawing diagrams. They only need to be very basic. Sketch one out really quickly on some scrap paper before you start, so you've got something to copy from, and make sure you label all the different bits of it really clearly.

b) Possible answers:
- Fewer physical cables are needed for a bus topology, making it more straightforward to set up.
- A bus network is cheaper as fewer cables are needed.

[1 mark]

c) Possible answers:
- A star network is often faster because there is an individual connection from the hub to each workstation.
- If the cable to one computer fails, it will not affect the operation of any other networked computers.

[1 mark]

As long as you know your network topologies, you'll be fine here. These "advantage" and "disadvantage" questions are really straightforward and a great way to pick up easy marks, so make sure you revise all the reasons thoroughly.

Section 10 — Data Capture and Organisation

Page 79 — Data Capture

1 a) Possible answers:
- The busy staff will be able to use their hands for other purposes whilst verbally creating messages.
- Faster data entry is possible if the typing skills of the staff are not very advanced.
- Any less time spent at the keyboard means a reduction in the risk of health problems such as RSI developing.
- It will be useful for any motor-impaired employees as they will not have to use a keyboard in order to create text.

[2 marks available — 1 for each sensible answer]

b) Possible answers:
- Background noise may interfere with data entry.
- The system will only work with people who have trained the computer to recognise their voice.
- It may prove slower to use the new system than it was to type, e.g. due to the computer mishearing words.
- Dictating to the computer may disturb other employees / create unnecessary extra office noise.

[2 marks available — 1 for each sensible answer]

Page 81 — Verification and Validation

1 a) Possible answers:
- House number
- Postcode
- Customer reference number
- Date

[2 marks available — 1 for each sensible answer]

b) Possible answers:
- Presence check to ensure the meter readings are present.
- Range check to check that the meter reading is equal to, or higher than, the previous reading.

[4 marks available — 1 for each of two check names. An additional 1 for each explanation]

c) Possible answers:
- The person reading the meter may have read the numbers incorrectly (e.g. they may have seen an 8 instead of a 3).
- The person reading the meter may have read the numbers correctly but made an error writing them down (e.g. they may have intended to write down 34153 but instead they wrote down 34513. The data validation software cannot pick up this sort of error.

[2 marks available — 1 for each sensible answer]

Page 83 — Databases

1 A primary key is a unique field in a table *[1 mark]* that is used to identify a record *[1 mark]*. A foreign key is a field in a table *[1 mark]* that is related to the primary key of a second table *[1 mark]*.

2 a) Product_ID *[1 mark]*
Cust_ID *[1 mark]*

b) Any two from:
Cust_ID in the ORDER table
Product_ID in the ORDER table
Supplier_ID in the PRODUCT table
[1 mark each for up to 2 correct answers.]

c) i) one-to-many / one customer may make many orders [1 mark].
ii) one-to-many / one supplier may supply many products [1 mark].

Page 85 — Databases (cont.)

1 Possible answers:
- Relational databases store data only once, which ensures data consistency (there's no danger of data being updated in one place, but not another).
- You can store a much larger variety of data than in a flat file database by organising it into separate linked tables.
- There is no redundant data / duplicated data because each data item is stored only once.
- Relational databases are less time-consuming to update.
- The DBMS can ensure that only authorised users are able to access certain parts (e.g. tables) of a relational database.
- Searching is quicker as all data is held in one place, and not in different independent files.
- It gives different views of the data to different users. This means users only look at the parts that are relevant to them.

[4 marks available — 1 for each reasonable advantage]

2 Possible answers:
- CUSTOMERS
- SUPPLIERS
- EMPLOYEES
- COMPLAINTS
- SERVICES

[3 marks available — 1 for each reasonable table]

3 Possible fields are: Pupil ID number, first name, surname, date of birth, tutor group, grade, address. Out of these the Pupil ID number would be the primary key.

[6 marks available — 1 each for 5 sensible fields, and another 1 for suggesting the logical primary key]

Wow — how easy is it to pick up marks on these questions! You'd be loving it if you got a question like this in the exam! They do come up, but beware of straightforward questions: it's sometimes all too easy to slip up on them...

Page 87 — Examples of Databases

1 Possible answers:
- PASSENGER (<u>passenger ID</u>, title, surname, phone number, address1, address2)
- COACH (<u>Registration number</u>, driver name)
- ROUTE (<u>Route ID</u>, destination)
- BOOKING (<u>Booking ID</u>, passenger ID, route ID, Registration number, seat, date, time)

[5 marks available — 1 for each of three suitable tables. An additional 2 marks for supporting information about relationships and keys]

Now remember guys — this kind of question is especially tricky, as it's not certain where exactly all the marks come from. The best thing is to make sure you don't skimp on the detail. Put in as much as you can about the tables (as long as you're not rambling on or repeating yourself) and you can be sure to pick up all the marks required here.

Page 89 — Normalisation / Data Dictionaries

1 Possible answers:
- Data type *[1 mark]*
- Data validation / Input masks *[1 mark]*
- Relationships between tables *[1 mark]*
- Primary keys identified *[1 mark]*
- Access rights e.g. edit / read only *[1 mark]*

[5 marks available — 1 for each sensible answer]

2 Possible answers:
- There is no primary key *[1 mark]* — no field contains unique data *[1 mark]*
- The fields are not atomic *[1 mark]*, they all contain data that could be broken down, e.g. the customer name field should be broken down into forename and surname *[1 mark]*.
- Repeating data *[1 mark]* held in the order field *[1 mark]*.

[4 marks available — 1 for each sensible answer]

Page 91 — Entering and Retrieving Data

1 Possible answers:
- Consistent layout to follow existing house / corporate style *[1 mark]*.
- Buttons / icons / menu options should be added to make it easier to use *[1 mark]*.
- The screen should only contain concise and relevant information *[1 mark]*.
- Layout of data entry screen should match layout of paper form with the source data *[1 mark]*.
- Error / help messages should be included to help the user enter the data correctly *[1 mark]*.

[4 marks available — 1 for each sensible answer]

2 a) In parameter queries, the user inputs the value to be searched for *[1 mark]*. It is used for a specific field / value *[1 mark]*. Example: All books about a specified subject *[1 mark]*.
[3 marks available — 1 for a brief description or 2 for a more detailed one and 1 for a suitable example]

b) A complex query uses more than 1 field and may be taken from different tables in the database *[1 mark]*. Complex queries often use logic functions such as AND, OR or NOT *[1 mark]*. Example: All books about ICT written by a specified author *[1 mark]*.
[3 marks available — 1 for a brief description or 2 for a more detailed one and 1 for a suitable example]

3 Possible answers:
- A CD-ROM holds a limited amount of information *[1 mark]*, whereas a website can hold larger amounts *[1 mark]*.
- Hyperlinks can be used on the web pages about each book *[1 mark]* and linked to related web pages on the company website *[1 mark]*.
- Increase in customer base *[1 mark]* as people may find the site through browsing the Internet *[1 mark]*.

[Maximum 6 marks]

Section 11 — Applications Software for Modelling Data

Page 93 — Modelling Software

1 Possible answers:
- They can be used to predict future financial events *[1 mark]*, using 'what-if' questions *[1 mark]*.
- They can be used to show trends *[1 mark]*, using graphs which change automatically as values are changed *[1 mark]*.
- No specialist software is needed *[1 mark]*, because spreadsheets are standard packages *[1 mark]*.
- There is less chance of errors occurring *[1 mark]*, because calculations are performed automatically *[1 mark]*.

Okay guys, six marks here. That means come up with three decent points and make sure you give full explanations of all of them.

2 Possible answers:
Functions:
- Functions are standard routines built into the spreadsheet package.
- They have wizards to help the user use them.
- Functions can be nested within other functions to create more complicated commands.

Examples of functions are:
- SUM, which calculates the total of a range of cells.
- IF, which returns one value if the condition specified is true and a different value if it is false.
- AVERAGE, which returns the mean or average value from a range of cells.

Formulas:
- Formulas are typed directly into the formula bar by the user.
- They use mathematical operators in order to prompt the computer to process the data in a particular cell.
- They're usually used for simple calculations.

Examples of formulas are:
- A3+(B7*RATE_VAT), which would multiply B7 by the RATE_VAT value, then add it to the A3 value.
- A3+B3+C3, which would add together each of the values in A3, B3 and C3.

Answers

[6 marks available — up to 3 for functions and 3 for formulas; 1 for an incomplete description or 2 for a full description, plus 1 for a suitable example]

Okay, simple — just break the six marks down into obvious components. It'll be 3 for functions and 3 for formulas — 1 for a lame description, 2 for a full description, then 1 for the example. Easy, eh?

Pages 95 — Spreadsheet Basics

1 a) *Possible answers:*
- A worksheet is part of a workbook, and can be stored and accessed as a single unit.
- Calculations can be performed, based on data from multiple worksheets.
- Worksheets can be used to break up related data in a logical way. For example, in a spreadsheet of sales data, there could be separate worksheets for sales volume, sales value, and sales graphs.

b) *Possible answers:*
- A workbook is a collection of worksheets.
- A workbook keeps related data in one file.
  For example, a chain of shops might keep a workbook containing information on the whole chain, while individual worksheets would refer to individual shops.

c) *Possible answers:*
- A cell range is a group of selected cells.
- Cell ranges often appear in formulas, e.g. the formula SUM (A3:B5) uses the function "SUM" and the range "A3:B5" to find the total of all the cells in the range.

[6 marks available — 1 for each of 3 full explanations, 1 for each of 3 appropriate examples]

There's only 6 marks here guys, and you have to give examples, so remember to make your explanations good or else you won't get the mark for each one.

2 a) *Possible answers:*
- Absolute referencing is where cells are copied without changing the value in the cell automatically, but are just kept the same.
- For example, a constant delivery charge or VAT rate on a spreadsheet that does not change during calculations.

[3 marks available — 1 for a partial explanation or 2 for a full one, plus 1 for a suitable example]

b) *Possible answers:*
- Relative referencing will copy the cells in such a way that the cell references change, either by row or column, in relation to where the copy gets placed.
- For example, adding up totals in a row or column.

[3 marks available — 1 for a partial explanation or 2 for a full one, plus 1 for a suitable example]

Page 97 — Customising Spreadsheets

1 a) Bar chart or line graph *[1 mark]*
b) Scatter graph *[1 mark]*

2 *Possible answers:*
- Label controls and error messages can be added to give the user guidance, e.g. error messages can be included in the cell validation.
- Macros can be linked to buttons, assisting the user in performing specific tasks.
- List boxes / combo boxes can be used, where users select from a preset list of options. These can be used for validation as the user is restricted to entering certain values.
- Option buttons can be used to select options where there is a pre-defined choice like the title of a person.

[4 marks available — 1 each for identifying 2 methods, an additional 1 each for a full explanation]

Section 12 — Software for Presentation and Communication

Page 99 — Using WP and DTP

1 a) *Possible answers:*
  Ask, Fill-in, If... Then... Else, Next Record, Skip Record If
  [2 marks available — 1 for each suitable word field]

b) *Possible answers:*
- Data can be taken from sources other than his original database.
- Unwanted data can be filtered out.
- Standard information, like the date the letter is being printed on, can be inserted.

[2 marks available — 1 for each suitable benefit]

c) *Possible answers:*
- Not having to type out every letter by hand simply saves a lot of time.
- Using a standard letter format means lots of letters can be created quickly, as he only needs to write one letter which can then be used as the template for the others.
- Using a standard letter format reduces the chances of error. As long as he proofreads the original letter, he knows the others will also be correct.
- It is important to be able to send letters with personalised information as every customer will have a different balance on their account.
- The fact that the data comes from an existing data source also means there is less chance of errors as no data needs to be re-keyed by him.

[4 marks available — 2 for each appropriately detailed description]

Obviously the key here is detail. Don't just write down impersonal blah — make sure you back up your answers.

Page 101 — Standard Documents

1 *Possible answers:*
- Large font
- Clear font
- Lots of white space on the page to help readability

[2 marks available — 1 for each suitable formatting suggestion]

2 *Possible answers:*
- All work done by each member of the team will follow the same consistent format.
- The initial work of setting up different styles can be done by one member of staff and then shared with others, so every member of the team does not have to waste time doing this.
- Formatting the document is faster and more straightforward, as team members can apply a pre-set style to a bit of text instead of having to format it the long way.
- Using paragraph styles means that global style changes can be implemented easily.

[3 marks available — 1 for each reasonable example]

Page 103 — Clipart and Graphics tools

1 a) *Possible answers:*
- Vector graphics are saved as a geometric equation.
- As vector graphics are saved as equations, it means the user has the ability to scale objects and calculate distances, which is very important for a map-maker producing accurate maps.

[2 marks available — 2 for a decent explanation with full supporting sentence]

b) *Possible answers:*
- Bitmaps could be used for icons / symbols on the map, as they will always appear at same size, superimposed on a geometric object.
- If photographs are used elsewhere on the map, bitmaps can be used for these.

[1 mark available]

2 *Possible answers:*
- Instead of having to hunt around for appropriate images and graphics to use in the journal, a large amount of the necessary images should be contained in the library and be easily accessible.
- Using a graphics library ensures that technical symbols and information used in the journal will look consistent and can be easily identifiable.
- It's much more efficient to insert ready-made images or graphics into a publication (where possible), rather than having to create brand new ones each time a new article is produced.

[2 marks available — 1 for each suitable advantage]

Answers

Page 105 — Clipart and Graphics Tools (cont.)

1 a) Possible answers:
- They could create the outlines of simple graphics by using line tools (either straight lines or drawing "freehand") and shapes tools (like squares and circles).
- They could use a "fill" tool to fill graphics in with colour.
- They could make the graphics look more sophisticated by using tools to add shadows or 3-D effects.
- They could use interactive fill tools to alter the shading within the graphic so that the fills change subtly from dark to light.
- The designers could copy and paste a single graphic many times in order to produce a montage where lots of images are layered over each other.
- Designers could use a transparency tool in order to layer one image over another without obscuring either.

[3 marks available — 1 for each suitable use]

b) Possible answers:
- They could use cropping tools to reshape the photograph and cut off any unnecessary details.
- They could alter the brightness, contrast or intensity of the colours in a photograph in order to make it more intense, or to bring out the features better.
- They could edit tiny details in the photograph, dot by dot, and remove unsightly things like red-eye.
- They could use shape and line tools to create a frame to put around the photograph, or they could add shapes to the image (e.g. stars or exclamation marks).
- They could apply built-in filters or effects to give the photo a sophisticated visual style, e.g. pastel, brush strokes, stained glass, watercolours, etc.

[3 marks available — 1 for each suitable use]

Page 107 — Multimedia Presentations

1 Possible advantages:
- It's very easy to move between slides.
- He's already familiar with creating and presenting OHPs so won't need new training.
- He already has his own equipment so will not need to buy any more expensive projectors or pieces of software.

Possible disadvantages:
- The transparencies can be easily damaged.
- Because new technology exists and is used so commonly, he runs the risk of making his own presentations seem very out of date.
- He has to change each slide by hand, which can be awkward.
- He can't use any added effects like video or additional sound, which might make the presentations boring.

[4 marks available — 1 for each of 2 suitable advantages, 1 for each of 2 suitable disadvantages]

Right — this one's quite tricky. Try not to get distracted by multimedia presentations and just focus on the good and bad things about OHPs.

2 Possible answers:
a) Slide Transition
- Different types of slide transition can be used to move from one slide to the next in an interesting way. For example, she could set it so that one slide faded into the next, making it look smart and professional.
- Slide transition moves the presentation from one slide to the next. The look should be kept consistent through the whole presentation to make it look more professional.

b) Buttons
- Buttons can be inserted into slides so that something happens when they are clicked on (e.g. activate a hyperlink which takes you to another part of the presentation). The number of these should be limited so that the presentation doesn't get too confusing.
- She can use buttons on each slide that will activate a hyperlink when you click on them. The buttons should be bright and clearly labelled in order to be effective.

c) Sound
- Sound can be used to emphasise an important point or the end of one part of the presentation. She shouldn't overuse the sound or else the presentation will become confusing.
- She can use pre-existing sounds or else record her own new ones for the presentation. She needs to think about the audience and make sure the sounds are not unclear or confusing.

[6 marks available — 2 for each fully explained and supported answer]

Page 109 — Creating Web Pages

1 a) Possible answers:
Advantages of web authoring software:
- The software is quite sophisticated, so exact effects can be achieved.
- The links can be checked and updated automatically.
- Web-authoring software can have other packages integrated into it in order to achieve more impressive effects, e.g. animations.
- You can choose to edit your page through what appears on the final screen (WYSIWIG) or by editing the HTML code directly.
- Specific wizards are included in the software, e.g. one could help the school create a site map for the web site.

Advantages of standard applications software:
- No additional software costs are involved, assuming that the school already has access to computers with appropriate software.
- Less extensive staff training on specific software is required.
- If documents which already exist need to be uploaded, then they can just be automatically converted to HTML.
- It is easy and quick to create web pages in this way.

[6 marks available — 1 for each of 3 suitable advantages of web-authoring software and 1 for each of 3 suitable advantages of standard applications software]

Wow — 6 marks up for grabs just for this one question. You'd best make sure you think about making 6 decent points here. 3 advantages for each sounds like a good start to me.

b) Possible answers:
- Using a consistent layout will help users become familiar with how the site works and they'll be able to navigate their way around it more easily.
- The consistency can make the site appear more professional.
- Following a similar template for each web page reduces the risk of certain elements being left out by accident, provided that the original layout is complete.

[4 marks available — 2 for each of 2 fully supported explanations]

2 a) Possible answers:
- A browser is a program that displays web pages in a human understandable form.
- A browser is an application that gives access to the Internet, displaying web pages in an understandable form, not in HTML.

[1 mark available]

Hey — don't say 'to search on the Internet', or use any company names here. Just tell it like it is.

b) Possible answers:
- A search engine is a web page that can be used to look for information and web sites.
- A search engine provides a way of searching the Internet, looking for specific information that the user chooses.

[1 mark available]

Index

Index

Index